"What I have discovered is neither a fortune nor a farthing, but a lump of ore containing a quantity of precious metal." That remark of Freud's sums up well wh... should be our attitude towar... psychology, particularly ... excitement over it is at la... an attempt is beginning ... evaluate it calmly, withou... tisanship. This book is a v...ble contribution to that evaluation.

Accepting Freud's work as a "classical beginning," it attempts to clarify just what psychoanalysis is; what are its characteristics and implications as theory and as a practical medical technique; where the dividing line comes between the observations of Freud and the personal philosophy by which he interpreted them; and so on. In addition to this examination of psychoanalysis as a system, both in theory and in practice, there is a discussion of it as concrete experience; of what it means for both patient and doctor; of how it is affected by the limitations which affect all human performance; of what can be expected of it and what cannot; of its relation to morality and to the development of personality. The book is a sound corrective to the views of both the fanatical Freudian devotee and the nervously angry debunker of psychoanalysis; the honest enquirer will find few more enlightening introductory guides.

S was born in Berlin, versity studies at Frei-)xford and Tübingen, ıte from the latter, and elberg. He is currently l Psychology and Psy- University of Mainz, an of the department. also Consultant to the ɔmmission for matters gy and psychoanalysis.

THE METHODS AND EXPERIENCE OF PSYCHOANALYSIS

THE METHODS AND EXPERIENCE OF PSYCHO-ANALYSIS

ALBERT GÖRRES

SHEED AND WARD–NEW YORK

Originally published as
Methode und Erfahrungen der Psychoanalyse
by Kösel-Verlag, Munich

LIBRARY OF CONGRESS CATALOG CARD NUMBER 62-15281

The author and publishers wish to thank Basic Books, Inc., for permission to reprint passages from *Studies on Hysteria* by Josef Breuer and Sigmund Freud.

MANUFACTURED IN THE UNITED STATES OF AMERICA

CONTENTS

FOREWORD

SOME TIME ago a popular Catholic television speaker and columnist in America stated that five minutes on your knees every day would save you five years on a couch. Ignace Lepp speaks of a prominent French psychoanalyst who remarked to him that he, the analyst, did not consider a treatment complete until the last vestiges of religious belief were eradicated in the patient.

Here are two irreconcilable worlds. And come to think of it, our entire life today is characterized by such Iron Curtains—not only the well-known geographic-political one.

However, when we consider those two remarks, we realize that it is not the chasm between believer and godless which startles us here. In the case of the first speaker it seems to be a matter of sheer ignorance. The man—he is, as I said, a Catholic and not a Christian Scientist—would never advocate five minutes of prayer per day as a cure for appendicitis. And if a psychiatrist could let him sit in on half a day of office work, he would soon understand that people with compulsive-obsessive symptoms, people with paranoid thoughts, men and women in the throes of melancholia, drug addicts and pathological arsenists, make up part of suffering mankind just like the patient with an "acute abdomen"—and that in order to help them one needs a technique, a well-defined craft and science.

Is it also a matter of ignorance in the second speaker? The remark is horrid enough. There is something daemonical about it, it has that unmistakable Stavrogin touch. We must realize that the speaker and a great number of his friends would advocate the same treatment not just for one patient but for mankind as a whole. We could leave him to his devices if it were not for the fact that he is in possession of a vast amount of truth. And this is the entire crux of the matter. The moral demand to search for truth and to accept it pertains to all truth, not only that of the spiritual order. The author of the Imitation of Christ and other spiritual writers seem to exhort us to despise worldly knowledge. However, when we scrutinize their doctrine we find that all they want us to do is to beware of the danger of pride which comes with the growth of science. "Every human being has an innate thirst for knowledge; but what is all knowledge without the fear of God? Indeed, it is better to be a humble and God-fearing fool than a proud scholar who, without taking care of his soul, plots the course of stars." We must keep track of the course of the stars *and* take care of our souls. We must seek truth, but before God there is no opposition difference between natural truths and spiritual truths.

The rise of psychoanalysis is one of the most dramatic events in the history of human knowledge. As a medical student in the Germany of the 'twenties I was taught pure "school psychiatry", i.e., the classical descriptive psychiatry of academic tradition. Today I live and work in the psychoanalytic era, and the only comparison I can find to illustrate the difference is that of someone who would have gotten all his physics from an Aristotelian schoolman, and then discovered the physics of Galilei and Newton. I have witnessed, in one lifespan, such transition. Whitehead described something comparable, referring, of course, to the big turning-point in modern science which came about through the Relativity Theory and Quantum Mechanics. "I was in Cambridge in the 1880's, first as an undergraduate, later as one of the staff. It was from two hundred to two hundred and fifty years since mathematics had had its fresh impetus from men like Descartes and Sir Isaac Newton; there were certain borderlands where affairs in that Science were considered indefinable, but in the main, mathematical physics looked sound and solid. . . . By the turn of the century nothing, absolutely nothing was left, not a single major concept. This I consider to have been one of the supreme facts of my experience."

As I said, with those of us who studied psychiatry in the 'twenties the experience was quite similar. The statement has to be modified a little, however. Firstly, it would be misleading to think that descriptive "academic" psychiatry can be discarded. The phenomenological and the physiological approach could still have their place. (Just as it would be misleading to think, on the basis of Whitehead's statement, that one should stop teaching Newton's laws.) Secondly, contrary to young Whitehead, we *did* know all the time that there existed something else. Our teacher in Munich, Geheimrat Oswald Bumke, took exactly one hour each academic term to talk to us about Freud, and to explain why he was rabidly opposed to him. I shall never forget how one of our professors used to make fun of the Freudian hypothesis that certain depressions in adults go back to bereavement and mourning in early infancy. He treated the idea as a big joke. Indeed, at first sight it did seem awfully speculative. For Freud never worked with small children. He drew his conclusions from the analyses of grown-ups. To surmise such early infantile depressions was comparable to the work of an archaeologist who, from a few bricks here, a few shards there, reconstructs the life of a vanished civilization. The only difference is that here we have scientific proof. Many years later René Spitz demonstrated the occurrence of deep melancholia in infancy precisely under the circumstances which Freud had theoretically reconstructed. He even took the trouble of using a movie camera so that you can *see* that Freud's assumption was correct.

Why had my teacher, before the scientific proof was furnished, regarded the hypothesis as a joke? I believe there are several reasons. Firstly, many of us have a dim notion that to be deeply disturbed about a loss you have to be able to appreciate your loss with the kind of intellect only an adult has. The idea is that a tiny creature too dumb to speak or to comprehend is not yet bright enough to become disturbed by the "external events" of life. The second reason is that, even if the baby did become disturbed, once grown up it could not very well go through the distressing experience again: for this would amount to a strange paradox—namely a kind of *reminiscence of the unremembered*. The third reason is that it seems scientifically somehow more appropriate to assume a pure biochemical or cytophysiological cause for a mysterious, unmotivated state of melancholia—the sort of thing one can eventually discover in the brain with the aid of laboratory methods. The solution seems somehow "cleaner".

If we consider these three reasons we notice that they have one thing in common. They are products of the Cartesian mind. They are prompted by an awfully rationalistic, compartmentalized approach to life. Human suffering is seen through a precision grid.

Sometime ago I had a conversation with a Moscow psychiatrist on the subject of psychoanalysis, and he told me that one of the reasons for which Soviet psychiatry rejects Freud is that he is "unscientific". If one means by "scientific", "verifiable", then my man was wrong. If one means by "scientific" the "precision grid", then he was right. For the precision grid is tumbled. Freud must have felt uneasy about this himself, very much as some contemporary physicists feel uneasy about shaking the principle of causality. And he held on to some kind of mechanistic determinism, although it contradicted the very essence of his discovery.

Here we come to an important observation. Freud's work is the first big turning-point away from a Cartesian view of life. It marks, not only the end of Cartesianism but of other Manichean currents which preceded Descartes for many centuries. Therefore, if properly understood, it confirms instead of denying the Christian concept of Man.

This is one of the points of the present book. The two men I quoted in the beginning represent two warring fronts. And people like Dr. Görres are negotiators with white flags who attempt to find some basis for a mutual understanding. A man who, white flag or no white flag, walks across no man's land is bound to be sniped at from both sides. Therefore a book like this one is not only a matter of intelligence but also of courage. The two instances quoted are extreme but, even more generally speaking, it is true that a Catholic psychoanalyst is regarded with equal suspicion by both his fellow-Catholics and his fellow-psychoanalysts. As though this were not enough, Dr. Görres teaches at a University in a country in which academic psychiatry, even today, is wary of psychoanalysis.

This apparent isolation, this state in between trenches, requires, as I said, courage, but it is the natural state of the seeker. Needless to say, it also makes for a position of strength. The alphabet game of bibliographies makes at times for strange bedfellows but rarely in literature do we find places in which "Bernard of Clairvaux—Bernfeld, Siegfried—Binswanger, Ludwig", or "Rahner, Karl—Rank, Otto—Reich, Wilhelm" find themselves bracketed. Behind this must be the same spirit of synthesis and discernment which prompted medieval thinkers to go out to the Arab and the Greek in their search for a deepened truth. Truth is a body with its own metabolic laws. To nourish it, requires discernment between the eatable and the non-eatable, the poisonous and the wholesome, that which can be assimilated and that which cannot. In the sureness with which a Saint Thomas plucked the fruits of antiquity to nourish the body of Christianity we have the perfect example of something like the natural instinct which enables an organism to distinguish between good and bad food. "None understand better the nature of real discernment than those who have entered into Unity". Commenting on this word of Tauler, Jacques and Raïssa Maritain say that "no-one enters into Unity save by Love." It is with these quotations that I should like to conclude my remarks, for this is precisely my impression of Dr. Görres' work—it represents a labour of discernment starting out from Unity.

Montreal, Christmas 1961

KARL STERN

INTRODUCTION

"PSYCHOANALYSIS" is a word which already has strong period associations, and if it is true that we are now witnessing the end of the modern world and entering upon a radically new period of history it may soon seem to belong to the past even more than it does already. And so it may be especially appropriate if this short introductory justification of psychoanalysis begins by repudiating the possible charge of antiquarianism.

There is no doubt that psychoanalysis in its original Freudian form has several serious weaknesses. It relies with unhesitating naivety on philosophical principles which, to put it as mildly as possible, are not in fact nearly as self-evident as they seemed to Freud. It relies on general psychological theories which were proved inadequate before his death; and its formulations are often unmistakably involved with the climate of thought of fifty years ago.

But it would be absurd, obviously, to dismiss psychoanalysis on account of these weaknesses as a matter of mere antiquarian interest—as dead as, say, Virchow's pathology. And not just absurd, but also rather barbarous. For once we have established that Freud's work really does contain original elements of lasting value, we can see plainly enough that there is no essential difference between dismissing Freud in this way and, for example, writing off Socrates or St. Augustine on the grounds of their antiquity. We may rank Freud lower than either, but his work, like theirs, is a classical beginning.

Something of the originality and value of Freud's work should appear in the course of the book, but we can make some preliminary suggestions here. Freud was the first to make a really intensive study of all aspects of the human individual. Before his time no doctor or psychologist or even priest had considered the whole sum of a person's individual experience either in such microscopic detail or with such painstaking exactitude. Moreover, Freud studied aspects of human behaviour which had received little attention of any kind. Psychoanalysis deals with behaviour which is apparently pointless, irrational and unaccountable. It investigates the inexhaustible field of distortions in the development of the personality, disturbances in instinctive behaviour, emotional inadequacy, self-deception, irrational attitudes, incongruous sensations, mental blockages, habitual misjudgement. Again, Freud's method of study was completely original. In the older psychiatry the patient was interrogated; and although this could produce valuable results, the answers were necessarily limited in scope. Freud discovered that one can find more by not directly looking for it. The analyst asks nothing, or as little as possible, and he lays down no boundaries of relevance beforehand. He directs the patient's attention inwards to the shifting movements of his own mind, and by this method he can discover more about the hidden, temporarily forgotten, and unconscious contents of mental and emotional life than he could by a series of definite questions.

Freud's work has a very wide relevance. It made an unintentional contribution to moral psychology by allowing the distinction between involuntary behaviour and mental illness, and moral degeneracy and culpability to be drawn with greater clarity and precision. With psychoanalysis more than with almost any other psychological method we can see man at once as an individual and in his relations with others, can see his personality both at a given point and over a long period of its development. And because psychoanalysis is concerned with the whole being of the individual, with the whole of his experience, it is naturally intolerant of any theoretical narrowness which tries to limit or distort its field of study. Psychoanalytical method is itself the rigorous critic of psychoanalytical theory.

If Freud's work does need careful and positive assessment, this is a favourable time for it. Scientists and moralists have had time to recover from the first rush of indignation which blinded them to any good in his work. Psychoanalysis has itself developed since the time when Freud's contemporaries and their immediate successors were so violent in their reaction. Our attitude today can thus come nearer Freud's own: "What I have discovered is neither a farthing nor a fortune, but a lump of ore containing an unknown quantity of precious metal."[1]

Like all branches of knowledge, psychoanalysis puts forward not only some certainly true and some demonstrably false propositions, but also some which may possibly be true and are in various degrees probable, yet can never be verified conclusively. Moreover, complete scientific objectivity is always a difficult, if not an impossible, ideal for an investigator to live up to. We can see today that a certain ambivalence in our attitude towards psychoanalysis is only reasonable.

But even now it seems particularly difficult to make an objective assessment of Freud's work. It still seems to be extraordinarily easy to be sucked down by either blind orthodoxy or violent and irrational hostility. Perhaps the most likely explanation for this is that Freud's work, for all its surface sobriety, has a fundamentally messianic character. It can be described without exaggeration as the last great secular prophecy of modern times, announcing a new road to salvation through the new gods Eros and Thanatos. This is not to deny that before Freud carnal love, at least, had taken on the attributes

[1] Sigmund Freud, *The Origins of Psychoanalysis. Letters to Wilhelm Fliess. Drafts and Notes: 1887–1902*, tr. E. Mosbacher and J. Strachey, London, 1954. Further references to Freud's works will omit his name.

of divinity and become an object of worship. We need only remember the extraordinary reaction to *The Sorrows of Werther*; the book described a new Passion, the suffering and sacrificial death of Eros's victim,[2] in language reminiscent of St. John's Gospel. But Freud's work provided, as it were, an elementary theology for the new religion. If for Boethius the end, perfection, and highest happiness of human life was the possession of God, "stabilis possessio summi et perfecti boni", towards whom all human desires consciously or unconsciously tended, for Freud the prime motive of all human actions is the achievement of sensual pleasure, "stabilis possessio delectationis sensualis". Man is condemned forever to worship the Golden Calf. His perpetual homage to the symbol of vitality and fertility[3] is really the expression of his own nature and the key to his self-knowledge. We have failed to understand psychoanalysis if we overlook its concealed claim to be a doctrine of salvation; we have misunderstood it if that is *all* we see.

But we must recall Freud's own balanced judgement once again. The lump of ore does contain precious metal; there is first the actual method, and then there is a mass of the kind of empirical evidence upon which any psychological theory must be based.

[2] Cf. H. Schöffler, *Deutscher Geist im 18 Jahrhundert*, Göttingen, 1956; H. Neumeister, "Säkularisierte Passion und Ketzerstolz", *Frankfurter Allgemeine Zeitung*, 28 Feb., 1957.

[3] The Golden Calf is a phallic god, not the symbol of wealth.

1

WHAT IS PSYCHOANALYSIS?

PSYCHOANALYSIS has three distinct meanings. It refers, first, to a particular method of psychological diagnosis and investigation which reveals psychic processes, relationships and structures not accessible to normal introspection.[1] Secondly, it is broadly used to describe a sum of psychological and psychophysical findings discovered both by the psychoanalytic and also partly by other methods of investigation. And thirdly, it refers to the system of theoretical psychology by means of which Freud attempted to interpret the phenomena which he had observed.

One of the fundamental difficulties of psychoanalysis, and indeed of all psychology, lies in drawing the boundary between the observed phenomena and their theoretical interpretation. If it is granted that every empirical science must begin by establishing facts, we are then faced with the problem of what constitutes an established fact in psychology. If the conjunction of sodium and chlorine in common salt is a fact, is, for example, a cheerful expression one too? Are narcissism and the Oedipus complex established facts? Or should we not rather reserve this status for the complex totalities of human be-

[1] "Psychoanalyse und Libidotheorie", *Gesammelte Werke*, London, 1940– , vol. 12, p. 211.

haviour from which such concepts are abstracted? In reality there can often be no sharp division between psychological observations and their interpretation; and the concepts employed in the interpretation are often rather vague. Trying to define these concepts can seem like trying to discern forms or faces or battles in the configurations of the clouds. The phenomena are naturally ambiguous and amorphous; psychology has chosen the most complex and mysterious of all objects of study, and it must in consequence be prepared to tolerate some ambiguity. If the exact scientist is over-suspicious of this ambiguity, then he has failed to realize that psychology, like the humanities, has its own kind of rigour.

In this study, therefore, we shall consider the discoveries of psychoanalysis rather than psychoanalytic theory. We do not, therefore, hold that psychotherapy needs no theory and can consist entirely of a mass of observations; nor do we intend to dismiss the orthodox Freudian theory out of hand, to deny that it contains both valuable and fruitful elements; nor, finally, do we believe that a philosophical analysis of existence can by itself make a sufficient theoretical basis for psychology.[2] If our experience is to increase our effective knowledge and wisdom, it will need both theoretical and general philosophical interpretation. But we shall emphasize the distinc-

[2] M. Boss, *Psychoanalyse und Daseinsanalytik*, Bern and Stuttgart, 1957.

tion between theory and findings here because in previous expositions it seems to have been obscured. There is a danger that we only see that part of the mental landscape which lies close to the theoretical railway-line; and this part has already been to some extent transformed by the effects of railway-construction. We are not far, at this point, from those pseudo-scientific Potemkin Tours of nature which are not genuine attempts to explain our experience, but rather triumphant progresses through intermittent and carefully fudged-up "illustrations" strategically situated along pre-existing routes of explanation. But certainly, as we shall show in what follows, the basic concepts of psychoanalysis have a definite value and basis in psychic reality.

Among German doctors and psychologists the weaknesses of psychoanalytic theory went a good way towards discrediting psychoanalytic method and the knowledge which it yielded. The situation was aggravated by the fact that the practitioners who employed the method often had the dilettante approach and were inexperienced. The importance of careful training was not realized. Thus disappointments were inevitable. But the inevitable reaction was not against theoretical exaggeration and dilettantism, but against psychoanalysis as such.[3] It was only very

[3] Only a few of the several hundred German doctors who now practise some form of psychotherapy have been properly trained in psychoanalytic method; and there are still no university facilities for such training in Germany.

gradually realized that it was essential for the therapist to be carefully trained, that the training should be partly theoretical and that the theory need not be completely orthodox.

But this does not quite mean that we want to throw the theory overboard in order to save the method. The ideal theory is in fact a system of co-ordinates which enables us to order our knowledge without distorting our evidence. It is legitimate to consider human life under one aspect at a time, provided that we do not lose the ability to see the other aspects. The fact that one is studying the development of human instinctual life does not entitle one to minimize, for example, the importance of human intellectual life. But provided we maintain a sense of proportion, we can gain valuable insight into the personality and its diseases from all the various theories and schools of depth psychology. Theories are like optical filters which separate out certain of the colours in a beam of light; and they only fail to help the progress of knowledge when we forget that they both select and refract.[4]

[4] On the theory of psychoanalysis see R. Dalbeiz, *Psychoanalytic Method and the Doctrine of Freud*, trans. T. F. Lindsay, London, 1941, 2 vols.; O. Fenichel, *The Psychoanalytic Theory of Neurosis*, New York, 1945; H. Hartmann, *Die Grundlagen der Psychoanalyse*, Leipzig, 1927; R. Heiss, *Allgemeine Tiefenpsychologie*, Bern and Stuttgart, 1956; P. Hofstätter, *Einführung in die Tiefenpsychologie*, Vienna, 1948; J. Nuttin, *Psychoanalysis and Personality*, trans. George Lamb, London, 1954; W. Toman, *Dynamik der Motive*, Frankfurt and Vienna, 1954.

Freud interpreted his observations according to certain philosophical principles: partly, as we should expect, according to the general principles of logic and scientific method, but partly also according to certain personal philosophical beliefs. Freud's world-view can be verified neither by the evidence produced by psychoanalysis itself, nor by any other empirical evidence, nor can its compelling superiority over other philosophical systems be demonstrated by abstract reasoning.[5] Though, therefore, we should be free to consider psychoanalysis as a world-view, it will be just as legitimate, and more helpful, to try to separate out those of its philosophical presuppositions which can be shown to be arbitrary or false.

Psychoanalysis is first and foremost a therapeutic method.[6] And it is precisely to its therapeutic character that it owes its success as a method of psychological investigation, even if

[5] As a young student Freud attended Franz von Brentano's philosophical lectures and seminars for several years. Although Brentano was an important teacher and drew some distinguished pupils to Vienna (among them Edmund Husserl, Alexander Pfänder and Carl Stumpf), there is no evidence that he had any influence on Freud's thought. Freud acknowledged that the physiologist Brücke had the most important single influence on his work (cf. E. Jones, *Sigmund Freud, Life and Work*, vol. 1, London, 1953, pp. 40ff.); he was responsible for Freud's lasting habit of thinking with analogies of physical models.

[6] This study will not contain a detailed account of psychoanalysis as a therapeutic and psychagogic method (i.e., method of restoring the patient's confidence in himself), and its efficacy; this will form the subject of a further investigation.

the two ends of healing and furthering scientific knowledge do sometimes conflict with each other. For few men would be prepared to reveal their most intimate thoughts and feelings purely and simply to further scientific knowledge; it is the hope of relief from illness and suffering which leads people to help science and themselves together.

PSYCHOANALYSIS AS A METHOD OF PSYCHOLOGICAL RESEARCH[7]

The chief aims of this study will be to try to describe the most important experiences, facts and relationships which psychoanalysis reveals. That is, it will describe those basic phenomena and structures which come under the pathology of personality and which can be most easily revealed by means of psychoanalysis; neurotic pathological symptoms in the narrower sense are not described, and reference can be made to any textbook of psychopathology.

We shall only deal with the really indisputable knowledge which has so far been yielded by psychoanalytic method, even though there is also a large body of important psychological knowledge which is either more or less certain, or which psychoanalysis indicates but cannot itself sufficiently explain, and which can be more

[7] E. Glover, "Forschungsmethoden in der Psychoanalyse," *Psyche*, 6 (1952–3); H. Stierlin, "Verstehen und wissenschaftliche Theoriebildung in der Psychoanalyse", *Psyche*, 6 (1952–3); see also p. 4, *n*. 4.

successfully investigated by other methods and hypotheses not within the scope of this book.

There would be some advantages in giving an exposition of psychoanalytic method and the knowledge it yields as they both stand at the moment without particular reference to Freud. But the disadvantages seem greater. For one thing, Freud himself gives accounts of both the fundamental phenomena of neurosis and the therapeutic method which would be difficult to rival in accuracy and vividness. For another, no alternative has been found to the Freudian theoretical framework; nor have the defensible elements of his system been definitively separated from the rest and incorporated in the body of established medical and psychological knowledge. And it is in any case a good thing to redress the balance insofar as progress in psychotherapy has tended to be at the expense either of denying the value of Freud's achievement or of failing to make use of it to the full. Thus we shall examine the results of psychoanalysis as Freud himself described them, and try to see the psychological realities to which his theories correspond, even when, taken in their literal sense, they may seem to obscure more than they illumine.

As early as 1946, V. E. von Gebsattel pointed out the need for some such attempt.[8] He wrote:

[8] "Sigmund Freud und die Seelenheilkunde der Gegenwart", *Medizinische Klinik*, 1946, p. 391.

"However pressing the need for a revision of Freud's theoretical and anthropological interpretation of his discoveries may be, it is equally important to arouse greater confidence in the value of the discoveries themselves. It is, of course, only to be expected that observation and interpretation will be more closely interwoven in psychology than, for example, in neurology, and it is difficult to see where the boundary between the two does in fact lie. With Freud's work the difficulty is to see the trees for the wood, the empirical observations for the total system of interpretation. The principles of this system, the mechanistic assumptions and the anthropological ideas, obscure empirical knowledge of the greatest importance. We may or may not agree with Freud's account of the sexual aetiology of neurosis, or with his doctrines of the unconscious, of the repression of drives and emotions, of transference and repetition-compulsion, of infantile sexuality, the super-ego and the id, the Oedipus complex, anal eroticism, castration anxiety and the rest. But whatever their apparent philosophical implications, Freud's formulations are undeniably based on valuable empirical evidence. Freud's intuitive power is likewise undeniable, whatever the weaknesses in his reasoning. In general, it is fair to say that a great many of his discoveries still need to be discovered."

If, partly for this reason, we shall restrict ourselves to the Freudian form of psychoanalysis, the restriction should not be taken to imply that other methods are worthless or unimportant. It is clear, for example, that many of C. G. Jung's valuable discoveries and insights would not have been so accessible to the Freudian method as they were to his own. There are grounds for an exclusively psychoanalytical approach to research and therapy insofar as some unity of method and principle is necessary for teaching purposes, to organic observations and to check mistakes. But there are no grounds whatsoever for demanding exclusive and absolute adherence to psychoanalytic orthodoxy. Even if, as Freud always claimed, the method were self-evidently convincing, there would still remain the need for some kind of external check on omission and distortion. And we may also doubt whether Freud's claim is justified. A scientific research method can only fulfil its function of furthering sure and systematic knowledge if its basic assumptions are both explicit and defensible. With psychoanalysis this is often not the case. There are times when we feel inclined to ask whether the assumptions do not already contain the discoveries which the empirical investigations are supposed to have made. And it is in fact a standard criticism that psychoanalysis merely digs up the old bones which it buried itself, though the matter is not as simple as that. Some of the confusion may be due to the fact that psychoanalysis serves the two masters of therapy and research at the same time.

The two chief kinds of emphasis in psychotherapy today were conveniently anticipated in the practice of Freud himself. At first Freud gave long theoretical explanations and interpretations of his procedure to his patients.[9] (In a letter to Fliess he tells him that he is feeling hoarse in the evening after talking for eleven hours!) But later he explained less and encouraged the patient to rely more on himself. Perhaps because it cannot be traced in his records of case-histories, which only go up to 1915,[10] this change of emphasis away from suggestion has not become common knowledge.[11] In the first kind of modern therapy, exemplified by Carl Landauer's passive technique,[12] and by Carl Rogers' non-directive psychotherapy,[13] and by a variation of Schultz-Hencke's procedure which he himself describes,[14]

[9] "A Case of Hysteria", in *Complete Psychological Works of Sigmund Freud* (Standard Edition) tr. and ed. James Strachey and others, London, 1953– , vol. 7, p. 7.

[10] From the "History of an Infantile Neurosis"; in *Works*, vol. 17, p. 145.

[11] There was a corresponding change of emphasis, also neglected by some psychotherapists, away from the analysis of the id and of instinctual drives to analysis of the structure of the ego and of repression. This appears in the later papers on technique, e.g., "Remembering, Repeating and Working Through," in *Works*, vol. 12, p. 145.

[12] "Passive Technik," *Int. Zschr. f. Psa.*, 10 (1924).

[13] *Client-Centred Therapy*, Boston, 1951.

[14] H. Schultz-Hencke, *Lehrbuch der analytischen Psychotherapie*, Stuttgart, 1951, pp. 224ff; cf. also "Die technischen

the psychiatrist intervenes as little as possible. Interpretations are only rarely and very carefully offered, and effective suggestion by the analyst is completely avoided. The patient must come to understand himself by his own efforts, apart from any psychological theory. The passive approach originally answered the needs of doctors investigating the little-known chronic psychosomatic illnesses and looking for a method of research which would yield reliable psychological knowledge without risk of harming the patient. The passive approach satisfied these requirements, and had in addition begun to prove its independent therapeutic power. It certainly takes time, but then, quick cures for neurosis or chronic psychosomatic illness are out of the question anyway. One cannot hope to straighten out the distorted growth of thirty or forty years, or even longer, in a matter of a few hours. There are some relatively mild neuroses which can sometimes be rapidly treated by strong suggestive therapy or some other non-analytical method. And often short-term psychological treatment can do much for severe crises, for neuroses which have reached a particularly important stage in their development. But whenever neurosis has deep roots in the structure of the personality or origins in childhood; whenever, that is, the whole personality must be, as

---

Schriften Freuds und die Weiterentwicklungen der psychoanalytischen Behandlungstechnik", *Zschr. Psychosom. Med.*, 2, (1955–6).

it were, transposed into a different key, then any lasting cure depends on extended treatment.

Opposed to these passive forms of analysis, we find Stekel's active analysis[15] and the method followed by Jung, in both of which interpretation and direction by the analyst play a much more important part. It is difficult to generalize about the relative efficacy of the two kinds of method. In certain cases it can be dangerous for the therapist not to intervene.[16] For example, in patients with depressive tendencies, non-intervention can exaggerate anxiety and guilt and feelings of hostility towards treatment until they become almost intolerable. But one can usually meet this danger without sacrificing the advantages of the passive method. As a rule these advantages are considerable, therapeutically; and from the point of view of research they are overwhelming. Of course it goes without saying that the psychoanalyst will always exert *some* influence on the patient, as in any relationship between two people, but so long as this is recognized, it need have no distorting effect.

The value of psychoanalysis as a method of diagnosis and research thus depends largely on the absence of unproved assumptions and suggestive distortion. It is now open to us to con-

[15] W. Stekel, *The Interpretation of Dreams*, trans. Eden and Cedar Paul, London, 1950 (2); *Technique of Analytical Psychotherapy*, trans. Eden and Cedar Paul, New York, 1943, 2 vols.

[16] F. Riemann, "Über neurosenspezifische Anwendung der psychoanalytischen Technik," *Psyche*, 6 (1952–3).

sider the results which would follow from offering the neurotic concrete suggestions and theoretical interpretations, and allowing him to reveal himself within this framework. If such a procedure were followed very carefully, it could produce valuable scientific results.[17] But it seems preferable on the whole to concentrate in what follows on what can be learnt about neurosis by the form of psychoanalytical method which avoids all suggestion. In the course of the exposition we shall see how far one can call such a procedure psychoanalytical at all. It remains to bear in mind, at this stage, that we are not offering an historical interpretation of Freud, but merely trying to see what useful knowledge he discovered; trying to find what his method can help us to see, not discussing what he himself saw.

Free Association

Freud laid down certain definite canons of theoretical orthodoxy to which, in his view, the genuine psychoanalyst must subscribe. These postulates and doctrines were for Freud at once the chief constituents of psychoanalysis, the basis of its theory and the canons of its orthodoxy: unconscious psychic processes, repression and resistance, the particular importance of sexuality, and the Oedipus complex.[18] But it is a curious

[17] Cf. "Constructions in Analysis," *Collected Papers*, vol. 5, ed. James Strachey, London, 1950, pp. 364ff.

[18] "Psychoanalyse und Libidotheorie," *Werke*, London, 1940, vol. 13, p. 225.

fact that he pronounced no dogma to guide the actual practice of the psychoanalytic method. His own practice was not completely consistent and reflected various aims, some of which we shall now try to distinguish.

We can best approach the task of reducing psychoanalytic method to its constituent elements by seeing it as a complex process determined by various factors which can be separately described. In the first place, Freud made his patients undertake to abstain from all conscious reflection; they were to shut out all other mental activity, sink below the surface of consciousness and peacefully follow their spontaneous train of thought. They had to report this to the analyst even if there seemed to be objections, even if the thoughts seemed, for example, too unpleasant, senseless, trivial or incongruous.[19]

But we cannot just imagine a solitary person given over to his spontaneous train of thought and say that this is an element of psychoanalytic method. Even when conscious reflection is cut down to a minimum the presence of a second person makes an important difference to the form of the train of thought; without in any way directly shaping it through hints or questions, the second person exerts a definite influence. He acts like the charge at the centre of a magnetic field. And if the second person does actively intervene to interpret what he hears, if

[19] "Kurzer Abriss der Psychoanalyse," *Werke*, vol. 13, p. 410.

he stresses some things and passes over others, then the procedure becomes so complicated and indeterminate that the sort of generalization we are attempting here becomes almost impossible. But we shall therefore leave this last objection aside for the time being, and take it as generally agreed that the analytic method involves free association and reflection in the presence of a second person who does not intervene but receives as complete a report as possible of the patient's train of thought.[20] Either the patient himself can choose some point of departure for his train of thought, or the analyst can suggest one. He may ask the patient what occurs to him when he considers such and such an event—some disappointment, dream, or detail of a dream; or when he considers his behaviour in a certain situation or towards certain people, his mother or father or the analyst himself. The patient is not to take any of these starting-points as a theme for conscious reflection, but merely to wait passively and see what psychic activity they stimulate. The analyst binds himself to complete discretion. He undertakes not to abuse his patient's trust by word or deed, by withdrawing his goodwill towards him, or by making unfavourable judgements on what he hears.

This simple method of free association, which at first strikes the patient as pointless, was Freud's most valuable and lasting achievement.

[20] *Introductory Lectures on Psychoanalysis*, trans. Joan Rivière, London, 1949, pp. 242–3.

It has been the basis of almost all the progress made up to now by all schools of depth psychology, Freudian or otherwise.

The discovery of the method was accidental. Before qualifying, Freud had been a friend of the Viennese doctor and research worker, Josef Breuer, and had heard from him the details of an important case which he had successfully treated in the 1880's. Breuer's patient, Anna O., who suffered from nervous hysteria accompanied by dramatic symptoms, had often uttered series of unconnected words during states of partial consciousness. Breuer hypnotized her and told her to elaborate on these words. She then remembered certain scenes which seemed to be connected with the symptoms of her hysteria. For a long period she had been unable to drink, even when extremely thirsty; and under hypnosis she recalled with disgust and anger an experience which had taken place before the emergence of this symptom. As a young girl she had had an English governess whom she had disliked. One day she went into the governess's room and saw her dog drinking out of a tumbler. She suppressed her disgust and anger at the time, and forgot the scene, but from then on she was unable to drink. After her recovery from what proved to be a cathartic hypnosis, the symptom disappeared.[21] It has since become clear that

[21] "Studies on Hysteria," *Works*, vol. 2, 21 ff. (Case (1), Fräulein Anna O.). After her cure, although it was incomplete, Anna O. played an important part in the development

Breuer's case was an illustration of one of the fundamental principles of psychotherapy: hysterical symptoms can originate in a forgotten experience which had a powerful emotional effect at the time, and an emotionally charged recollection and mental re-enactment of the experience can remove the symptoms it produced.

Freud was greatly impressed by Breuer's account of Anna O.'s case and immediately began to experiment on the same lines. In 1889 he travelled to Nancy to perfect his hypnotic technique under the famous suggestion therapist Bernheim. But Bernheim himself admitted the limitations of hypnotic therapy, and Freud came to rely more and more on Breuer's so-called "cathartic method".[22] The disadvantage of catharsis was that it depended on hypnosis, which was not successful with all patients. Freud overcame this by developing a special suggestive technique, the "pressing procedure". He pressed the patient's brow with his hands and assured him that some image or word would occur to him which was connected with the traumatic origin of his symptom.[23] By this means he could bridge the gap between the symptom

---

of social welfare organization in Europe. (See E. Jones, *Sigmund Freud, Life and Work,* vol. 1, p. 245.) In 1955 a German stamp was issued in her honour.

[22] "The Mechanism of Hysterical Phenomena", *Collected Papers,* vol. 1, trans. Joan Rivière, London, New York and Vienna, 1924, p. 24.

[23] "Psychotherapy of Hysteria", *Works,* vol. 2, pp. 267ff.

and the forgotten trauma. Once five apparently unrelated words occurred to a patient. Freud describes what happened in his treatise "On the Psychotherapy of Hysteria"[24]:

> When I asked the lady whether she had seen anything or had any recollection under the pressure of my hand, she replied: "Neither the one nor the other, but a word has suddenly occurred to me." "A single word?" "Yes, but it sounds too silly." "Say it, all the same." "Concierge." "Nothing else?" "No." I pressed a second time and once more an isolated word shot through her mind: "Nightgown". I saw now that this was a new method of answering, and by pressing repeatedly I brought out what seemed to be a meaningless sequence of words: "Concierge"—"nightgown"—"bed"—"town" "farm-cart". "What does all this mean?" I asked. She reflected for a moment and the following thought occurred to her: "It must be the story that has just come into my head. When I was ten years old and my elder sister was twelve, she went raving mad one night and had to be taken into town on a farm-cart. I remember perfectly that it was the concierge who overpowered her and afterwards went with her to the asylum as well." We pursued this method of investigation and our oracle produced another series of words which, though we were not able to interpret all of

[24] *Works*, vol. 2, pp. 275–6.

them, made it possible to continue this story and lead on from it to another one. Soon, moreover, the meaning of this reminiscence became clear. Her sister's illness had made such a deep impression on her because the two of them shared a secret; they slept in one room and on a particular night they had both been subjected to sexual assaults by a certain man. The mention of this sexual trauma in the patient's childhood revealed not only the origin of her first obsessions but also the trauma which subsequently produced the pathogenic effects.

The peculiarity of this case lay only in the emergence of isolated key-words which we had to work into sentences; for the appearance of disconnectedness and irrelevance which characterized the words emitted in this oracular fashion applies equally to the complete ideas and scenes which are normally produced under pressure. When these are followed up, it invariably turns out that the apparently disconnected reminiscences are closely linked in thought and that they lead quite straight to the pathogenic factor we are looking for.

The next stage in the development of psychoanalytic method came when Freud gave up his suggestion technique and the concentration on the symptom as the starting-point for the spontaneous thoughts:

> . . . since the date of the Studies psychoanalytic technique has been completely revolutionized. At that time the work of analysis started out from the symptoms, and aimed at clearing them up one after the other. Since then I have abandoned that technique because I found it totally inadequate for dealing with the finer structures of a neurosis. I now let the patient himself choose the subject of the day's work, and in that way I start out from whatever surface his unconscious happens to be presenting to his notice at the moment.[25]

Thus we can see how free association depended at first on the model of the cathartic method and its assumptions: the spontaneous thoughts which occurred to the patient, like his symptoms, were determined by suppressed experiences or "strangulated affects",[26] and "subconscious complexes of ideas".[27] The analyst gathers thoughts as clues leading to traumas.

Once it was realized that the spontaneous thought was related to the trauma, it was natural to suppose that it also stood in other, non-traumatic, psychological relationships. And once this step had been taken, psychoanalysis was emancipated from Breuer's catharsis. Free association no longer depended entirely on traumas; it

[25] "A Case of Hysteria", *Works*, vol. 7, p. 12.

[26] "The Mechanism of Hysterical Phenomena", *Works*, vol. 2, p. 17.

[27] "Studies on Hysteria", *Works*, vol. 2, p. 69*n*. (Case (2) Frau Emmy von N.)

appeared as the key to all psychic life, past, present and to come. The cathartic investigation of traumas became the psychoanalytic method of free association.

This was much more than a mere change of technique. Psychoanalytic method had developed from an instrument for diagnosing and treating a particular form of neurosis into a completely unprecedented means of self-knowledge and self-adjustment.

It is true there are ancient and well-tried ways to self-knowledge which in many respects go further and deeper than psychoanalysis, restricted as it is to a specific sphere of human life; and not all people respond equally to psychoanalysis. But psychoanalysis nevertheless represents a very great advance.

The patient will not usually begin his treatment with much precise knowledge of psychoanalysis. The analyst starts by not only giving him permission but also requesting him to say anything that enters his mind. This means that the doctor[28] is prepared to hear the whole

[28] Insofar as the psychoanalyst's job is to heal the mentally —and often, in consequence, the physically—sick, he is a doctor, despite the fact that his competence is more psychological than medical in the normal sense. Thus we shall sometimes substitute "doctor" for "analyst" or "psychotherapist" in what follows. But we should also bear in mind this statement of Freud's: "Psychoanalysis falls under the head of psychology; not of medical psychology in the old sense, nor of the psychology of morbid processes, but simply of psychology." ("Postscript to a Discussion on Lay Analysis", *Collected Papers*, vol. 5, p. 251.)

life history of the patient, and everything that occurs to him, in the minutest detail. And it also means that the patient has already been accorded a degree of respect for his person and condition which he has probably never encountered before. This respect allows him to enter into a new kind of relationship both with himself and with his doctor. Because the doctor has undertaken to hear him out there already seems to be some hope.

At this point a difficulty arises which must be carefully dealt with. By recommending the patient to note carefully, and faithfully report, his train of thought, however startling or painfully shocking its contents may be, the doctor necessarily goes beyond his purely professional competence, giving the patient definite grounds for conscientious objection. The doctor cannot consider this part of his treatment purely and simply under the aspect of its therapeutic efficacy. He must be clear that he is making a moral judgement which is by no means self-evident; he must therefore exercise the greatest discretion, particularly as no authority in matters of conscience has been committed him.[29] And he must be prepared to explain the moral legitimacy of his procedure, to explain to the patient that the analytic method is not condoning what it reveals simply because what may later be judged must

[29] For a careful ethical analysis and justification of "abreaction", see Nuttin, *Psychoanalysis and Personality*, pp. 148ff.

first be revealed, or because motives for some later judgement may themselves be examined in the light of what is revealed.

Not only does the doctor promise the patient freedom from danger or practical harm as a consequence of what he reveals, but he can also promise him a certain freedom from anxiety. The neurotic tends to have groundless feelings of guilt, because he is often unable to distinguish between spontaneous pre-personal psychic events and a responsible personal attitude towards them, between temptation and guilt, between *sentire* and *consentire*; he confuses the good man with the unspontaneous man. And it is a new and liberating experience for him to be able to recognize, for example, malicious or egotistical impulses and yet to realize that they do not mean that he is a hopelessly malicious or egotistical man or bound to become one. The doctor creates a situation in which the patient's lost primitive trust in the goodwill of his fellow men can be revived.

The experience is liberating, but it is also in a sense disturbing. The patient finds that in this situation his customary mode of behaviour is inappropriate. The transition to a new mode is assisted by the external arrangements for psychoanalysis. The patient lies on a couch and the analyst sits beside or behind the end where the patient's head lies. This makes it easier for the patient to free himself from habitual attitudes which would determine his behaviour in conventional conversations. He is less tempted to modify what he says according to the impression it makes on the analyst, to watch for signs of approval or disapproval, and so more likely to report his train of thought accurately. It can seem to the patient as though he were lying in the state between dream and reality where no thought or act is really binding or fully deliberate; and this feeling can help to remove some of the inhibitions which are part of complete consciousness. But any chance of successful treatment depends on the absolute truthfulness of the patient. It is perhaps only rarely that we can form real-life relationships in which one person can unburden himself without fear of injuring the other, or hearing his moralizing, or his excuses, or bearing his ambiguous silence; rarely that a man can find so detached an audience for his intimacies, a confidant as free from any suspicion of ulterior motives, as the psychotherapist.

One of the fundamental principles of psychoanalysis is that the analyst offers no advice or directions on his patients' future conduct. The patient must redevelop his own responsibility and independence after their growth has been checked or distorted by neurosis. The neurotic fluctuates between falsely trusting childish obedience and falsely independent childish rebellion; the analyst refuses to encourage the tendency of the neurotic to see him either as an all-wise or as a tyrannical father. He does, however, insist on certain rules or conditions of treatment. The patient must try to give exact and truthful information about his psychic life; during analysis he must try so far as possible to avoid taking important decisions on marriage or divorce or change of occupation; he must not discuss his problems or his treatment with others while the analysis is still in progress; he must abstain from all neurotic compensating activity.[30] The patient must continue to do his normal work or some other work—his psychological condition must not become his sole preoccupation; and he must pay for the cost of the treatment out of his own income. These rules are in fact no more than maxims from past experience of successful analyses; and the analyst will always draw the patient's attention to their infringement and try to explain why their observance is necessary.

Free association affects the patient in two distinct ways. It enables him to attain the passive state of mind which otherwise eludes him; and at the same time it demands from him constant and healthy self-discipline. A great deal of ill-temper, vanity, over-sensitiveness, self-indulgence and general fear and egoism have to be overcome in order for the truth to be seen and kept in sight. Psychoanalysis is a school of moral courage and will-power; some fail.

Once the patient has grasped what his proper

[30] For Freud's conception of the "abstinence rule" see "Lines of Advance in Psychoanalytic Therapy," *Works*, vol. 17, p. 157.

relation to the analyst should be he will gradually take over more and more of the initiative. Alternatively, he may take the initiative from the beginning and immediately pour out the details of his present difficulties and problems. These will become gradually tinged with memories and anxiety, or optimistic hopes and sudden, unconnected thoughts[31] will erupt into the flow of speech. When he begins to trust the analyst the patient will be able to relinquish conscious control over his train of thought. But as soon as anything too strange or painful occurs to him, he will begin to comment on it. There is a fluctuation between half dreamlike immersion in the spontaneous train of thought, and its conscious consideration from outside; or, as you might say, a dialogue ensues between nature and person.

The course taken by the analysis will depend not only on the extent to which the rules are observed and on the nature of the particular case, but also on the motives for which analysis is undertaken. A man may be a suffering neurotic, he may think that neurosis is fashionable, or he may have been consigned to the analyst as a commercial unit due for overhaul. He may suspect the existence of childhood traumas or of

[31] Not just spontaneously occurring thoughts of any kind but "the involuntary thoughts (not infrequently regarded as disturbing elements and therefore ordinarily pushed aside) which so often break across the continuity of a consecutive narrative." ("Psychoanalytic Procedure," *Works*, vol. 7, p. 251.)

an inferiority complex, expect to recognize his previous mistaken decisions, or to contemplate "archetypes". Thus in at least some cases the therapist will need to correct exaggerated general expectations about the efficacy of analysis or distorted ideas of its implications, and we must bear in mind that the information which he will give will have some effect on the course of treatment. But usually it is enough if the doctor makes it clear to the patient that provided certain rules are followed, a picture of his personality will emerge from the details of his train of thought; that certain aspects of his personality will be related to his illness and its symptoms; and that by clearly perceiving and reporting his train of thought without himself trying to form a complete picture, the patient can expect a good deal of relief from the tension, inhibitions and anxiety from which he has been suffering.

The analyst directs the attention of the patient towards what he is experiencing and how, rather than why, he is experiencing it. While, naturally, no patient will completely ignore the question of the origin and nature of his condition, it is neither the first nor often the most important object of psychoanalysis to establish the exact structural and genetic form of a neurosis. Often a clear perception of the contents of the train of thought is a sufficient stimulus for the patient to begin to reach the understanding of his own development which can cure his illness.

For a long time the analyst will remain no more than a passive observer; his task is not to suggest possible interpretations of what he hears, but to make certain that what he hears is a clear and accurate account of the facts.

We have tried to describe the conditions for successful psychoanalytical therapy, not the factors which can diminish the scientific value of observations made in the course of treatment. But it is worth emphasizing that regardless of the great importance which Freud attached to sexual problems, the atmosphere of his own analyses always remained exceptionally healthy and indeed antiseptic. Freud himself must have possessed to an extraordinary degree the two attributes of the ideal doctor, complete objectivity and positive goodwill; and he succeeded in imparting something of these personal qualities to the method which he introduced. Thus psychoanalysis belongs to the best medical traditions. There is nothing of the inquisitorial scientist about the analyst. He is as frank and receptive towards the patient as the patient must learn to be towards himself. Both must wait patiently until unconscious and hidden psychic life begins to speak for itself.

This approach rests on the assumption that all psychic disorder and disturbance takes place within the framework of a pre-existing and partly surviving natural order. And the analyst holds that this natural order, as perhaps in normal life, can come to prevail more easily if there is room for a certain over-expansiveness of good intention. And it is good to record that academic psychology supports this assumption, even if it does not recognize the antiquity of its origin. Metzger writes:

> Among the various kinds of process, there are some which independently observe their own particular order. There is no tendency for this order to disintegrate; and in certain conditions—not necessarily exceptionally or only temporarily—a higher degree of order can be independently reached. Order can in certain conditions arise without any external intervention; and under the same conditions it can maintain itself independently of the power of some determinate mechanism. It can change itself in response to changed conditions —and indeed must, if it is to maintain itself without the help of rigid mechanistic switchboards, or of vitalist traffic-police. Finally, because of the absence of protective mechanisms the order can be more easily disturbed, but it can restore itself completely after the disturbance. And it is here that its enormous superiority over externally imposed order lies: the same forces and conditions account for its origin, its continuance, its adjustment to changed circumstances, and its recovery after a disturbance.[32]

[32] W. Metzger, *Psychologie, Die Entwicklung ihrer Grundannahmen seit der Einführung des Experiments* (Darmstadt, 1954 (2)), p. 209.

2

THE DIMENSIONS OF ANALYSIS

DEPTH psychology views its subject-matter in three different ways; psychoanalysis can mean the analysis of psychic life under any of three different aspects. We can consider psychic (i.e., mental and emotional) and psychological phenomena, psychic structures, and the origin and course of development of these phenomena and structures.

ANALYSIS OF THE PHENOMENA OF EXPERIENCE AND BEHAVIOUR

As the first sense of psychoanalysis, this deals with the changes in and relations between those phenomena which lie below our relatively conscious experience.

It is important to be clear at the outset about the ambiguity of the ideas of surface and depth in this context. With neurotic people, what occurs in the depths of the unconscious is often of supreme importance, and must be carefully brought to the surface by psychotherapy. With them, "the reason we can fathom is no true reason, the meaning we can grasp, no true meaning, the name we can name, no true name."[1] But

[1] *Tao-Te-King,* trans. Richard Wilhelm, Jena, 1911, p. 3. Wilhelm translates "Tao" as "meaning".

in other cases a man's conscious experience can influence his whole being so deeply that his unconscious experience appears relatively unimportant by comparison. Completely conscious, and so in one sense superficial, decisions can determine the whole course of a person's life. Thus "depth" in depth psychology may refer to no more than the comparative remoteness of the unconscious, and it certainly does not imply that unconscious is in some way more profoundly important than conscious life. This is one of the doctrines of romantic pseudo-mysticism, and it has no place in scientific psychology.

This first kind of analysis tries to establish the complete content of psychic experience as it appears to the investigator in the first instance. The phenomena are approached from two points of view. First, an attempt is made to establish the complete psychic context of experience and behaviour, and, second, to establish the previous course of development of the experience and behaviour in this context. We try to hear, as it were, both the harmonies and discords which accompany the melody of experience, and of which we are at first unaware, and the whole sequence of the melody and its harmony. What F. Sander has termed *Aktualgenese*—that is, the growth from the embryonic stage to completion of actualized or apparent organization in psychic life—also falls into this category insofar as it can be observed through psychoanalysis.[2]

[2] Freud refers to "images *in statu nascendi* before they can

Only a small part of the enormous complexity of psychic life is accessible to conscious reflection. Much only becomes visible when critical attention shifts away. Phenomena of this kind are often so difficult to see that they can legitimately be called unconscious even though they can clearly be experienced as the lasting psychic structures and the less stable structural dispositions cannot be. When Freud talks of unconscious ideas, tendencies and so on, his usage is not always consistent. Sometimes he is referring to what we called the harmony of the melody of conscious experience, but sometimes to psychic structures—that is, to the basic determinants of experience as distinct from its direct content. And lastly but not less often he is referring to hypothetical psychic processes which cannot be said to be in any way experienced—"processes occurring outside consciousness—they may be presumed but they cannot be proved by any clinical psychological procedure"[3]—perceptions, estimations and expectations, moods, desires and emotions often tone our experience in a diffuse, intangible way; but they are extremely difficult to consider in abstraction from their context. We recognize them as the man does who can hear the composite sound of a symphony but is unable to distinguish its constituent parts.

---

be noticed by consciousness". ("Formulations on the Two Principles of Mental Functioning", *Works*, vol. 12, p. 223.)

[3] "The Defence Neuro-Psychoses", *Collected Papers*, vol. 1, p. 67.

There are all kinds of atmospheric feelings which are recognizable enough but still elusive: intuitions, premonitions, indeterminate fears and desires. When we meet an old friend, we know at once, without consciously formulating the knowledge to ourselves, his origins, occupation, character, attitude towards us; what pleases, hurts and irritates him. All this knowledge is implicit in our feelings at the moment of meeting and determines our behaviour from then onwards. We can see this just by comparing a meeting with someone we know well with a meeting with a stranger. In that case there will also be more or less unformulated feelings and attitudes, but they will be quite different ones. We encounter every situation with expectations and attitudes of which we become conscious only when disappointment, for example, shows them to be false.[4]

These implicit feelings are especially important in valuing and assessing. Each person or thing which we encounter appears to have good and bad features which we often unconsciously register. Sometimes we know the worth of an object by intuition, and succumb to its attraction even when our conscious mind rejects it. Our experience and behaviour are highly stratified and full of contradictions about which we may know

[4] Cf. Max Scheler's remarks on "unconscious spheres of inner perception" in *Der Formalismus in der Ethik und die materielle Wertethik, Gesammelte Werke*, vol. 2, Bern, 1954, p. 402.

little or nothing. This unconscious ambivalence of experience was Freud's first, and one of his most important, theses.[5] Objects of human desire must always have two sides. When such an object is perceived and desired, we can suppose that at the same time the shadow side of the object either splits conscious experience or gives a negative tone to the semi-conscious experience we have just referred to. And the subject can, furthermore, draw attention towards or away from this process itself.

Embryo psychological tendencies which, if given an uncontrolled course of development, would cause conflict both within and with the outside world, are among the most important of Freud's "unconscious ideas". We can scarcely perceive these tendencies; they are like faint, disturbing, only intermittently audible drum-beats in a work for full orchestra. But they can set the rhythm of the whole; they can cause excitement, tension, abnormal behaviour and physical symptoms. Freud described them in his essay "Screen-Memories".[6] (The screen-memory he uses as illustration is one of his own discovered in self-analysis.)

Thus depth-psychology in this first sense

[5] The thesis was put forward in the first of the treatises on the psychology of neurosis, "A Case of Successful Treatment by Hypnotism", *Collected Papers,* vol. 5, p. 33.

[6] *Collected Papers,* vol. 5, pp. 47ff. This essay is important because it contains a clearer account of the central concept of "unconscious fantasy" than can be found in any of the later writings.

chiefly comprises the careful illumination of hidden experience and of hidden tendencies in semi-voluntary behaviour. And we have also seen that terms like "unconscious idea" refer with Freud to an area of experience which cannot strictly be called unconscious without some imprecision and over-simplification.

Insofar as the conscious ideas imply unconscious cognition they will arouse the suspicions of the phenomenologist. Cognition would necessarily seem to require consciousness, at least of the automatic kind which accompanies all experience,[7] or of the kind which attends sensing or intuition.[8] But there is nevertheless a legitimate sense in which the experience to which Freud was referring can be called unconscious, or at least preconscious,[9] for the experiences are unrelated to the subject's self-consciousness; even when the psychoanalyst does not mean precisely this, the patient usually understands his references to unconscious impressions, feelings, desires and so on to be to something which has actually been experienced, but without the concomitant knowledge that it was being experienced.

[7] ". . . in der Weise des unbemerkten, ungewussten 'schlichten Erlebens'." (P. Lersch, *Aufbau der Person*, Munich, 1954 (6), p. 530.)

[8] On the "Feinbewussten", see D. Feuling, *Des Leben der Seele*, Salzburg, 1940, p. 86.

[9] The terminological distinction between consciousness and experience has also been adopted in phenomenological psychology. See Lersch, *Aufbau*.

Whatever its ambiguities, the doctrine of the unconscious idea has been a stimulus to research into the remoter areas of psychic life. Freud himself illustrated the concept with observations which could hardly be included within its logical limits. He frequently emphasized in later years that the doctrine was in no sense conclusive or definitive. He admitted the possibility that the phenomena might eventually be expressed as material compounds in a chemical formula. Or equally, that unconscious ideas might make up a distinct psychic species requiring their own specific form of description. The view to which he inclined in the meantime was that unconscious and conscious reality were both of essentially the same kind; they both consisted of streams of impressions, impulses and feelings. The basic principle of his thought was that psychic reality can only be considered in terms of impressions and perceptions; and reality as a whole consisted either of such impressions or of matter. Freud had no psychology of unconscious psychic life, but rather, as it were, a psychology of the consciousness of the unconscious.

There seems to be a psychic tendency towards the definite verbal and conceptual formulation of semi-conscious experience; but apart from this, actual psychotherapy can afford to neglect many of the psychic processes which, according to Freud, remain completely unconscious in the sense that they are not experienced. But even though we agree with Freud that such events are purely hypothetical, even though their existence "cannot be demonstrated by any clinical psychological procedure",[10] the hypothesis is an important part of psychoanalytical theory. We shall therefore now turn to consider whether unconscious psychic processes exist which are in no way experienced but nevertheless determining experience and physical behaviour.

The concept of the unconscious idea or impression originated in the experiment in post-hypnotic suggestion which Freud had borne in mind since the time of his studies under Charcot and Bernheim.[11] Freud interpreted hysteria as a condition similar to that of a person carrying through some instruction received under hypnosis. He observed that an hysteric unable to quieten her child "behaves as if it were not her will to feed the child on any account . . . this will evoke in her all the . . . symptoms . . . "[12] Her behaviour thus showed an unconscious opposition to the conscious intention, a "counter-will"; and Freud developed the doctrine of the unconscious counter-will out of the analogy which he suggested between hysteria and hypnosis. As Freud said in his *Preliminary Report* of 1892, his teachers Charcot and Bernheim supported the hypothesis that hypnosis was a form of artificial

[10] "The Defence Neuro-Psychoses", *Collected Papers,* vol. 1, p. 67.

[11] "Kurzer Abrisz der Psychoanalyse," *Werke,* vol. 13, p. 407.

[12] "A Case of Successful Treatment by Hypnotism," *Collected Papers,* vol. 5, p. 40.

hysteria.[13] In the interpretation of the "case treated by hypnotism" he reversed the terms, at least implicitly, and described hysteria after the model of post-hypnotic suggestion as a kind of natural auto-hypnosis; and in the *Preliminary Report* published at about the same time the analogy appears quite clearly.[14] Here he even suggests that a trauma must be experienced in a hypnoid condition in order for it to produce hysteria. This idea originated with Breuer and was in fact later abandoned by Freud. But he did not abandon the basic analogy.

In the ideal case of post-hypnotic suggestion the patient is given some instruction under hypnosis which he forgets on recovering full consciousness but carries out in his own time without knowing that he is in fact acting under the influence of his previous hypnosis. And it is natural enough to describe his action as determined by an unconscious idea. If we wanted to put the point more cautiously, we should say that in post-hypnotic suggestion complex experiences and actions can be determined by a psychic entity which is neither experienced nor conscious, but itself formed under the influence of a conscious idea, namely the suggestion of the hypnotist. And this unconscious psychic entity continues to exist and operate until it can be

[13] "Report on the Mechanism of Hysterical Phenomena", *Works*, vol. 2, pp. 12ff. Cf. also "Kurzer Abrisz der Psychoanalyse", *Werke*, vol. 13, p. 407.

[14] Cf. also "Kurzer Abrisz der Psychoanalyse", *Werke*, vol. 13, p. 407.

expunged or modified or turned back into a corresponding conscious idea or memory under hypnosis. A gramophone recording makes the simplest analogy; we can only hear what has been recorded when certain conditions come into operation; but the record is not a storehouse of unhearable sounds.

We shall return to the question of unconscious psychic processes when we come to deal with structures. For the time being we can say that the unconscious psychic reality to which psychotherapy refers can be handled as if it were conscious experience. The entities dealt with in psychoanalysis which are unconscious, in the strong sense of "unexperienced", are chiefly effective experiences once conscious but now forgotten.

Freud thought that psychic entities like the counter-will and unconscious counter-expectations and fantasies exercised an influence over bodily conditions distinct from that of the conscious will. And he applies the hypnotic analogy here as well. Physiological processes can be altered and pathological conditions can be produced and removed by suggestions and autosuggestive ideas. These possibilities can be exploited in therapy. It would not be surprising to find that the patient remembered emotionally charged ideas of an autosuggestive kind and was obliged to admit that he had anticipated his symptoms in anxious fears or even in wish-fantasies. Perhaps he would also remember that such thoughts had crossed his mind and then been violently repressed. Or on the other hand, the analyst might be able to discover, with the aid of hypnosis, inner experiences which corresponded to the external symptoms. In fact, a careful observation of the anamnesia accompanying the symptoms often enables him to identify either conscious or unconscious processes ("ungewusst-unbewussten Vorgängen" (Lersch))—for example, counter-expectation and unconscious fantasies. Unconscious and repressed experience can cause everlasting and manifest tension and disturbance in the organism.

Freud's counter-will is really much more than a disturbing antithetical idea. Like the conscious will, it organizes means to achieve definite objects. It controls the body by means of simulated but conscious ideas; indeed, according to Freud, "... the counter-will exercises greater control over the body than does conscious simulation..."[15] In an analogy relating to unconscious life, it would resemble the organizing principle in the development of the embryo. It is not merely manifest in bodily changes; it does not merely exercise an influence over them; it should be seen as a principle which orders structures and functions of all kinds towards ends as distinct as those formed and reached by the "determining tendencies" of the conscious will.[16] So that granted that there is an unconscious

[15] "A Case of the Successful Treatment of Hysterical Phenomena", *Collected Papers*, vol. 5, p. 40.

[16] N. Ach, *Analyse des Willens*, Berlin and Leipzig, 1935.

psychic principle which counters in this way the intentions of the conscious mind, we can say that it can not only, as it were, form potential schemes of action, but also, under certain conditions, carry them through, in the way that we have already seen in connection with post-hypnotic suggestion. It may also be worth noting that Adler's psychology is constructed on this basis. According to him, symptoms originate by way of autosuggestive fantasies which are used as parts of plans for the achievement of definite ends. The neurotic is essentially autosuggestive, and psychotherapy consists in dissolving the autosuggestion.

Psychoanalysis is concerned not just with the experience of the patient but also with his behaviour and its effects. Each patient reacts to the analytical situation in his own individual way. His report gives the analyst a picture both of his daily routine and of the general features of his way of life. When the picture is examined closely, characteristic patterns appear; in any period, whatever its length—a year, a week, an hour—behaviour takes certain typical forms.[17] The theory of history shows us how the historian's account of persons and periods depends upon the criteria by which he makes his selection from the range of possibilities open to him. Simi larly, in the course of a session the psychothera-

[17] Cf., for example, "Character Types Met With In Psycho analytic Work, (II) Those Wrecked by Success", *Works,* vol. 14, pp. 316ff.

pist will notice different patterns and sequences according to whether he is a follower of Freud, Jung or Binswanger. In any case he will, of course, need good judgement, accuracy and interpretative power. The method only shows things to people with eyes to see them.

Only a few psychologists are able to discover new patterns for themselves. And the significance of the various schools of depth psychology lies in the fact that recognition from text books is easier than discovery. The patterns which the therapist recognizes are made up out of distinct and unambiguous pieces of evidence as well as vague and equivocal ones. And partly because some of this evidence can so easily be overlooked the limited perspective offered by each individual school of depth psychology has a certain heuristic value; it concentrates attention on certain lines of thought which might not be so exhaustively pursued by the uncommitted investigator. The orthodox Freudian misses a good deal, but he also sees things which might escape an observer free from theoretical preconceptions. So far as practical psychotherapy of any school is concerned, it is difficult to decide between the respective merits of exhaustive narrowness and shallow breadth.

Finally, phenomenological analysis considers the performance of the patient, the adequacy and appropriateness of his behaviour. It considers whether his emotions are adequate, whether his memory and perception of external objects are reliable. And as we shall show later, it has to employ a criterion of normality which is indispensable but extremely difficult to establish.

Structural Analysis

We turn now to the analysis of psychic structures, the general determinants of psychic phenomena.[18] We can imagine structures as situated in concentric layers built round the centre of the person; some have a more general influence on experience than others.

Nineteenth-century psychology often limited itself to the investigation and classification of phenomena; today we go behind the phenomena and consider the subject, person, being, body-soul who *has* the experience rather than describe some object which *is* the experience. Modern psychology tries to see a person's structural dispositions in such a way that they explain the form which his experience and behaviour take. We might say that whereas nineteenth-century psychology tended to concentrate on the shape of the Cheshire Cat's disembodied grin, we are today more interested in why it is that the hypothetical cat should be grinning at all. Man does not consist entirely of his experiences; they

[18] Cf. to what follows: F. Krueger, *Zur Philosophie und Psychologie der Ganzheit*, ed. E. Heuss, Berlin, 1953; Lersch, *Aufbau der Person*; A. Wellek, *Das Problem des seelischen Seins*, Meisenheim, 1955 (2), and *Die Polarität im Aufbau des Charakters*, Bern, 1950.

presuppose a subject, and therefore a structure of body and soul which contains the proper subject of psychology.

It is true that Freud did not explicitly or consistently distinguish between phenomenon and structure. Although, for example, for him the ego is a group of mental events,[19] and, like some of his other definitions, this has a phenomenological air, he nevertheless used concepts which at least suggested structures: for example, "id", "ego", "super-ego", "instinct" and "instinctual system", "sexual organization", "complex" and "defensive reaction". Other psychoanalytical terms denote both processes and their results, for example "structural characteristics": "fixation", "inhibition", "regression", "identification", "splitting of the ego", and so on. Still others refer to the manifestations of structures in processes: the tendency towards projection appears in "transference", defensive attitudes appear in "repression" and "resistance". Thus analysis reveals the structures which underlie the patient's experience and behaviour, his complexes and "mechanisms", in short, the unconscious effective psychic reality which underlies and determines conscious life. As a method for investigating characterological structures, as a tool for "concrete characterology" (Wellek), it is in fact the most reliable and fruitful available.

It might seem as though the division of psychic

[19] Charcot, *Collected Papers*, vol. 1, p. 20.

life into structure and phenomenon makes it unnecessary to postulate unconscious, unexperienced psychic events in order to complete the interpretation of psychoanalytical observations. But this is really the case only if we think of the structure as in some way rigid. Ontologically, a structure is a *potentia activa*; it is distinguished from its mechanical analogue in that it does not consist of unalterable parts moved by an agent, but can be seen as a living picture which can change itself while its essence remains unchanged by moving from potency to act. It is useful to keep the division between structure and phenomenon, provided that we remember that the structure can grow and develop, sometimes in a way which is invisible to consciousness. It would not be accurate to equate the distinction between structure and phenomenon to the ontological distinction between being and acting. In general psychology, memory phenomena and the empirical findings of depth psychology are interpretated with the concept of the "dispositional unconscious".[20] This is a concept of a structural kind; and it clearly covers not just a sum of stable conditions, but a living psychic entity constantly shifting and changing, influencing and being influenced by experience but more than an object of experience when it is experienced. Every conscious thought, act of will, intention or impulse influences unexperienced structures and the dispositions affecting

[20] Cf. Lersch, *Aufbau*, p. 531f.

memory, and itself depends on, and can be modified by, instinctive tendencies, even when the latter remain unconscious. When we say that structural life and growth are not directly experienced we are not, of course, saying that there are such things as unexperienced ideas or ideas which are not thought by a subject. Psychoanalysis does not go any further towards a precise definition of unconscious, unexperienced psychic processes. The most convincing evidence for such processes is to be found in Freud's *Psychopathology of Everyday Life* (vol. 6 in the *Complete Works*) and in his *Introductory Lectures on Psychoanalysis.*

Psychoanalysis is completely flexible, a kind of testing-bed which can be adjusted to each individual case. Each patient responds in his own way to the analytic situation. He does not himself organize his free association; it is for the analyst to find the principles in the chaos of detail, and without weakening any further the patient's capacity for independent thought and action. Analysis shows how the patient thinks, feels and suffers, how he approaches other people and how he regards himself; it shows his vices and virtues, his talents and difficulties, his habits and gestures; and it shows all this in relation to the underlying tendencies which are at work in his personality. In the long run, it reveals the defects, weaknesses and tensions as well. When one considers what could happen when a person was called upon to give an accurate report of his stream of consciousness, it is natural to wonder just how beneficial and wholesome the method really is. But however much emphasis one may lay on the possibilities of suggestion and self-deception, one must admit, even at this point, that the method is fruitful for characterology and character pathology. Its value in this direction has hardly been recognized. Structural research in characterology has been neglected, partly because the typological characterologies which have been built up in psychiatry are not very useful to the psychotherapist. They contain some arbitrary theoretical presuppositions,[21] and can only occasionally be applied to the psychotherapist's patients, who come to him not just via psychiatry but from all the departments of clinical medicine. This is not to deny that these typologies can be useful to the psychiatrist. But even he is only rarely obliged to make a characterological diagnosis of, say, a patient suffering from ulcers, or an asthmatic. Moreover, these typologies do not take

[21] Karl Jaspers and Kurt Schneider have both offered convincing criticisms of E. Kretschmer's well-known typology. Schneider's own system is based on a conception of psychopathy which, unlike most current definitions (cf. below pp. 67ff.), includes neurosis, but in so doing denies it any separate existence. His conception of disease in general—"disease is always in the physical"—is in itself doubtful and in any case too narrow to be of use to psychotherapy. (K. Jaspers, *Allgemeine Psychopathologie,* Berlin, 1946 (4); K. Schneider, *Die psychopathischen Persönlichkeiten,* Vienna, 1943 (6) (quotation from p. 8) and *Klinische Psychopathologie,* Stuttgart, 1952.)

into account either the genetic approach or that of individual or "concrete" characterology. Finally, many typological expositions of psychosomatic research have been seriously damaged by empirical tests and theoretical criticism. It now seems that there is no such thing as an ulcer type, or a typical asthmatic or hypertonic. The features which people suffering from these diseases undoubtedly have in common are not sufficient to constitute characterological types.[22]

Lersch describes the structural analysis of personality as follows: "The study of structures aims at *structural reduction*, that is, the reduction of all discernible qualities to ultimate organizing principles which determine all aspects of a person's psychic life. From this point of view the personality can be seen as a hierarchy of distinct characteristics; there are both central and peripheral characteristics in the sense that two characteristics, A and B, will be peripheral to characteristic C when their presence can be shown to follow from that of C according to what Rieffert calls the laws of 'psychic logic'. Working on this principle one can eventually find characteristics which do not follow from others; and these are termed characterological primary qualities."[23] As an example Lersch gives an account of a structural reduction leading to the

[22] H. J. Weitbrecht, *Kritik der Psychosomatik*, Stuttgart, 1955; K. Kolle, "Zur Kritik der sogenannten Psychosomatik", *Mschr. f. Psychiatrie und Neurologie*, 126, 341 (1953).

[23] Lersch, *Aufbau*, p. 48.

identification of lack of self-confidence, or rather an account of the formation of a personality rooted in this lack:

> The man lacking in self-confidence tends to be dissatisfied with life, and this shows in depression or ill-temper. He tends to be anxious. He tends to react to disturbance and danger with alarm, excitement, or nervous irritation. The risk is that by reacting in this way to any kind of change he will eventually become completely paralysed and lose all judgement and initiative. He is unable to take risks and responsibilities. The world threatens him, disaster seems certain. He is naturally weak-willed, timid, inhibited, and vacillating. He lacks all impulse to formulate personal aims and objects for himself because he has no confidence in his power to achieve them: he is much more prepared to accept ready-made suggestions and instructions from others. Under certain circumstances his dependence on others can increase to the point of blind faith in their authority. He lacks the courage to contradict or offer resistance; pliancy and obedience come more easily. Sometimes he will resort to deceit and pretended virtue. He invariably tries to escape any difficulties which confront him by following the easiest line of retreat, whereas the man with a normally full measure of self-confidence needs some opposition to call forth his powers of will. In his

relations with other people he tends to be shy, inhibited, embarrassed, although he may construct a compensatory façade of stridency and ostentation. Even in their mildest form these characteristics suggest a flight from, or at least a lack of close contact with, reality; and in severe cases the sufferer can become completely absorbed in his own carefully constructed world of fantasy or surrender unconditionally to paralysing introspection."[24]

We can see from this description how a dominating primary quality forms secondary qualities and through them determines the form of experience and behaviour. We can see how it organizes repression and defensive attitudes, for example against suspected aggression, and attitudes of rejection and expectation which determine personal relations and so the whole course of life; in sum, how an emotional structure gives rise to a complete complex form of life. Preliminary approaches to structural reductions are to be found, in so many words, in what Freud calls "ego-analysis", and also in some earlier writings (for example, "A Case of Successful Treatment. . . ." (*Collected Papers,* vol. 5, p. 33)): he does seem to have been trying to explain neurosis in terms of primary qualities.

Psychoanalysis postulates certain instinctive tendencies and ego-structures, both inborn and determined by external circumstances, which

[24] Lersch, *Aufbau,* pp. 280ff.

correspond to these primary qualities and organize secondary qualities. For example, the lack of self-confidence described above would roughly correspond in psychoanalysis to castration anxiety and the castration complex. Transposing a structural reduction onto the genetic plane in this way is a typical procedure in psychoanalysis. This is a perfectly legitimate procedure. But this kind of transposition depends upon a satisfactory structural reduction. For example, we saw above how submissiveness to authority (say, that of the analyst) can be explained by general lack of self-confidence. If one were looking for some genetic explanation for the submissiveness, apart from the primary quality to which it can be reduced, one might, for example, suggest the influence of a tyrannical father. But an explanation on these lines would not necessarily be valid. The submissiveness might have had this direct root, but equally it could have arisen from some injury to the person's self-respect which had nothing to do with parental authority and could not have been prevented even by the best father. It might be due to indirect causes acting by way of a general weakening of self-confidence and not recognizable as direct causes of submissiveness. Equally, structural reduction can go wrong when it tries to derive qualities with their own particular origin from some other hypothetical primary quality.

Characterological diagnosis aims at structural

reduction and insight into the complete structure of the personality, but only rarely achieves this aim. One must usually be content to see all the individual parts: to see all their interrelations is a more difficult matter. It is enough if the analytic method can help us, as it usually can, to see the primary and secondary qualities which explain a particular neurosis.

The broad category of structural analysis covers two fundamentally different procedures. The first, which we can call "structural understanding", involves no more than grasping fairly obvious relationships and therefore hardly amounts to analysis in the strict sense. Lersch's description of a structural reduction would make an example—he shows how a psychic condition gives rise to certain characteristics according to the laws of "psychic logic"[25]; we can ourselves understand without much difficulty how ill-temper, anxiety, indecision, and dependence can arise from a lack of self-confidence. But there is another form of structural analysis which uses a less obvious kind of explanation. It considers psychisms (or "psychic mechanisms") rather than easily recognizable motives. One can very easily understand an experience of fear if one knows that danger is present or that the person concerned tends to imagine that situations like the one he is in are dangerous. But a condition of

[25] Rieffert, *Methoden und Grundbegriffe der Characterologie, Bericht über den 13. Kongresz der Deutschen Gesellschaft für Psychologie,* Jena, 1934.

anxiety caused by unconscious libidinal blockage, for example, cannot be understood in the same way. The anxiety does not have a conscious motive, but a cause which cannot be recognized as such by the subject. In this case a causal hypothesis is put forward to account for the observed sequence of two events or situations; a psychic mechanism is postulated to account for the observed regularities. The psychoanalytical interpretation of symptoms, experiences and forms of behaviour employs both of these two forms of structural analysis.[26]

Psychoanalysis has not made much contribution to the psychology of motivation in the sense of discovering new kinds of motive. All the motives with which it deals had already been seen at work in conscious life; and it is in fact a psychoanalytical principle that nothing can be unconsciously desired that is not also the basic object of the conscious will. But it has shown that certain apparently strange, perverse, criminal, and generally impenetrable motives long known to psychopathology can exert a hidden and unsuspected kind of influence on both neurotic and normal people. Apart from concentrating attention in this way on certain kinds of motives, and so on the types of personality formed by such motives, the most valuable service rendered by psychoanalytical research has

[26] Cf. also the discussion on "indirect understanding" (*mittelbare Verstehen*) in R. Heiss, *Allgemeine Tiefenpsychologie,* Bern and Stuttgart, 1955.

been to describe psychisms or "psychic mechanisms", and to explain genetic relationships.

Genetic Analysis

In general Freud relied more on the biographical and genetic approach to psychic life than on the kind of natural ordering of psychoanalytical observations described above. Genetic analysis tries chiefly to discover the events and influences which have formed psychic structures, and to establish the history of pathogenic partial structures—such as, for example, the so-called "complexes". All experiences and structures have important historical roots; in the study of motivation we see how present behaviour and experience can arise out of past situations; in *Aktualgenese*, we see the process by which articulated and developed forms of experience and behaviour grow out of amorphous embryo tendencies; and in the same way the maturing of the adult personality-structure depends on the foundations laid in childhood and adolescence.

The three aspects of psychic life which we have been considering are naturally complementary. Structures and primary qualities are not necessarily the ultimate psychic categories, and they should be distinguished from each other. In the diagnosis of psychopathy in particular, this distinction is frequently not made. A man with weakened and inhibited self-confidence will be put down simply as a psychopath lacking self-confidence as a result of his inherited disposition.

But whereas psychoanalysis is completely agreeable to the reduction of experience and behaviour to primary qualities, it does not hold that these qualities are ultimate from the point of view of psychic life in all its aspects. The next step is from primary qualities to the inherited constitution. And in order to reach the inherited constitution we must first consider formative processes. Or, in Freudian terminology, we must consider ego-formation, identification, repression, fixation, deprivation, traumas, and other processes forming the instinctual constitution.

According to Freud this was the final step in genetic analysis which led one back to the source of development. But it is only the final step if we have some determinist reason for limiting the scope of psychoanalysis. If we leave such prejudices on one side, we can go on to consider the influence on the development of the personality which is exercised by the conscious operation of free-will.

At this point we must introduce a distinction between development and history.[27] Animal organisms develop according to biological laws, which, within certain limits, leave room for the formative influence of environment. For example, dogs can, within the limits of their nature, be influenced or trained to behave in certain ways. Man, an organism consisting of

[27] Cf. A. Portmann, *Zoologie und das neue Bild des Menschen*, Hamburg, 1956.

body and soul, develops in an analogous way: the development of inborn tendencies is modified by external influences and impressions whose effects can be generalized in what we referred to above as the fundamental determinants of the primary qualities. But man not only develops but also has a history which he makes for himself. He does not see his environment simply in terms of potential pain and pleasure. He also sees attainable ends, meaning, values. In its own way his environment offers him the chance to understand himself and the whole of reality. Natural development and formative processes are complemented by education in the widest sense. Working from the basis of nature and environment, education inculcates certain habits and reflex actions. One can consider the process of psychoanalytic therapy as a kind of re-education, as a process in which certain induced distortions in the personality are replaced by a critical understanding of reality which can lead to a more healthy experience and behaviour.

The infant receives impressions passively and cannot respond freely to them. The educator who introduces the child to the world of meaning and value must allow for a much broader range of independent action. Even the three-year-old child is no longer completely passive and determined by his inherited disposition and environment. He already has the occasional possibility of comparing hints of meaning with each other.[28] He can thus doubt and criticize and to some extent reject, for example, his parents' judgements of value, and decide for one alternative against another. Small children will sometimes say, "I want to be naughty, why shouldn't I be naughty?"

It is rather doubtful whether Freud recognized any difference between development shaped by natural laws and outside influences, and free personal history shaped by the conscious exercise of the will and co-operation with others, between formation and education. But he did show in his applications of psychoanalytic method the necessity for careful investigation of the world of human values and its early history. As Freud saw, psychoanalysis not only tries to reveal hidden impulses and their direction, but also the range of ideas, objects, and values, the order according to which the patient tries to regulate his behaviour. And he therefore formulated the concept of the ego-ideal.[29] He saw the ego-ideal as the origin of motives for behaviour which consist at least partly of feelings of duty as distinct from those motives—for example, pleasure motives—which amount to no more than inclinations to act in a certain way. The feelings of duty arising from the ego-ideal often have very little

[28] Thure von Uexküll sees the origin of freedom in man's ability to doubt the interpretations of existence which are offered him. ("Die Naturwissenschaften und unsere Vorstellungen von der Seele", *Psyche*, 11 (1957–8).)

[29] *The Ego and the Id*, trans. Joan Rivière, London, 1950, p. 44.

connection with objective moral duties. A person can feel he wants to be something fairly dubious. The ego-ideal of the fourteen-year-old boy can reflect the panache of the gentleman crook or the loud mouth of the school bully.

The ego-ideal has three distinct roots: shaping models, accurate or distorted personal insights and conscious choices between alternative models and values. The ideal self partly consists of the system of values inculcated in the passive child by parental authority, and is partly shaped by conscious choice, affirmation and denial.[30]

When we examine the motives for a given choice, we see that they are determined by the personality-structure of the subject. But not completely determined. Often an alternative choice would have been equally consistent with this structure. Certainly there are situations in which the structure is such that a particular choice could have been predicted with almost complete certainty. But there are also other situations where the act of choosing is autonomous; I can choose to co-operate with any of my structural tendencies, and to make my choice on the basis of whatever general beliefs I prefer. There is no point here in trying to identify the strongest motive, for in such cases it is not specific motives which are the preponderant influence, but a general attitude adopted by a free person.

[30] Cf. G. Siewerth, *Metaphysik der Kindheit,* Einsiedeln, 1957.

3

PSYCHIC HEALTH AND SICKNESS

THE object of all medical diagnosis is to find out the ways in which the performance of the patient is unsatisfactory. But whereas in other branches of medicine the doctor diagnoses by tests of his patient's organic performance the psychoanalyst constructs a picture of his patient's personality by discovering the extent of his ability to perform, or experience and behave, as he would naturally wish and intend. Neurosis is a disease which weakens or destroys this ability, and psychotherapy begins by establishing the destructive factors.

In order to recognize unsatisfactory performance, the psychoanalyst must clearly have both some criterion and some knowledge of satisfactory normal performance.[1] Just as there can be no pathology without physiology, so there can be no psychopathology without knowledge of the constitution of the normal personality. But we do need to stress that "normal" here is not synonymous with "statistically average"; there are such things as collective neurosis and the pathology of civilizations. No-one will suggest

[1] Cf. G. Bally, *Der Normale Mensch,* Zürich, 1952; F. Duykaerts, *La Notion du normal,* Paris, 1954; H. Kunz, "Zur Frage nach dem Wesen der Norm," *Psyche,* 8, (1954–5), pp. 241f.; H. Müller-Suur, *Das psychisch Abnorme,* Berlin, 1950.

that tuberculosis becomes less of a disease or homosexuality more normal the more prevalent it becomes. Nor are carious teeth healthy merely because most people suffer from them. And while it would be equally mistaken to understand normality as some kind of ideal image demanding conformity in all respects,[2] we cannot hope to grasp it apart from some judgements of value. Psychotherapy is more than description and classification; its aim is to restore health, to achieve an end judged good.

There are certain kinds of behaviour which are obviously disordered because they are completely inappropriate. What would have been healthy and natural behaviour in a child often denotes sickness, or at least immaturity, in an adult. Again, we can see easily enough that if a hungry man feels disgusted, instead of even hungrier, at the sight of food, his experience contradicts the natural order of sensation; or that if a man can only experience erotic and sexual feelings towards other males, his experience contradicts the natural order in sexual life. There is a similar natural order in emotional life; certain things are naturally and obviously attractive and pleasant, others repulsive; and therefore certain reactions are, in relation to the natural order, appropriate.[3] "Sapiens est, cui

[2] Kurt Schneider sees only this kind of norm and thus not unnaturally rejects the concept of the norm altogether. (*Die psychopathischen Persönlichkeiten*, p. 2.)

[3] Cf. O. F. Bollnow, *Das Wesen der Stimmungen*, Frankfurt am Main, 1956 (3).

res sicut sunt sapiunt",[4] and we can often clearly see that the neurotic does not experience things as they are. We can further see that the incongruity of his experience can be either quantitative or qualitative; a reaction appropriate in kind can nevertheless be too weak or too strong. We take it as a sign of mental imbalance for a person to fly into a violent rage at the slightest provocation; and we know what constitutes a sufficient provocation even if we are each provoked by different kinds of things.

But there are other cases in which it is by no means clear that behaviour is disordered. And in order to judge these cases, and in order to distinguish clearly, as we must, between moral and psychic order and neurosis and natural human weakness and disorder, we need a more theoretical criterion of normality. Health presupposes life. A man can only be healthy if he is alive and capable of falling ill or dying. Health is, therefore, connected with order in the processes involved in living and in the conduct of life. Moral conditions and acts belong to the conduct of life; but this does not mean that health is equivalent to goodness or evil to sickness. Man is good insofar as his free desires and acts correspond, together with all their implications, to the essential order which is immanent in human nature. Goodness is consistency with

[4] Bernard of Clairvaux, *Sermones de Diversis,* 18, 1 (Migne, *Patrologia Latina,* 183, 587), quoted in J. Pieper, *Die Wirklichkeit und das Gute,* Leipzig, 1935, p. 9.

reality.[5] Order in the conduct of life can be achieved despite psychic disorder, and psychic order will not necessarily produce order in the conduct of life. Order in the sphere of free human decisions and attitudes is more than health, even though it is in a mysterious way connected with health.

The distinction between psychic and moral order can be made clearer if we situate it in some kind of scheme. We can consider the human person as made up of three spheres, each subject to disorder. First, there is the vegetative-physical sphere, the preservation of order in which is the object of anatomy, physiology, pathological anatomy and pathological physiology. Secondly, there is the sphere of personal being and action. Its order depends on attitudes freely formed through the intelligent perception of reality and on the free exercise of the will; and the fluctuations in its order are described by ethics in terms of the four cardinal virtues of prudence, justice, fortitude, and temperance. When this order is stable, man is good. And thirdly, there is the pre-personal or psychic sphere. This comprises, first, various more or less involuntary "mental" experiences and events—for example, memories, fantasies, spontaneous or impulsive trains of thought; psychisms. Then, various more or less involuntary emotional experiences: pain, fatigue, natural impulses, general feelings and moods, likes and dislikes. And second, the dis-

[5] J. Pieper, *Wirklichkeit*, p. 9.

positions, talents and deficiencies which make up what we think of as a man's equipment for life[6]; and his personality as it has been formed by environmental influences apart from its original inherited structure and his own conscious efforts to shape himself. This sphere becomes disordered when it is extended so as to restrict the possibilities of order in the other two spheres; that is, when it produces psychosomatic disease in the physical sphere and unduly reduces the area of free personal choice in the personal sphere.

Every free act of the will presupposes and is preceded by spontaneous, involuntary psychic events. All free acts without exception will be influenced by the subject's individual qualities. And because of this close practical relationship[7] it is important to see clearly that the distinction between free action and involuntary occurrence is not the same as that between the spiritual and rational, and the material. There can be spontaneous involuntary movements towards understanding and insight. Not every movement of the will presupposes a free and rational decision. Man's corporal nature is involved in both his rational insight and his spiritual tendencies; and equally there can be no perceptions or instinctive and emotional movements which are un-

[6] G. Pfahler, *Der Mensch und sein Lebenswerkzeug. Erbcharacterologie,* Stuttgart, 1954.

[7] K. Rahner, "Zum theologischen Begriff der Konkupiszenz", in *Schriften zur Theologie,* vol. 1, Einsiedeln, 1954.

connected with his spiritual and intellectual nature. If man is essentially, and therefore in all his experiences, a rational animal, this rationality cannot be divorced from his senses and instincts, nor will it be restricted to conceptual thought and conscious self-determination, even though it is here that it may be most clearly manifested.

Thus we can say that a person is psychically healthy when the influence of his psychic sphere does not extend to producing physical disorder or to limiting his ability to experience and perform to a satisfactory degree those conditions and acts which are essential to the development and fulfilment of his human nature.[8]

A man's state of health can be seen first in his organic performance and disposition, and then in the experience and behaviour which he is capable of and disposed towards. Thus, as a rational being he is naturally disposed to understand the whole of reality, just as he will tend to perceive forms and colours because he has eyes. Psychic health requires a healthy judgement, or ability to perceive reality without undue distortion. As a spiritual and corporeal being, man tends towards understanding the meaning, value and implicit possibilities of reality as a whole. As a social being man depends

[8] If I understand M. Boss correctly he takes psychic disorder to be a disturbance in the person's ability to exist in and cope with the objective world. ("Beeinträchtigung des In-der-Welt-sein-Könnens", *Sinn und Gehalt der sexuellen Perversionen*, Bern, 1952, p. 99.)

on other individuals and on the community and must meet threats from others. To be able to love and fight, to trust others, to sacrifice oneself and to assert oneself, is necessary for life and therefore to psychic health. As a sexual being, man needs the fulfilment and assistance brought by marriage. The emotions of sexual love transcend the individual partners and generate the warmth necessary both for their own growth and for that of their children. Where the ability to love is lacking, psychic health is, at the least, imperfect.

The definition of psychic health must take human defects and weaknesses into account. Some restriction of freedom, some disorder in the pre-personal sphere, is too much a part of human nature to be considered psychopathic or neurotic. Moreover, pre-personal disorder can be due to distorted moral attitudes and natural faults of character not in themselves neurotic. In the matter of suffering Freud distinguished between "normal unhappiness" and "hysterical misery".[9] We need to make the same kind of distinction between impropriety and wickedness in the psychically healthy, on the one hand, and the symptoms of neurosis, on the other. Man is good when he desires what belongs to a full human life; he is healthy insofar as he is capable of it.

But psychic health is not just a matter of *doing* things. Many of the psychically sick can do as

[9] "Psychotherapy of Hysteria", *Works*, vol. 2, p. 305.

much as healthy people. The difference is that they cannot stop doing things. They cannot bear any kind of rest or leisure. Their activity is breathless and hunted. And where activity has no still centre, no axis around which to revolve, people are enslaved to false sophistication and are degraded to inhuman robots.[10] In the same way, the psychically healthy man is capable of bearing things. He can bear deprivation, temptation, disappointment, injury and sorrow, and these not just as passing situations, but even when they darken the whole future with fear and anxiety. He has reserve capacities of courage and selflessness on which he can draw in need.

It will have become clear by now that the concept of health used in psychoanalysis inevitably involves metaphysical assumptions about the nature of man. The practising psychotherapist can, no doubt, do his work without having any conscious philosophy of man, but if he has not, then unconscious prejudices will rush into the vacuum. His alternatives are either to construct some arbitrary private philosophy to help order his observations, or to take over more orthodox philosophical principles of the kind presented above. The psychotherapist will in any event need to rely often enough on rough common sense, and fortunately for his patients this common sense is a good deal healthier and more reasonable than many current psychologi-

[10] E. Michel, "Zur anthropologischen Deutung der Hysterie", *Stud. Generale*, 3 (1950).

cal theories. As we should expect, no general criterion of psychic health is of much value unless the man who interprets it in practice has a good sense of proportion and plenty of experience, unless he possesses the virtue of prudence and the spiritual gifts of discernment and understanding.

Neurosis

Psychic disorder can originate in four distinct ways. First, it can be produced by particular physical causes; for example, delirium can be produced by fever and psychosis by poisoning. Second, it can be produced by disorder in the personal sphere, by free and conscious attitudes and acts of the will; for example, certain psychic dispositions can be produced by habitual self-indulgence and neglect of duty, or by the habitual insincerity of a life based on lies and self-deception.

The third kind of disorder is the inherited malformation or deficiency of the psychic structures. This is characteristic of so-called psychopathic conditions. "Psychopathic" is often used broadly to cover neurosis in general. But we shall limit its use here to the description of those inherited psychic malformations which, even given favourable circumstances, would have prohibited healthy development. One can rarely be absolutely certain whether one's diagnosis of psychopathy in this sense is in fact correct, but one can often be sufficiently sure. Although we do need some proper term to describe inherited psychic malformation, there is another reason for restricting the use of "psychopathic" in this way. Any doctor who has to deal with psychically sick people and possesses no psychotherapeutic knowledge will be tempted to disguise his ignorance. And a broad, vague use of "psychopathic" makes it easier for him to obscure the distinction between what is really incurable and what he is merely himself unable to cure.

The fourth kind of disorder is also structural; malformation and distortion are produced by the absence of the conditions which are necessary for the healthy development of the personality, and by positively harmful environmental influences. We shall define this kind of disorder, for which the person has no moral responsibility, as pure neurosis. The analytic method deals with the symptoms, forms and determinants of these "diseases of the personality"[11] under the three aspects considered in the last section—the phenomenological, the structural and, where possible, the genetic.

There is no *a priori* method of identifying pure neurosis. Psychoanalysis must use free association to reconstruct the life-histories of all kinds of patients—psychopathic, perverted, corrupted, psychotic, psychosomatically ill or just afflicted by everyday inhibitions and weaknesses of character—and then evaluate the evidence

[11] A. Wellek, *Die Polarität im Aufbau des Charakters*, Bern, 1950, p. 20.

about the origins of the patient's condition. The conditions which are most often purely neurotic are the psychoneuroses, certain neurotic dispositions which resemble psychoneuroses, and the chronic psychosomatic illnesses.

When we are diagnosing actual patients we find these conceptually distinguishable forms side by side and combined in a single personality. We have good grounds for supposing that pure neuroses do exist; we can find malformation in an originally sound personality which has not been produced by free personal decisions or direct physical causes. But we have no sure empirical means of distinguishing the psychopathic, personal and neurotic elements in the development of the personality. A person can be neurotic in the pure sense and also be in some degree psychopathic, and have helped to destroy or disturb his psychic health by his own responsible acts. An unbalanced personality is much more likely to become neurotic than a personality with inherited stability. But also personalities which, although completely healthy, are endowed, for example, with a highly refined sensibility, will be particularly prone to neurosis and will need careful upbringing under especially favourable circumstances.

The definition of neurosis above is in fact too narrow for our present purpose; and for the time being we shall describe as neurotic all the distorted developments, diseases and symptoms which experience tells us can be cured permanently by psychological methods of treatment. Neurosis, in this sense, could be produced by deficiencies in the inherited psychic constitution, and also—and especially—by the absence of the necessary environmental assistance for development[12] and personal failures to deal with experience and come to terms with reality.[13] It will include conversion- and anxiety-hysterias, phobias and compulsive neuroses, manias and perversions, the various conditions which are now rightly regarded as psychosomatic (for example, certain forms of abdominal and duodenal ulcer and of bronchial asthma), and the pure "character-neuroses" without medically ascertainable symptoms; we assume that all these conditions are structurally similar. Patients suffering from any of these conditions can be cured by analytic psychotherapy, although one cannot, of course, guarantee success in every case. We are well aware of the danger of broad categories of this kind; schizophrenia, for example, covers a wide variety of distinct *entia morbi*. But we have found that there are good grounds for considering the psychoneuroses, the chronic psychosomatic illnesses, and distortions in the development of the personality, under a common

[12] Cf. G. Gueux, *La névrose d'abandon*, Paris, 1950; A. Mitscherlich, "Oedipus and Kaspar Hause, Tiefenpsychologische Probleme der Gegenwart", *Der Monat*, 3 (1950), p. 11.

[13] Cf. E. Speer, *Der Arzt der Persönlichkeit*, Stuttgart, 1949, pp. 23ff.

perspective. The legitimacy of this viewpoint is being more and more frequently confirmed.

There would, of course, be no point in denying that inherited psychopathic dispositions are often important in neurosis. The term is not negative or exclusive but emphatic. We shall thus speak of "pure neurosis" where we have grounds for supposing that the clinical picture is essentially determined by the changes which life has produced in an originally healthy personality.

Interpretations of the Neurotic Personality

Ludwig Klages was one of the first writers to try to determine the essential characteristics of the "psychopathic personality" (the term is used here in a broad sense to include neurosis).[14] He believed that neurosis consisted essentially in an attachment to self-deception which had gone so far as to become indispensable to the conduct of life. Since then the question has received a good deal of attention from psychotherapists. Alfred Adler[15] claims that feelings of inferiority and compensatory masculine protestation can as a general rule be found at the root of neurosis. The formula is: "I am only a woman and I will become a man at any price." Adler holds that the

[14] "Bemerkungen zur sogenannten Psychopathie", *Nervenarzt*, 1 (1928), p. 201.

[15] A. Adler, *The Neurotic Constitutions*, trans. Bernard Glueck and John E. Lind, London, 1921.

concrete personality is a system of tactical positions maintained as part of a strategic plan for the reconquest of self-respect. Fritz Künkel[16] has shown how far this idea can be applied in characterology. In this view the life of the neurotic man is ruled by the quest for security. Failures of all kinds are feared because they injure the neurotic's self-respect even more and confirm his "basic anxiety" (Horney). His energy is largely invested in "insurance policies".

Karen Horney[17] has recently shown some of the limitations of this fundamental idea of individual psychology. The desire for self-respect, self-confidence and recognition is certainly very strong in all men, and particularly in neurotics. But Adler's formula does not measure up to the general variety of the phenomena, and is in fact often completely inapplicable. Often it obscures the one vital feature of the personality which would complete the explanation of the symptoms.

Carl Gustav Jung does not attempt to subsume the particulars of the neurotic personality under any simple formula, but draws attention to general characteristics which can usually be

[16] *Let's Be Normal! The Psychologist Comes To His Senses*, trans. Eleanore Jensen, New York, 1929. (A translation of *Einführung in die Charakterkunde*, Leipzig, 1934(6).)

[17] *The Neurotic Personality of Our Time*, New York, 1937; *New Ways in Psychoanalysis*, New York, 1939; *Our Inner Conflicts, A Constructive Theory of Neurosis*, New York, 1945; *Neurosis and Human Growth*, New York, 1951. For criticisms of Horney's work see W. D. Grodzicki, "Neue Wege in der Psychoanalyse?", *Psyche*, 10, (1956–7).

found in neuroses. The emphasis in his theory, diagnosis and therapy is characterological. He has no precise doctrine on symptom-formation, no genetic theory of neurosis. Jung has his own picture of man, made up from Gnostic, Romantic and biological elements as well as from psychological observations. On the basis of this picture Jung looks for an aspect of his personality which the patient could have developed but has not, an aspect of himself from which he is alienated, and tries to stir it into growth through recollection and meditation. Thus, for Jung, the neurotic is above all the man whose psychic potentialities have been only one-sidedly fulfilled. He shrinks from total fulfilment because the process of integration or "individuation" involves trouble, sacrifice, pain and anxiety, whereas partial development can follow the line of least resistance. It is, of course, outside the scope of this work to give an exposition of Jung's characterology and typology. It should be enough to say that despite his neglect of the specific aetiology of neurotic syndromes, Jung's concentration on the more central structural relationships has had an important influence on the theory of neurosis. Neurotic symptoms are deeply bound up with the total personality, and casual analysis of these symptoms needs to be complemented by a characterological structural analysis of neurotic cases in a broad context.

It is not far from the partially developed man of Jung's "complex psychology" to the "inhibited man" of the so-called neo-psychoanalysis, as represented by Harald Schultz-Hencke[18]: Freud's concept of repression, and his complementary idea of the defensive reaction, already referred in part at least to the structural aspect of the personality. But Schultz-Hencke largely rejects such generalizations in favour of a concept of inhibition which depends on structural assumptions. The "inhibited man" seems to make the most inclusive formula of all; but the theory of neurosis and the characterology on which it depends is not securely based. Schultz-Hencke offers no real proof for his thesis that "neurotic symptoms are manifestations of repressed instinctive life".[19] He hardly succeeds in his attempts to establish a connection between his theory of neurosis and general psychology, and to bring the analysis of symptoms and the analysis of personality under a unified system, though no doubt his work offers broad and careful descriptions of neurotic phenomena which are not influenced or distorted by his theoretical assumptions. The form of inhibition of instinct which he describes, and what he calls "bearing" ("Haltung") (that is, the emotional manifestation and effect of inhibited instinctive life at the unconscious level of expectation and pretension and in a diffuse tingeing of the whole of experience) are important aspects of neurosis. But the

[18] *Der gehemmte Mensch*, Stuttgart, 1947 (2).

[19] *Lehrbuch der analytischen Psychotherapie*, Stuttgart, 1951, p. 16.

restriction of the term "bearing" to the neurotically inhibited personality does seem rather unfortunate.

Apart from this, the neurotic is not just an inhibited man. He is also a driven man. The behaviour of every man is in part uncontrolled, passionate. Schultz-Hencke himself emphasizes these aspects of behaviour; his mistake is to try to derive them entirely from inhibition. Finally, in his polemic against the "nomothetic" procedure of Adler and Jung he does seem to have overlooked the arbitrary philosophical ideas embedded in his own "autonomous therapy".[20] The most obvious of these is a dogmatic ethical relativism. In the same way the "attitude of tolerance towards the instincts" which he recommends to the therapist presupposes principles which would be by no means self-evident to, say, a Buddhist or a neo-Platonist. Schultz-Hencke's anti-puritanism is a philosophical and theological matter.

We are indebted to Felix Schottlaender for, among other things, a formula which penetrates deep into the heart of neurosis: "The way of neurosis is the way of rejection." The neurotic protests against the determinate nature of existence. "He is essentially divided against himself, unconsciously unreconciled to the unalterable."[21]

[20] Schultz-Hencke, *Lehrbuch,* p. 13.

[21] "Die Welt der Neurose", *Schriftenreihe für Ganzheitsmedizin,* Geissen and Stuttgart, 1950, course 1, vol. 7, pp. 47, 56. Cf. further, "Das Ich und seine Determinanten", *Psyche,* 5 (1951–2).

It does seem true that analysis can find this habitual rejection of basic realities in every neurosis. And quite possibly such rejection would be the ultimate characteristic which the structural reduction of the neurotic personality could reach.

Igor Caruso[22] and Wilfried Daim,[23] following up (not without some oversimplification) ideas first put forward by Scheler and Von Gebsattel, have taken psychoanalysis beyond characterological observation in the narrower psychological sense to consider character in the moral sense. They have attempted a transvaluation of psychoanalysis. Their formula is: The neurotic is a man who culpably makes relative values absolute. This idea needs to be treated with the greatest caution. Other writers with similar ideas, such as Jores[24], Journier[25] and Bovet,[26] and Frankl[27] have had only an indistinct or overextended concept of guilt. Here we may perhaps rightly ask whether the neurotic tendency to make spontaneous pre-personal occurrences equivalent to free decisions has infected the analyst. Even Freud had occasional lapses in this direction, but his great service was to replace moral judgements on the physically ill by scien-

[22] *Religion und Psychotherapie,* Innsbruck, 1946, p. 10; *Psychoanalyse und Synthese der Existenz,* Freiburg, 1952.

[23] *Umwertung der Psychoanalyse,* Vienna, 1951.

[24] "Was ist Krankheit?" in *Medizin Heute,* 1 (1952).

[25] *Krankheit und Lebensprobleme,* Basel, 1955.

[26] *Die Person, ihre Krankheiten und Wandlungen,* Bern, 1946.

[27] *Arztliche Seelsorge,* Vienna, 1947.

tifically impartial investigations of their condition.[28] One must be careful not to blacken the character of the sick in the eyes of their fellows, and as a rule healthy public opinion is only too apt to dismiss the neurotic as dishonest and antisocial. To say this is to object to the misuse of the theory, not to the theory itself; and certainly not to represent the intentions of the writers mentioned above. But in the nature of the case the onus of proof should weigh on them in particular.

However, these writers give us more than merely a vulnerable theory; they give us valuable observations and insights of a new kind. And their formula has a characterological content which we can extract and state in this way: the neurotic is a man with an over-rigid, undiscerning and obstructive control over his emotions. We are not very far here from Freud's idea that the neurotic is afflicted by fixations—but the difference is that whereas Freud held that the neurotic was ruled by instinct, for Caruso and Daim the fixation is situated in the personal sphere. In both interpretations the neurotic is entangled with certain values or apparent values, and with certain people, so that he cannot reach the measure of detachment and free action which is necessary for the development of a mature personality. Neurotic inhibition has to be distinguished from the kind of self-control on which

[28] "Die sittliche Verantwortung für den Inhalt der Träume", *Werke*, vol. 1, p. 565.

any real depth or strength of character depends. A neurotic inhibition is usually found in inverse proportion to genuine self-control, though they can both be found together.

What is the basic characterological formula in the Freudian theory of neurosis? Psychoanalysis provides two answers to this question. The first is theoretical and the second derived from the actual observations made with the psychoanalytic method. According to Freud,[29] the neurotic is a man whose libido is so fixated as to obstruct the course of his life. He is tortured by wishes which he can neither abandon nor hope to satisfy. The neurotic has an unfavourable "sexual" instinctual constitution. His "component instincts" are so disposed, or hardened in such an early stage, that they can only reach the mature genital stage of organization under exceptionally favourable circumstances. The neurotic tends to form instinctual fixations in that phase of development which is controlled by his most marked component instincts. (For the theory of phases of development see below, pp. 247ff.) This tendency towards fixation can often be confirmed by external circumstances or events—as, for example, traumas. Even a favourable inherited disposition can be forced towards fixation in certain circumstances. As a child the neurotic absorbs his elders' disapproval

[29] Cf. for what follows; "Three Essays on the Theory of Sexuality", *Works*, pp. 122ff.; *Introductory Lectures on Psychoanalysis*, London, 1949 (2), pp. 286ff., 301ff.

of his "sexual behaviour". (The process is described as introjection and is in turn determined by instinctive identification.) Absorbing this disapproval, he builds within himself defensive attitudes (super-ego) which split his instinctual disposition into two parts. The parts stand in permanent tension and conflict, and repression becomes necessary. There is also a fixation on these defensive attitudes—an application of the concept which is often overlooked.

Freud understood all neurotic symptoms, and all aspects of the personality, either as direct, adapted or sublimated expressions of libidinal drives and the defences erected against them. We hold that so far as this doctrine covers the whole human person, it is not worth serious discussion as a theoretical hypothesis, and still less as a supposedly experimental psychoanalytical discovery.[30] We certainly do not want to deny the importance of the mass of observations and insights which lead Freud to formulate his thesis, and which still call for a theoretical interpretation. But we cannot consider the ramifications of Freudian theory here, even though it contains many hypotheses relevant to characterology, because this would take us far beyond the actual findings of psychoanalysis. In general, Freud's procedure is the reverse of Jung's; he begins with

[30] Cf. among others P. Matussek, *Metaphysische Probleme der Medizin,* Berlin, 1950; Karen Horney, *New Ways in Psychoanalysis*; J. Nuttin, *Psychoanalysis and Personality,* London, 1954.

symptoms, tries at first to ignore the personality, and is only drawn into its analysis in spite of himself.[31]

In conclusion, we should perhaps point out that we are not concerned so much with determining the essence of neurosis or the common characteristics of all neurotics, as with the description of some of the acquired structural distortions which can be found particularly clearly in cases of neurosis. The progress of the exposition will not depend on whether there actually is some definite single disease called neurosis. It is just that as a matter of convenience we shall assume for the moment that such a disease does exist.

[31] "Character and Anal-Eroticism", *Collected Papers,* vol. 2, trans. Joan Rivière (London, New York and Vienna, 1924), pp. 45ff.; "Instincts and Their Vicissitudes", *Works,* vol. 14, pp. 109ff.; "Some Character Types", *Works,* vol. 14, p. 309; "Über libidinöse Typen", *Werke,* vol. 14, pp. 507ff.

4

PHENOMENA AND STRUCTURES OF THE DISORDERED PERSONALITY

General Neurotic Performance: Disorders in Perceiving, Feeling and Willing

Before the psychotherapist turns to the detailed study of less obvious phenomena, structures and genetic relationships, he finds his bearings by a general diagnosis of his patient's performance. And equally he must measure performance when he makes his detailed analysis. In what follows and in a way which will explain itself performance will be extended to cover experience and behaviour, the other two aspects under which psychic phenomena can be considered.[1]

When we consider the intellectual performance of neurotics, we generally find a tangled mass of errors and illusions, which distort their experience and behaviour. They have no clear view of things, no sound judgement; they often approach people and situations with extraordinarily false ideas and expectations and are badly set back by the disappointments which they receive. The careful examination of a neurotic's life-history usually reveals that he has constantly misunderstood the real state of affairs, although this misunderstanding is not always evident at

[1] K. Bühler, *Die Krise der Psychologie*, Jena, 1927.

first sight. On the other hand, neurotics can often compensate for this deficiency by finding and exploiting, in some intuitive way, the appropriate counter-neuroses which enable them to avoid disaster. Moreover the partial psychic paralysis which characterizes the neurotic—his inability to understand life or his fellow men (Schultz-Hencke), his inability to enjoy experience freely, his tendency to distort reality—can be counterbalanced to some extent by high intelligence.

But even highly intelligent neurotics cannot always turn their gifts to good account. One can often see astonishing practical stupidity joined with high intelligence, and demonstrated for example in the choice of profession or marriage partner. The neurotic frequently marries a partner whom he has completely misunderstood and to whom he is entirely unsuited. He takes up a profession for which he has no talent whatsoever. If one happens to meet people who have previously been described to one by neurotics one is astonished to find how completely inaccurate their description turns out to be. This, of course, makes for difficulties in treatment, for the doctor depends on the information given him by the patient. But he can often discover the grosser gaps and distortions. If the doctor has the opportunity to treat brothers or sisters or others in close contact with the patient at the same time, then the inability of the neurotic to grasp situations, people and relationships without distortion appears with particular clarity. And apart from this, the doctor can usually build up a fairly accurate picture by means of his patient's own unconscious self-contradictions. The patient may describe his father-in-law as mean and greedy. But not very long afterwards it may transpire that his father-in-law recently made him a birthday present of a television set, and that for years he has been making him a generous monthly allowance. Among compulsive neurotics particularly, we find sticklers for truth who scrupulously weigh up every insignificant word and fact. But however accurate the details may be, the total impression they give is invariably distorted and deceptive: they leave out vital facts and emphasize the wrong things.

In many cases prejudice and fixed ideas prevent any free exercise of personal opinion. There may be superstition and hyper-scepticism. General attitudes and tacit opinions are often completely unbalanced. Neurotics may expect individuals, or even the world in general, to obey them blindly. Analysis reveals a whole system of opinions on what is and what should be, opinions which appear self-evident to the neurotic but which, objectively considered, are far from self-evident, and indeed highly distorted. Experience and behaviour follow certain patterns which are sometimes explicitly formulated, but are mostly semi-conscious, unreflective and emotional. The neurotic will often indignantly reject the attitude which his behaviour implies.[2] What the normal man wishes and hopes for, the neurotic claims by right. He reacts to trivial everyday misfortunes with bitter anger, self-pitying resignation, or even desperation.

There are also distortions and failures of memory. In extreme cases of chronic hysteria, large gaps appear in the memory of the comparatively recent, as well as of the more remote, past. When an hysteric relates the events of the previous day, he often forgets the very event which affected him most deeply, or at least he will leave out events of obvious importance. He is especially liable to forget what happened just before the onset of his illness. Often he only remembers decisive events—disappointments, injuries, deprivations, troubles, temptations—after thorough interrogation or, as the case may be, lengthy psychoanalytic treatment. Gaps in the memory are filled by mistakes. Not only hysterics, but most neurotics and sufferers from psychosomatic illnesses, tend to forget important events and relationships in their lives. They place the onset of their symptoms at a certain time, but the analyst may discover later from reliable sources that the disease definitely began at another time and in conjunction with some important event. Whereas the hysteric uncon-

[2] Newman was concerned with unconscious opinions and maxims of this kind in his doctrine of "first principles", which is therefore important for depth psychology. See *The Grammar of Assent* (1870).

sciously falsifies, the obsessive neurotic distorts by way of understatement: he suppresses the emotional content of the memories.

The normal man constantly depends on his pre-personal nature in the ordinary process of living—on feelings and spontaneous tendencies, without which reasonable, accurate thought becomes extremely difficult or even impossible; and one merely distorts the doctrine of free-will if one forgets this fact. But the neurotic's course of life is obstructed by incongruous feelings and tendencies, or by the failure of emotions to manifest themselves where they would have been helpful or necessary. Spontaneous nature refuses to respond or opposes itself to conscious intentions. Its motions and acts are apparently irrational. It is like an autonomous, apparently arbitrary, tide, ebbing and flowing over the free, conscious, personal sphere. There is a limit to every man's control over his own nature; but for the neurotic inner experience is an unknown land.

The neurotic is disturbed in his emotional relationships with himself, with other people and with the world in general. His attitude towards his own spiritual and corporal nature and existence lacks any kind of tolerance or flexibility. He cannot say, with St. Francis de Sales, "I praise the Lord in the countenance he gave me." He objects to just those parts of himself which give him no grounds for discontent; he objects to natural limitations and dispositions which he neither can nor is obliged to alter. He does not like himself. He can acquire none of the legitimate self-confidence and self-respect necessary for existence. This is a particularly striking characteristic; and Adler interpreted it in his doctrine of the inferiority complex and made it into the point of departure for his whole theory of neurosis. Even in his first psychological treatise,[3] Freud already saw it as a characteristic of the neurotic disposition. He noted other associated disturbances in his writings on the super-ego: neurotics very often have unfounded feelings of shame and guilt,[4] tend towards self-criticism and self-hate, make exaggerated demands on and have exaggerated expectations of themselves, quite outside the rational context in which the healthy man places his ideals. Irrational guilt is a very common neurotic burden; people may feel guilty even for existing or having a body or sexual faculties. Sometimes the neurotic feels guilty about acts and decisions which are really quite legitimate. Sometimes the feelings are based on an objectively valid guilt, but the guilt is transferred to other objects and acts so that it becomes unintelligible.

However much the neurotic may despise himself, he can still be narcissistic, in love with himself, tending to overvalue, spoil and pity him-

[3] "A Case of Successful Treatment by Hypnotism", *Collected Papers,* vol. 5, pp. 38ff.

[4] "Das Interesse an der Psychoanalyse", *Werke,* vol. 8, p. 418.

self. Neurotic self-love and conceit have little to do with the equally repulsive kind of pride which can go with psychic health. They can represent an attempt by the neurotic to compensate for or cover up a profound conviction of his own worthlessness. Freud's distinction between narcissism and egoism[5] (the former is an expression of the autistic libido, the second is an expression of the ego-instinct) is now hardly used in psychoanalytical theory. The concept of narcissism is now very broadly used to cover what is normally called egotism; egocentric, selfish behaviour.

Disorders in the general moods underlying experience and behaviour are extremely common: especially general debility or absence of feeling, an oppressive lack of joy. Depressive tendencies can frequently develop out of neurotic lethargy, a lack of all capacity for effort. Also there are often moods involving general discontent, tension and a craving for pleasure, fashion and distraction (E. Michel). Neurotics are never relaxed and contented.

The neurotic has a poor appetite in the most general sense; he cannot respond fully to the variety and savour of the earth; he finds no joy in a blossoming twig, a smiling child, a song, a friendly word. He receives intellectual information rather than life-giving contact. "It is not to

[5] On the distinction between narcissism and auto-eroticism cf. "The Disposition to Obsessional Neurosis", *Works*, vol. 12, pp. 320–1

know much, but it is to understand and savour the matter interiorly that fills and satisfies the soul"—this sentence from the Exercises of St. Ignatius of Loyola[6] refers primarily to the meditation of spiritual matters, but it applies equally to our relations with earthly realities. This "understanding and savouring of the matter interiorly" is impossible when the faculties of the soul are clogged and constricted. The neurotic cannot reach the heart of things; his knowledge is not animated by the breath of contemplation: his thought is no more than a barren arrangement of concepts, his outlook a *cloisonné* of fragmented experience. It may well be that this fragmentation and barrenness is more a matter for cultural pathology than for psychological research into the individual. For large numbers of people are afflicted in some such way, and they can hardly be called neurotic because they have reached a mass-adjustment to their condition, and have no symptoms involving pain or suffering. But we can almost always find this characteristic in psychic diseases. And there seems to be a greater chance of curing such diseases if one can awaken a contemplative responsive relationship to the world. The constrictions of neurosis can be loosened when what is understood as a meaningful pattern, as natural, as a gift not merely intellectually recognized

[6] *Spiritual Exercises,* trans. John Morris and others, London, 1952 (5), p. 2.

as such but accepted with active thanks.[7] And although psychoanalysis cannot induce this kind of attitude, it can go some way towards making the right conditions for its development. Josef Pieper has given us a lucid and beautiful description of the way the soul draws energy from the contemplation of the world.

> Above all there is a contemplative way of seeing the things of creation. I am speaking now of actual things and of seeing with the eyes; I mean also hearing, smelling, tasting, every type of sense-perception, but primarily seeing.
>
> A man drinks at last after being extremely thirsty, and feeling refreshment permeating his body, thinks and says: "What a glorious thing is fresh water!" Such a man, whether he knows it or not, has already taken a step towards that "seeing of the beloved object" which is contemplation. How splendid is water, a rose, a tree, a human face—such exclamations can scarcely be spoken without also giving tongue to an assent and an affirmation which extends beyond the object praised and touches upon the origin of the universe. Who among us has not suddenly looked into his child's face, in the midst of the toils and troubles of everyday life, and at that moment "seen" that everything is good, is loved and lovable, loved by God! Such

[7] This idea of acceptance is one of the main themes of Charles Morgan's novel *The Voyage*.

certainties all mean, at bottom, one and the same thing: that the world is plumb and sound; that everything comes to its appointed goal; that in spite of all appearances, underlying all things is—peace, salvation, *gloria*; that nothing and no-one is lost; that "God holds in his hand the beginning, the middle and the end of all that is." Such non-rational intuitive certainties of the divine base of all that is can be vouchsafed to our gaze even when it is turned toward the most insignificant-looking things, if only it is a gaze inspired by love. That in the precise sense is contemplation.[8]

We can see from this the extent to which neurosis is really a deficiency-disease. The neurotic is disordered in his relations with other people. He finds it difficult, and often impossible, to love another person, to maintain his individuality, or to come properly to grips with opposition. He cannot establish a proper relationship with the community; he either sinks into the mass or becomes a lonely outsider.[9] American psychologists have tried to interpret neurosis as chiefly a matter of social maladjustment, and this point of view is important in psychoanalysis as well.[10] No sphere of human life

[8] *Happiness and Contemplation,* trans. Richard and Clara Winston, London, 1959.

[9] "Das Interesse an der Psychoanalyse", *Werke,* vol. 8, p. 418.

[10] Cf. Horney, *New Ways*; H. Sullivan, *Conceptions of Modern Psychiatry,* Washington, 1947.

is in principle immune from neurosis; but there are certain spheres in which emotional disorders appear particularly clearly; the most important of these is the person's human relationships. The neurotic is seldom capable of warm, lasting love and friendship. Irrational, uncontrollable impulses of mistrust, jealousy, hatred, disgust, irritation, force themselves to the surface, or feelings of warmth and friendship painfully sicken and die. For the disorders are concerned with the sensitive kinds of body-soul experience which are involved in the various natural processes of emotional development. Thus we find that most neuroses are accompanied by sexual disorder. The neurotic can build up no stable relationship to his workmates or employers, subordinates, neighbours, acquaintances, relatives. He is isolated, though this isolation, especially in hysterical cases, may be disguised by a wide superficial acquaintanceship. He can never approach others as an equal; his demands and expectations are too high or too low; he is too much either their aggressive competitor or their humble servant.

The neurotic is egocentric, sometimes autistically bound up with himself and imprisoned in himself. He cannot consider the interests of others; his own problems and difficulties are too pressing to be forgotten for even a moment. This egocentricity and lack of contact with others are among the most important neurotic symptoms.

Freud studied neurotic emotional life chiefly

in relation to transference and resistance—that is to say, chiefly in relation to the patient's disordered relationship to the doctor. But he also saw the extent of neurotic disorder in extra-analytical situations; he saw especially how the neurotic's relationship to his own family is always extremely difficult, how intense are his feelings of love and hate towards parents, brothers and sisters.

The pre-personal sphere of spontaneous emotion and instinct extends itself under these forms whenever neurosis is present. This has to be stressed, because disorder can be overcome by the exercise of reason and will at the centre of the person without the removal of all the neurotic symptoms and tendencies. Equally, despite what has been said above, some neurotics have a high capacity for genuine love. In such cases the diseased part merely overlies reservoirs of health which remain uninfected.

Neurotics often, but not always, find it difficult to establish proper relationships to things—to art, work, property. The neurotic finds it difficult to concentrate his energies, he lacks what Charles Morgan calls the "impersonal passion".[11] But this is not always true; and sometimes the neurotic can distinguish himself brilliantly in his own field. It may be that the neutral world of things offers outlets for his energy which are less liable than others to be clogged up by his emotional disorders.

[11] *The Flashing Stream*, London, 1948.

Anxiety is one of the most important of the unnatural, inappropriate feelings with which we have been dealing. It can appear in a great variety of forms, not all of them easily recognizable. It can be generalized or attached to certain objects or situations; and it is always a heavy burden for the neurotic.

Often psychoanalysis must completely change the outward face a man puts to the world. One of its chief tasks is to classify the incidence of fear and anxiety in all its forms and equivalents, abortive or chronic. As Rudolf Allers so rightly points out, "There is no case of characterological anomaly either in children or in adults, no case of dissociation, as in neurosis, no case of difficult upbringing or of childish shortcomings, in which open or variously disguised fear does not lurk; it is a never-failing symptom of faulty adaptation to the actual conditions of life."[12]

The neurotic does not take proper measures to deal with his anxiety; his commonest reactions are flight, repression, or uncontrolled and pointless aggression. He fears anxiety and its consequences but finds it impossible to pluck up any courage and optimism. He is not just anxious but also cowardly, particularly in direct encounters with other people. He is very rarely frank and is often incapable of unconstrained behaviour in the good sense. This is why psychoanalysis is so valuable, requiring as it does a

[12] R. Allers, *The Psychology of Character*, trans., with an introduction, by E. B. Strauss, London, 1939, p. 115.

measure of courage and honesty on the part of the patient.

These basic feelings of insecurity and anxiety and the defensive attitudes which follow from them can be partly explained in conjunction with neurotic *aggression*. This covers not merely assault on others but also various other kinds of active self-assertion. Here, also, the neurotic cannot control his behaviour, cannot measure his behaviour to the situation. He is either inhibited by his aggressive tendencies or so fixated on them as to be incapable of maintaining his independence and exercising his influence in a peaceful and moderate way. We do, of course, find numerous varied forms of inhibited, repressed, unconscious aggression apart from anxiety.

There is an Italian proverb which says, "How delicious water would taste if it were a sin to drink it!" This often applies to neurosis. Often positive, healthy feelings can develop only if certain false or *unnatural* conditions are fulfilled. Thus, many neurotics are only capable of loving someone insofar as they feel it is against their conscience, or insofar as it involves a radical rejection of others—parents, for example. Others, again, can feel tenderness only so long as there is no question of a sexual relationship; and some can experience sexual feelings only if they know that these feelings are onesided. The so-called perversions also depend on unnatural conditions in this way.

The freedom of the neurotic to aspire to and will things is unduly limited. Schultz-Hencke has described the most notable forms produced by inhibition of natural instincts.[13]

The neurotic is unable to exercise proper control over psychic forces and movements, and his behaviour is consequently over-disciplined or uncontrolled, or impossible to control even partially. Often these two apparently opposed forms, of rigid self-control and complete lack of control, occur together and overlap in the same person. The neurotic cannot bear to know that by making a choice he is excluding possible alternative choices, that every gain is also a loss. "You cannot have your cake and eat it",[14] and this is what he finds it so difficult to bear.[15] He wants to be a man but also to remain a child, to be a good husband but unfaithful at his convenience, to do great things but avoid exertion, to enjoy both the peace of a good conscience and the sensations of vice. Every decision implies the denial of a wide range of possibilities, but the psychically healthy can bear this implication without heroic virtue. They take it as a matter of course.

We have now a very rough sketch of the performance of the neurotic. We shall work it over and fill in the details in what follows, so that at

[13] *Der gehemmte Mensch,* Stuttgart, 1947 (2).

[14] Or as the German proverb has it, "You can't dance at two weddings with one backside."

[15] I. Caruso, *Psychoanalyse and Synthese der Existenz,* Freiburg, 1952.

the end we may have a fairly complete picture of the three aspects of psychic life investigated by psychoanalysis.

The Pathology of Personality: Elementary Psychoanalytic Findings

The neurotic or psychosomatic patient tells the analyst his sufferings, difficulties, symptoms; his life-history, his present experience with family and profession, his expectations, hopes and fears of the future. He confides his fantasies, his thoughts on God and life, his attitude to other people and to himself. Gradually the analyst constructs a picture of his patient's personality. And even allowing for all the variety of individual experience, neurotic personalities show certain common characteristics which are much more strongly marked than in normal personalities which show no psychopathological or clinically observable neurotic symptoms. These neurotic characteristics are largely the findings of psychoanalysis; empirical findings, not Freudian interpretations.

Peculiarities in the course of experience and behaviour are particularly susceptible to analytic investigation, and it is here particularly that we can expect some progress in the future. We can answer questions such as, Under what conditions does aggression occur with this person, this type, this neurosis? When does anxiety appear? When do feelings of guilt appear? In what connections do we find lapses, ill-humour, greed and passion? How does a man react to demands, attacks, injuries, disappointments, temptations? How does he reach his decisions, important or trivial, right or wrong? When do conflicts show, how are they resolved, when do they remain unresolved?

The reputation of the psychoanalytic method has suffered because its findings have been built up into theories which it is unable to sustain. But the method itself is not to blame for the exaggerated demands which have been put on it. It gives us facts and interrelations between facts; it directs our attention to a wide and important sphere of human experience and creates favourable conditions for its observations; no more and no less.

Freud's phenomenology and theory of structures is built around his doctrines of conflict, defence, repression and inhibition; and these doctrines form the point where theory and description intersect. Neurosis is misplaced self-denial, excessive in extent and inappropriate in form. The theory of defence and repression describes objects, motives, means and effects of neurotic self-denial. And every finding of the psychology of neurosis comes under one or other of these four heads.

We can begin with the negative findings which Freud thought were effects of failure to control instincts properly. They are discontinuity, lapses and gaps, lack of spontaneity, disintegration.

DISCONTINUITY, LAPSES AND GAPS

The first finding of analytic investigation is that neurotic experience and behaviour show striking discontinuity[16] and are constantly interrupted by apparently unmotivated moods, feelings, ideas and tendencies. When we observe the course of neurotic experience we find extraordinary lapses. The most striking lapse is hysterical amnesia. But in other neuroses as well, continuity of memory and the intellectual perception of relationships between events and situations are destroyed. There are no sufficient motives for behaviour, sometimes no motives at all. In many situations the natural and appropriate feelings and movements are lacking. Thus, the experience and behaviour of the neurotic become unintelligible both to himself and to others.

Free association sometimes restores the completeness and continuity of experience by suddenly bringing up the missing elements which fill the gaps. There is an analogous common experience. Most people have at some time woken up in a bad temper which seems inexplicable until they suddenly remember some bad dream of the previous night. Perhaps this use of free association is best illustrated by the case of Freud's which has been mentioned above (pp. 17ff.).

As analysis works through the course of daily

[16] "Psychotherapy of Hysteria", *Works,* vol. 2, pp. 292ff.

experience, gaps in the memory are gradually filled. And as the gaps are filled the analyst can make out certain connections between the forgotten things. They may be disappointments, deprivations, temptations, conflicts, or certain forms of anxiety. Interrelated weaknesses in psychic constitution appear for the first time. An attack of asthma or persistent depression can, for example, regularly occur after professional setbacks; and the patient may not himself see the relationship between the two events.[17] Thus the psychoanalyst carefully notes the gaps in the course of experience, in memory, and in relations between motives and behaviour. And he therefore works on the assumption that psychic and intellectual life, despite all its emotional irrationality, is determined by meaningful interrelations. Freud writes[18]:

> ... if we examine with a critical eye the account the patient has given us without much trouble or resistance, we shall quite infallibly discover gaps and imperfections in it. At one point the train of thought will be visibly interrupted and patched up by the patient as best he may, with a turn of speech or an inadequate explanation; at another point we come upon a motive which would have to be described as a feeble one in a normal person. The patient will not recognize these deficiencies

[17] Cf. W. Bräutigam, "Über die psychosomatische Spezifität des Asthma bronchiale," *Psyche*, 8 (1954–5), pp. 481ff.

[18] "Psychotherapy of Hysteria", *Works*, vol. 2, p. 393–4.

when his attention is drawn to them. But the physician will be right in looking behind the weak spots for an approach to the material in the deeper layers and in hoping that he will discover precisely there the connecting threads for which he is seeking with the pressure procedure. Accordingly we say to the patient: "You are mistaken, what you are putting forward can have nothing to do with the present subject. We must expect to come upon something else here, and this will occur to you under the pressure of my hand."

For we may make the same demands for logical connection and sufficient motivation in a train of thought even if it extends into the subconscious, from an hysterical patient as we should from a normal individual. It is not within the power of a neurosis to relax these relations. If the chains of ideas in neurotic and particularly in hysterical patients produce a different impression, if in them the relative intensity of different ideas seems inexplicable by psychological determinants alone, we have already found out the reason for this and can attribute it to *the existence of hidden unconscious motives.* We may thus suspect the presence of such secret motives whenever a break of this kind in a train of thought is apparent or when the force ascribed by the patient to his motives goes far beyond the normal.

The gaps in neurotic experience and behaviour are often inconsistent. The findings shift and contradict each other. A man largely dead to all feeling can be at times very deeply moved. A man usually lacking any concentration, bored by everything, is sometimes capable of long periods of eager and intense work. In certain circumstances a weak-willed man develops surprising energy. A man unable to establish contact with others makes an encounter which realizes all his potential ability to love. On occasion a narcissistic introvert develops suddenly into an open, prudent man of action. Shy and modest people develop unusually high pretensions, softness and shrinking turn to violent aggressiveness, over-abstraction to a luxuriant excess of feeling which makes decisions much easier to reach. These are not just exceptional cases of a man acting out of character—a phenomenon which is common enough. It is rather that a second, latent or repressed character is showing through the gaps in the manifest mode of behaviour. One can also look at these findings from another point of view. One can make out a more or less systematic inventory of the instincts and feelings of the healthy man. As Lersch has shown us,[19] this can be done with great precision by the phenomenological method. If we make an inventory of neurotic experience and compare it with an inventory of normal experience, the former will seem full of gaps.

[19] In *Aufbau der Person,* Munich, 1954 (6).

And these gaps do not represent inherited defects, but deficiencies which can be explained by lack of early care, absence of the necessary processes of stimulation, learning, education, and by general distortions and disturbance of psychic forces.

Lack of Spontaneity

Lack of spontaneity is an invariable neurotic characteristic. Some of the findings we have already described suggest a general lack of this kind. "Even if no manifest incapacity for life results, there almost always follows a loss of power to make free use of the energies of the mind."[20] Whole areas of the personality which were once living become dead, frozen, inaccessible; the free play of vital forces is restricted. The person cannot control his "psychic organs" (A. Pfänder),[21] his "component structures" (A. Wellek). Vitality, instinct, emotion, memory and imagination, mind and heart, all seem oppressed, congested, their development obstructed; we can find inhibition of spontaneity in all aspects of the personality. This is much more than Schultz-Hencke's inhibition of instinctive life. Often some parts of the personality are powerfully active whilst others are restricted. A vivid imagination can go with the inhibition

[20] "Sexuality in the Aetiology of the Neuroses", *Collected Papers,* vol. 1, p. 247.

[21] *Die Seele des Menschen,* Halle, 1933 ("Seelenorgane").

of instincts and behaviour; when memories referring to certain periods or themes are shut out, the mind may be overwhelmed with memories of a different kind.

If the analytic method is properly used it can stimulate and release all kinds of spontaneous processes and regenerate petrified psychic structures. Thus the lapse or apparent lack of spontaneous experience in certain spheres has to be seen as an effect of inhibition and not as an inherited dispositional deficiency. The kind of experience and behaviour which in healthy people can easily mount to passionate intensity is also the kind which is most likely to be inhibited in neurotics. As Schultz-Hencke has shown, the chief themes of neurotic conflict and inhibition are firstly the person's relationship to his possessions in the widest sense—that is to everything, including forms of experience and behaviour that he wants to preserve. And then his aggressive tendencies; and finally his human relations, his power to love, to sacrifice himself, his sexual potency.

The neurotic usually lacks spiritual spontaneity; he is alienated from the natural springs of religion. Religious experience can lead to passionate inner conflicts; many kinds of anxiety and feelings of guilt can be due to unresolved difficulties in this sphere. Neurotics often lose their natural religious vitality and courage. And the consequent incoherence of their general outlook can itself cause further disturbance.

Lack of spontaneity is indeed the most striking neurotic characteristic of all. Every neurosis is a form of "psycho-sclerosis" in which all parts of the personality, but chiefly the feelings and emotions, can become more or less rigid and brittle. Freud first formulated this finding in his theory of the "strangulated affect".[22] He held that a virtual experience, or psychic reality which is not yet experienced and cannot yet reach full consciousness, produces a tension which often disturbs conscious life until it does in some way itself become conscious: "... *it follows from the existence of a symptom that some mental process has not been carried through to an end in a normal manner so that it could become conscious* ..." That is the fundamental pathogenetic principle of psychoanalysis.[23]

Ambivalence

A strong and often hidden tendency to ambivalence in feeling and wishing is the third important negative characteristic of neurosis.[24] Like discontinuity, this characteristic was described by Freud at an early stage. We can often

[22] "The Mechanism of Hysterical Phenomena", *Works,* vol. 2, p. 17.

[23] *Introductory Lectures on Psychoanalysis,* London, 1949 (2), pp. 247–8.

[24] "A Case of Successful Treatment by Hypnotism", *Collected Papers,* vol. 5, pp. 33ff.; *Introductory Lectures,* pp. 356ff., 369ff.; "The Dynamics of Transference", *Works,* vol. 12, p. 170.

find an undertow of counter-expectations, antithetical ideas, and counter-intentions (the "counter-will") below conscious expectations, hopes and fears, wishes and intentions, likes and dislikes. This split in the impulses and emotions which the neurotic feels towards persons, things, ends and values, is often disguised by a deceptive simplicity at the beginning of analysis and only appears as strong resistance, usually at first in the form of "transference" (see below) onto the analyst. Ambivalence causes high tension because one part of the split is rejected and forcibly relegated to the "dispositional unconscious". After this the part which is able to remain conscious develops out of proportion. (Cf. "A Case of Successful Treatment by Hypnotism.")

The term "ambivalence", taken over from Bleuler, originally referred to the fact that contrasting instinctive pairs, for example sadism and masochism, are formed in approximately the same way.[25] But today the normal sense is the one used above. Thus, neurotics are said to be ambivalent because they often feel intense love and hate towards the same person; the same object is at once feared and longed for.

Instinctual Disintegration

Every neurotic has an unbalanced instinctual

[25] "Three Essays on the Theory of Sexuality", *Works,* vol. 7, p. 199; "Instincts and their Vicissitudes", *Works,* vol. 14, p. 131.

life. The instincts are not integrated into his human life as a whole; they have not yet found their proper place, or they have lost it. Individual tendencies have asserted themselves at the expense of the whole, have established a tyranny which suppresses other parts of the personality.[26] Instinctual atrophy and hypertrophy are closely associated in neurosis. This is true of all instinctual life, but especially of sexual life, which is usually disordered and distorted by perverse tendencies. In hysteria particularly, but also in other neuroses,[27] we find both an over-valuation of sexual life (which is often disguised by its anxious depreciation)[28] and the dangerous coincidence of abnormally high sexual needs with sexual over-abstinence.

Infantilism and Fixation

The first form of fixation, which was already known to Breuer, is fixation on the trauma.[29] The hysteric suffers from his memories[30]; some past experience proves so indigestible that the traumatic scene is repeatedly brought up in the form of symptoms and reacted against symbolically. Freud saw that this was only a particular case of the general rule that neurosis implies

[26] "The Unconscious", *Works,* vol. 14, pp. 194–5.
[27] "Three Essays on Sexuality", *Works,* vol. 7, p. 165.
[28] "Observations on Transference-Love", *Works,* vol. 12, p. 170.
[29] *Introductory Lectures,* pp. 231ff.
[30] "The Mechanism of Hysterical Phenomena", *Works,* vol. 2, pp. 8f.

not only a fixation on a particular trauma, but also an inescapable adherence to many different kinds of past experience.

Neurotics show infantile or juvenile characteristics in great variety. Experience and behaviour are partly retarded and follow childish patterns. "Fixation can be described in this way. One instinct or intellectual component fails to accompany the rest along the anticipated normal path of development, and, in consequence of this inhibition in its development, it is left behind at a more infantile stage."[31] Neurotics are often prepared to do only the things that would be expected of a child, and continue to expect the world to treat them as if they were children. Neurosis does not lead to a complete standstill in the way that melancholy does, but as Von Gebsattel has pointed out, it leads to activity and thought which go round in circles.[32] The neurotic does not move in an ascending spiral; he makes an endless, noisy song and dance which leads to nothing. In Freud's terminology, he is afflicted by "repetition-compulsion".[33]

Infantile fixation appears in many forms: in slavery to the "pleasure-principle",[34] or to specific

[31] "An Autobiographical Account of Paranoia", *Works,* vol. 12, p. 67.

[32] "Störungen des Werdens und des Zeiterlebens im Rahmen psychiatrischer Erkrankungen", in *Prolegomena einer medizinischen Anthropologie,* Berlin, 1954.

[33] *New Introductory Lectures on Psychoanalysis,* trans. W. J. H. Sprott, London, 1949, p. 137.

[34] *Introductory Lectures,* p. 299.

kinds of pleasure, in "oral" and unnaturally high demands and expectations of other people, in inability to abstain even for a short time from instinctual satisfactions, in attitudes of defiance, in excessive identifications with parents or others, in an exaggerated need for protection, security and authority.

The neurotic is usually so fixated on ideal images that he is largely alienated from himself. Without knowing it, he tries to be completely the same as, or entirely different from, some ideal figure left over from childhood. Primitive layers of the personality sometimes establish an impregnable dominance and remain uninformed by a mature personal superstructure; instead, the pre-personal sphere is surrounded by the super-ego, a rough scaffolding itself constructed out of material from the primitive layers. The emotional life of the neurotic is dominated by the kind of negative feelings which properly belong in the nursery: dependence on others, impotent defiance, envy, rivalry, insecurity and fear of punishment, of loneliness and of not being loved. These feelings are always powerful, but usually repressed. The word "fixation" (in the sense of the previously formed structure rather than the formative process) itself suggests that there is nothing childlike in the good sense about neurotic infantilism; it is nearer the kind of petrified rigidity which appears in second childhood. What is lacking in neurotic infantilism is the child's ability to learn, to discover new realms of experience and eagerly explore them—in a word, to develop; and the vitality of the mature man depends on this ability as well. Neurosis prolongs or halts the course of development. The neurotic does not want to grow. He is content to remain at the stage he has already reached. With healthy people, infantile fixations dissolve when new stages of development bring new joys and sorrows, values and objects. According to Freud, fixations remain intact when the impulse to maturity is injured or blocked or burdened with feelings of anxiety and guilt after the person has entered a new stage of development. In these conditions the impulse is repressed, and the person begins to inhabit an unreal world. His behaviour is determined by infantile fantasies, imaginary pleasures and fear of the punishment which is supposed to be due for these pleasures.[35] Under analysis these things force their way into consciousness. Profound autistic regressions can result from this; the patient no longer tries to resist his infantile fantasies and impulses but surrenders to the world which he has created for himself and becomes alienated from reality.

In every analysis we find things which are common to neurotics of all kinds; but we also find experience and behaviour which are typical

[35] Anna Freud, *The Ego and the Mechanisms of Defence*, trans. Cecil Baines, London, 1937, pp. 3–4.

of normal human nature everywhere. It is therefore very easy to confuse the common human condition with the neurotic condition. Fixation was discovered by Freud. In the cave allegory Plato described man as bound by chains to shadows; in a sense he described the inhibited, fixated man. But this slavery to the εἴδωλα, this "making the relative absolute",[36] is not the same as Freud's fixation. The term is ambiguous; or, more precisely, it is analogical, referring to different things or different levels of existence. The fixation of a vital instinct is not the same as the fixation of the choosing centre of the person on what it has chosen. It is different from a binding of heart and faith made by a mature and physically healthy man. A man can be vitally, libidinously fixated on a certain object, but nevertheless be personally free in his relations with that object. And even when the centre of the person supports and adopts the fixation of the libido as it appears in a distorted inclination (this may be much more often the case than not), the personal attitude and the libidinous fixation are still essentially distinct. Disorder in a person's attitude towards values, and in the habitual dispositions of the choosing centre of the person, is not the same as disorder in the pre-personal sphere of emotions and tendencies. The first is a matter of good and evil, the second a matter of health and sickness. If a neurotic is hungry but nevertheless experiences disgust and nausea at

[36] I. Caruso and W. Daim; see above, pp. 76–7.

the prospect of food, then his pre-personal order of sensation is clearly upset, and we shall be able to discover traumatic and infantile fixations. And in most cases we shall also be able to find distortions in personal attitudes—the relative will have been made absolute. But the coincidence of these two kinds of neurotic characteristics does not, of course, allow us to deduce any causal connection between them. A man suffering from anorexy may achieve the highest degree of central personal order. Such order does not immunize him against neurosis any more than personal disorder necessarily leads to pre-personal disorder. Witches and bad men burn in the fairy stories, but not always in reality. On the contrary, we can quite often see how an increase in personal order must be paid for by neurotic disturbance, by a revolt of pre-personal nature. As we have already said, there is order in the personal sphere which makes a man good. And there is order in the pre-personal sphere which makes a man psychically healthy. If we can find neuroses in animals, and in children too young to choose freely between moral alternatives, then we see that psychic sickness need not be due to personal guilt. The point was laboriously made by Freud, but it still needs to be emphasized. Although, as a person, man has some limited control over himself, as a natural being he is determined by all kinds of laws and causal interrelations over which the centre of his person has no control.

Anthropology is more than the science of the free and responsible human person.

LATENT PERVERSION[37]

In connection with his theory of infantile fixation, Freud developed the idea of neurosis as perversion. He held that neurosis was due to repressed and unacknowledged perversion,[38] and to the tendency to repress such perversion. The theory was badly received, but it contained a kernel of truth. No-one denies that gross and humiliating perversions do exist. But most people prefer to imagine that only a few psychopaths are afflicted in this way. They find it unpleasant to be told that traces of perversion, often very distinct traces, are to be found not just in neurotics but also in the fantasies and behaviour of the ordinary healthy man.

Freud's thesis was based on a broad range of empirical observations. The first of these was that neurotics are only rarely capable of full and mature heterosexual love. They cannot forget themselves and turn with inspired tenderness to another. They cannot become one flesh with

[37] Cf. M. Boss, *Sinn und Gehalt der sexuellen Perversionen*, Bern and Stuttgart, 1952; O. Fenichel, *Perversionen, Psychosen, Charakterstörungen*, Vienna, 1931; Von Gebsattel, *Prolegomena einer medizinischen Anthropologie*, Berlin and Heidelberg, 1954; H. Kunz, "Zur Theorie der Perversion", *Mschr. f. Psychiatrie*, 105 (1942), p. 1.

[38] "Three Essays on the Theory of Sexuality", *Works*, vol. 7, p. 165; "My Views on the Part played by Sexuality in the Aetiology of Neurosis", *Works*, vol. 7, pp. 271ff.

another and so find happiness and peace. Sexuality by itself can only give a hint, an incomplete sketch, often an ugly caricature, of human love as it can and should be; full and genuine love can dissolve the inner anxiety and resistance which lead to its travesty and obstruct its progress.

Freud's second observation was that the conscious and unconscious fantasies, which disturb the neurotic and which he tries to repress, include wish-fantasies of a more or less perverted sexual kind. These fantasies often occur in childhood or youth and can only be suppressed with the greatest difficulty.

Many of the preconscious fantasies associated with neurotic symptoms have a sexual significance. For example, hysterical disturbances affecting eating can be accompanied by conscious or preconscious fantasies in which the mouth appears as the organ of conception. Occasionally harmless childish ideas of oral conception, or less harmless seduction scenes, occur to hysterical patients without any previous suggestion. One can also find coprophagous (excrement-eating) impulses. Frequently sexual sensations either can only be experienced in the oral zone or cannot be experienced in this zone at all. Findings of this kind formed the basis of Freud's theory of oral sexuality.

Neurotics often tell the analyst of sadistic or masochistic[39] experiences, and also of the sexual

[39] "A Child is Being Beaten", *Works,* vol. 17, pp. 175ff.

sensations to which Freud was referring when he talked of the production of pleasure from the stimulation of erogoneous zones,[40] for example the pleasure produced by defecation and its associated activities. We may also find tendencies towards sexual exhibitionism and the voyeur's perversion among the instinctual forms which have been relegated to the dispositional unconscious.

These tendencies usually only become conscious or semi-conscious insofar as they are legitimized in professional, scientific or aesthetic interests. And fixation on these more or less hidden tendencies is among the most important of neurotic characteristics.

In many psychoanalytic case-histories what Freud called "latent homosexuality" appears as the real key to the patient's condition. According to Freud, "What men essentially repress is their paederastic element",[41] and "analysis shows that in every case, a homosexual attachment to an object has at one time been present and in most cases has persisted in a latent condition".[42] But Freud seems to have used "latent homosexuality" in a sense to cover a variety of things

[40] Cf. "Three Essays on the Theory of Sexuality", *Works,* vol. 7, pp. 123ff.

[41] *The Origins of Psychoanalysis,* London, 1954, p. 204; cf., against this, "A Child is Being Beaten", *Works,* vol. 17, pp. 200ff., and further, "From the History of an Infantile Neurosis", *Works,* vol. 17, pp. 1ff.

[42] *An Outline of Psychoanalysis,* trans. J. Strachey, London, 1949, p. 14.

not strictly connected with homosexuality at all; for example, anxious submission to the father and his successors due to broken self-regard, or identification and abortive identification. But it is nevertheless certainly true that the neurotic is often unable to solve the problems presented by the homosexual feelings which naturally appear at certain human phases of development. We can see these feelings in, for example, girlhood crushes or adolescent hero-worship. Homosexual fixation is the result of a complex and obscure process which can be determined by a variety of external influences. Both homosexual tendencies and fear of homosexuality are often met with in analysis, and it is easier to heal the neurosis if they can be brought under control.

According to Freud auto-eroticism, particularly in the form of childhood masturbation and the fantasies which accompany it, is of the greatest importance for an understanding of the genesis and psychology of neurosis. Even where there is no actual masturbation, analytic investigation leads to the discovery of behaviour, often unconscious, which seems to suggest the act of masturbation or at least to suggest a repressed wish to masturbate. Perhaps because of the resemblance, such forms of behaviour afford a certain amount of pleasurable satisfaction or, even when they are not pleasurable, at least some release from tension. Occasionally one can observe that such symptoms begin immediately after the habit of masturbation has been successfully conquered.[43]

One of the difficulties of the analytic method appears here. We have good grounds for accepting that a repressed impulse can reappear in a form of behaviour which is similar to the original impulse, and that this resemblance can afford satisfaction to the subject. But we have to be extremely careful when it comes to applying this principle. Outward resemblance does not necessarily imply an inner relationship of any kind, and nothing is easier to find than an analogy.

If we were determined in advance to see things in this way, we could see almost all human behaviour as an analogical expression of perversion. If he wants to, the analyst can see the journalist's pleasure in writing as the sublimated expression of an urethral or sexual tendency to soil himself. On the other hand, it is not really possible to reduce psychoanalysis to an absurdity, as people often try to do, by multiplying examples of this kind. There are in fact cases of constrictions in writing where independent evidence as well as outward resemblance seems to justify a sexual interpretation. It can be that the neurotic wants to abstain from what he unconsciously equates with the illicit pleasure of soiling himself. But it is the independent evi-

[43] "Analysis of a Phobia in a Five-year-old Boy", *Collected Papers,* vol. 3, trans. Alix and James Strachey, London, 1925, pp. 149ff.

dence which justifies this kind of interpretation and makes it convincing. Suppose, for example, an hysterical seizure takes a form resembling some sexual act, or the act of giving birth. One would need to know from free association or hypnotic exploration that the patient experienced corresponding fantasies before or during the seizure in order to be able to interpret the symptoms on the basis of the resemblance.

Kretschmer's attempt to explain hysterical seizures on the analogy of fits of excitement in the lower animals shows how carefully one must proceed when making this kind of explanation. His explanation only stands if very broad theoretical assumptions are granted.

Throughout his work and especially in his case-histories and lectures and in the *Psychopathology of Everyday Life*, Freud offers interpretations of, for example, errors and compulsive rituals, on the basis of their similarity to sexual or pregenital behaviour. Some of these interpretations are far-fetched and unconvincing. But others help to reduce extremely complex behaviour to order, and give convincing explanations of what the behaviour really expresses.

Inclinations and dispositions which merely show similarities to perversion are perhaps more important than actual sexual perversion. Sadism is, strictly speaking, a perversion in which sexual pleasure is sought for in, and gained from, the infliction of pain; but apparently neurotics often also gain non-sexual pleasure from pain. Many neurotics are cruel, quarrelsome and feel strong impulses to destroy things and to criticize, subject and humble others. But this is not the place to answer the questions, "What precisely is the origin and nature of this desire for pain?" and "What has sadism in this sense to do with sexual sadism?"[44] Masochism is a perversion in which sexual pleasure is derived from suffering pain. Pleasure is also derived from humiliation, often of the grossest kind. The instinctual impulse is matched by a tendency to spiritual self-torture, to self-humiliation; and to seek unpleasant treatment, situations and circumstances and make no attempt to escape from them. The subtle pleasure derived from this kind of behaviour is often as obvious to the observer as the sexual pleasure derived from the actual perversion. We have, of course, no right to derive one kind of behaviour from the other genetically just because they resemble each other; and every tendency to punish or despise oneself is not necessarily sublimated (sexual) masochism. But the resemblance remains, and it needs some theoretical explanation.[45] An explanation is also necessary because traces of manifest perversion are sometimes found in conjunction with dispositions which merely resemble those of per-

[44] Occasionally Freud described sadism simply as an instinct to dominate. ("Three Essays on the Theory of Sexuality", *Works,* vol. 7, pp. 193, 199.)

[45] H. Kunz, *Die Aggressivität und die Zärtlichkeit, zwei psychologische Studien,* Bern, 1946; M. Boss, *Sinn und Gehalt der sexuellen Perversionen.*

versions; there are all kinds of transitional forms. A particularly harsh employer may recognize sadistic fantasies in himself; or a man who is too hard on himself may remember sexual-masochistic images, temptations or experiences of pleasure.

The same applies to other perversions. Exhibitionism is matched by pleasure in spiritual self-revelation which can seem decidedly perverted to the observer. Some patients obtain a distinct pleasure from analysis, and relate their sexual experiences with shameless freedom at unnecessary length. It is not that the patient is showing particular care in observing the rules of analysis; on the contrary, he is placing a powerful obstacle in the way of successful treatment. Neurotics can try to involve the inexperienced or over-theoretical analyst in their neurosis and make him into an accomplice by drenching him in sexual revelations, or by leading him back by coquetry and assumed prudishness into their sexual past. By such means they cover the traces of the really important hidden distortions.[46]

For theoretical reasons Freud also included under the heading of sexual perversions forms of behaviour which yield no perverted sexual pleasure and which do not even resemble sexual perversions. Freud held that these forms of behaviour were related to sexual perversions

[46] We have already dealt with narcissism, one of the fundamental distorted dispositions which resemble perversion.

simply because they were compulsive and because they yielded pleasure of some kind. The course of neurotic experience is at once driven and blocked or tortured by fantasies, impulses, motives, and forms of pleasure which seem unintelligible, strange and repulsive to the neurotic himself. These movements sometimes appear in striking contrast to the neurotic's usual cultural, ethical or aesthetic character. They break into his conscious experience with uncontrollable force, and in this respect they are formally similar to perversion. Almost all neurotics are plagued by sudden, unintelligible invasions of avarice or greed, or unmotivated envy, suspicion, inconsiderateness, by destructive urges or irruptions of burning ambition, by unaccountable delight in obscenity or vulgarity, torturing sensitiveness, unfounded fears of all kinds, unreasonable feelings and impulses.

Before we turn to Freud's fourth group of observations, it may help to make some preliminary observations from the genetic and theoretical points of view. Freud held that sexual impulses can be found in very young children. The experiences of children, he maintained, contain an element of physical pleasure which is really a particular form of sexual pleasure.[47] We can find this pleasure in sucking at the breast, eating and drinking, thumb-sucking, in tactile

[47] "Three Essays on the Theory of Sexuality", *Works,* vol. 7, pp. 204, 205; "Psychoanalyse und Libidotheorie", *Werke,* vol. 13, p. 220.

sensations produced by washing, cuddling and smacking, in the sensations produced by rocking in cradle or arms, by pot-training, and when the child exercises its muscles and plays with its own body. Apart from this, any strong emotion tends to produce sexual movements. According to Freud all these forms of experience and behaviour have a sexual content; in all these cases, as he puts it, "pleasure is produced by the stimulation of erogenous zones".

But these experiences also have a spiritual and intellectual content. In some of them the child is experiencing his parents' love and care for him, or becoming aware of values which are concerned with more than the gaining of sensual pleasure. The activities themselves, and the experiences of the child, amount to more than just pleasurable or unpleasurable stimulations and reactions. They are *signs* which have a meaning. And we have to analyse the meaning of oral or anal experience and behaviour, as well as analyse the sensual pleasure which it can produce. We can illustrate this by an example from Freud.

> Children who are making use of the susceptibility to erotogenic stimulations of the anal zone betray themselves by holding back their stool till its accumulation brings about violent muscular contractions and, as it passes through the anus, is able to produce powerful stimulation of the mucous membrane. In so doing it

must no doubt cause not only painful but also highly pleasurable sensations. One of the clearest signs of subsequent eccentricity or nervousness is to be seen when a baby obstinately refuses to empty his bowels when he is put on the pot—that is, when his nurse wants him to—and holds back that function until he himself chooses to exercise it. He is naturally not concerned with dirtying the bed, he is only anxious not to miss the subsidiary pleasure attached to defecating. Educators are once more right when they describe children who keep this process back as "naughty".

The contents of the bowels have other important *meanings* for the infant. They are clearly treated as part of the infant's own body and represent his first "gift"; *by producing them he can express his active compliance with his environment and, by withholding them, his disobedience.*[48]

So we can move on from the sensual aspect of anal behaviour to consider its possible meanings. We can consider its relations to human existence in the widest sense; how it illustrates defiant self-assertion, obstinacy, willing or unwilling co-operation with the desires of others, and the early experience of the contrast between law and freedom. We can also see impulses to save for

[48] "Three Essays on the Theory of Sexuality", *Works,* vol. 7, p. 186. (Our italics.)

oneself and to give up one's own property. The second impulse may certainly imply the sacrifice of erogenous stimulation, but it is clear that we are dealing here with experiences which are not sensually pleasurable as such. Thus Freud's concepts of anal and oral eroticism refer to a variety of different findings. And he had himself already moved from the analysis of sensual pleasure to the analysis of the meaning of the experience which produces it. Modern work is concentrating more and more on the latter kind of analysis.[49] When modern psychologists say that the depressive is orally determined and disturbed, they mean much more than that his condition is due to a frustrated desire for sensual pregenital pleasure from the stimulation of the mucous membrane of the mouth.

Thus Freud's concepts of latent perversion, oral and anal[50] eroticism and the Oedipal (dealt with below), refer to findings which extend beyond the striving for pleasure from the stimulation of erogenous zones. Neurotic tendencies are concentrated around certain characteristic motivational themes, and the neurotic is led to overvalue these motives by his fear and unsatisfied longings. Neuroses are "distorted forms of

[49] There are some fundamental analyses of the meaning of the experiences of young children in G. Siewerth, *Metaphysik der Kindheit,* Einsiedeln, 1957.

[50] A more detailed description of the significance of oral and anal themes is given in the section on "The Formation and Development of the Personality in the Light of Psychoanalysis", below, pp. 235ff.

the impulse to love" (W. Heinen) in the widest sense.

Thus we do not have to take the thesis that neurosis is perversion only in a literal sense. We can also take it to mean simply that there are passionate instinctual movements and feelings which can cause the neurotic to behave in ways which seem to him wrong, ugly or unworthy, and which he therefore refuses to admit. Behaviour of this kind is normally forbidden by ostensibly healthy people; in some cases it is counted as definitely criminal. But common norms are not infallible, whether they are held by groups of individuals or by whole civilizations. They are influenced by individual feelings and by cultural assumptions.

Neurotics often repress desires or feelings simply because they *feel* that they are inadmissible. Freud's thesis was an attempt to understand neurotic behaviour by finding its predominant motives. He held that the neurotic is unable to accept his own predominant motives, and that the most important group of motives, at once rejected by him and determining his behaviour, consists of perverted tendencies. Thus for Freud one of the chief aims of analysis is the revelation of perverse (and genital) instinctual elements in neurotic symptoms and behaviour.

The chief question raised in the controversy over psychoanalysis is whether perverted motives can give a sufficient explanation of neurosis. And in fact all kinds of other motives were revealed by Freud's own analysis. For example the desires for power, recognition and security and the desire to be independent of others. But Freud held that sexual force was attached to these motives from their origins and that it was only by virtue of this force that they could lead to neurosis. Adler opposed this with the thesis that the really important cause of neurosis was not so much the sexual motive as the desire for power and recognition. Schultz-Hencke represents a third position. He claims to have discovered several characteristic, or, rather, predominant, neurotic motives. He holds that the motives which actually explain neurosis are ones that bring the neurotic into conflict with the surrounding world and with himself. The formula comes from Freud. Schultz-Hencke himself emphasizes the ultimate nature of these motives—they cannot be reduced to others. The most important ones are the desires for property, for recognition and for love.

We can now sum up the properly established findings of psychoanalysis on perversion. First, any extended analysis of the neurotic reveals perverted tendencies and defences erected against them. We find them in memories, fantasies, dreams, fears, in manifest and often very powerful impulses, and in other outward forms of behaviour. Conflicts produced by perverted sexual tendencies and incestuous tendencies (see below) are very common in neurosis; and the neurotic's approach to them and the way in which he tries to master them have an important influence on his psychic condition. We must therefore conclude that these perverted tendencies are of fundamental importance in neurosis.

Freud also gave us valuable descriptions of some of the distortions of the impulse to love which are characteristic of neurosis. For theoretical reasons he counted them as manifestations of sexuality, and this must be rejected. But the most general formulation of Freud's findings can be accepted: neurotic disorder is produced by the repression of uncontrolled and passionate feelings and desires which can be neither accepted nor renounced nor cast in any acceptable form.

The doctrine of the structural and genetic relationship between neurosis and perversion is one of the most fruitful working hypotheses in psychoanalysis. If the sexual emphasis is one of the weak points in psychoanalysis considered as theoretical science of man, it is one of the strongest points in its empirical doctrine of neurosis. But it is important not to overstate the case. Even if man were sexually neutral, without sexual instincts and erogenous zones, we could probably still find fixation, repression, inhibition, instinctual tension, anxiety, aggression, conflict, and disordered psychic development.

Finally, in actual experience we can find many neuroses which are very largely determined by sexual disturbances. And it is also true that there is scarcely a single neurosis in which the sexual sphere remains unaffected. But so far as we can see, there are also neuroses in which the main problems are non-sexual. Yet according to Freudian theory all neuroses are sexual because all forms of love (taken to include not just love for persons, but also love for things and values—love of home, truth and justice) are derived from the sexual instinct and its embryonic forms.[51] The arguments for this seem few and poor.

NEUROTIC COMPLEXES

In the most popular account the neurotic is a man suffering from complexes. Freud's first use of the term is in the phrase "subconscious complexes of ideas".[52] This describes a mental content which is repressed and inaccessible to memory, a structural disposition which has mainly a disturbing influence on present experience and behaviour and causes the person in question to react emotionally against certain situations and objects. The disposition is impressed into the unconscious mind by some wounding experience or trauma (cf. Breuer's patient Anna O. and her inability to drink, above pp. 16–17).

Psychoanalysis originated with the discovery of traumatic complexes of this kind. It appeared after this, that partial structures formed by the

[51] See below p. 251.
[52] "Studies on Hysteria", *Works,* vol. 2, p. 69*n*.

powerful effect of single traumas were much less important in the genesis of neurosis than great distortions of the whole structure of the personality formed over a long period of development. The findings which are described by the terms "Oedipus complex" and "castration complex" are concerned with these long-term distortions.

The relevant findings, insofar as they are surely based upon and easily accessible to analytic investigation, are as follows. The analysis of neurotics shows that a disturbed emotional relationship to the father and the mother is an important, and sometimes the most important, theme. Neurotics are either passionately attached to their parents or they passionately reject them, although they frequently disguise their feelings by assumed coldness or indifference. The neurotic's emotional life is governed, often up to old age, by his hatred and defiance of his parents, and by his fear of them, subjection to them and exaggerated dependence on their image or efforts to win their love and approval. When analysis dissolves inhibitions and liberates spontaneity, an ambivalent attitude towards the parents appears. The ambivalence is often highly aggressive and is sometimes erotically or sexually tinged. We can often find feelings of hostility and envy towards the parent of the same sex, tender overtures towards the parent of the opposite sex, and heavy feelings of guilt towards both parents. Relations with older people and with people of the opposite sex are, to some extent, governed and upset by parental relations; we can see this particularly in the choice of marriage partner and in marital relations, and also in other matters, such as the choice and conduct of a career. The memories and observations which lead us to assume the existence of Oedipal influences in childhood will be dealt with in the section on the genesis of neurosis.

The findings which Freud described under the heading of "castration complex" are of various kinds. Most neurotics have an ambivalent attitude towards their own sexual natures and feel insecurity about their sexual roles. Male neurotics tend at once to fear and long for everything which seems especially masculine; neurotic women are unsure about their womanhood. The neurotic feels that he or she is unmasculine or unfeminine, and this involves conflicts and difficulties.[53] The male neurotic may be afraid of his emotions because he is not sure of his masculinity. Sometimes a neurotic woman will exaggerate her rational capacities to show that she lacks none of the attributes of the other sex. Apart from the neurotic's ambivalent attitude towards his own particular sex, we find that in most cases he is ambivalent towards sexual experience in general. His attitude is a mixture of anxious rejection and gross over-valuation. Tenderness,

[53] This is well exemplified both in and by Simone de Beauvoir's book *The Second Sex*, trans. H. M. Parshley, London, 1953.

love, sexual feelings are destroyed by fear or disgust; sometimes they are never present at all. Sexuality is not integrated into the neurotic personality. The neurotic is ridden by powerful feelings of guilt. Sometimes these are due to real disorders in sexual behaviour which are often to be found; sometimes they are unfounded and attached to sexual life as such. The unconscious philosophy of the neurotic is Manicheism; a rejection of the body and the sexual faculty, often accompanied by a subterranean luxuriance of sexuality. The opening sentence of Porphyry's Life of Plotinus could be applied to many neurotics: "Plotinus was a man who was ashamed to be in a body".[54]

Together with this general intolerance of sex and general fear of sex inadequacy, we can often find a specific fear of mutilation or castration which appears in fantasies and dreams. Freud believed that the desire to confront other men in a passive, feminine, "castrated" role lay at the root of every male neurosis, and that the neurotic woman was similarly dominated by the desire to become in some way the sexual equal of the man. Freud held that he could find these motives in everyone. But it seems to be true that although there are certainly traces of these motives in everyone, it is only the neurotic who

[54] *Porphyrii Vita Plotini*, in *Plotini Opera*, ed. P. Henry, S.J., and H. R. Schwyzer, Paris and Brussels, 1951, vol. 1, p. 1.

becomes fixated on them and for whom they make an insoluble problem.

In healthy people we do not find discontinuity, lapses and gaps, lack of spontaneity, psychosclerosis or fixation. And therefore the elements of latent perversion which may be present in healthy people can produce no powerful effect on their personalities. A healthy young girl may have a strong Oedipal link with her father. But she can nevertheless turn her feelings towards another man, whereas her neurotic sister will never be able to forgive her husband for not being her father. In the sister's case the old feelings are strong enough to prevent the growth of new ones.

What reasons have we for supposing that the motives and structures which Freud describes are the most important neurotic characteristics? Other investigators using the same analytic method have found other motives and conflicts and interrelations which seem equally essential to neurosis. If we follow Freud's interpretation, what guarantee have we that we are not overlooking the essential, and exaggerating the significance of the unimportant? Freud himself admitted in his old age that the essential nature of neurosis was still a mystery to him. The psychoanalytic method cannot by itself give us the answers to these questions. We can find phenomena and structures in neurotics which occur so regularly that they could well be considered as essential neurotic characteristics. But the psychoanalytic method is always open to the discovery of new facts and interrelations. Adler, Jung, Binswanger and Gebsattel, of the generation following Freud, and other investigators of a later generation, not only reformulated Freud's discoveries, but used the method to reveal aspects of psychic sickness which were unknown to him. Freud never claimed that he saw all there was to see; the only claim that the psychoanalyst is entitled to make is that what he sees is really there.

NATURE AND DETERMINANTS OF NEUROTIC EMOTIONAL LIFE

When we analyse the course of neurotic experience we can see various patterns which are structurally determined. One of the most significant of these patterns is made by peculiarities in the course of emotional experience. The peculiarities are especially significant because they appear very frequently in analysis and they can be easily discerned as abnormal. Research into neurotic emotional development by both the psychoanalytic and other methods grows in detail and volume every year[55]; and we cannot cover all the findings here. Therefore, instead of

[55] J. McV. Hunt, "Experimental Psychoanalysis", in Harriman's *Encyclopaedia of Psychology*, 1946; *Personality and the Behavior Disorders*, New York, 1944; K. Lewin (ed.), *Untersuchungen zur Handlungs- und Affektpsychologie*; F. Hoppe, *Erfolg und Misserfolg*; T. Dembo, "Der Ärger als dynamisches Problem", in *Psyche. Forschung*, 14 (1930) and 15 (1931).

dealing with all the various ways in which neurotic emotions can be displaced, disguised or reversed, we shall only consider *deprivation*, a particularly important determinant of emotional life, as an illustration of the way in which this aspect of neurosis can be studied by the analytic method.

When a small child is refused what he wants, there are many ways in which he can deal with the refusal. If he cannot get his train set fetched from the cupboard, he can comfort himself with a ball or with a sweet. Or he can cry or scream or hit his mother. Or he can run out of the room and sulk on his bed and deprive his parents of the joy of his company. No-one has taught him these possible reactions; they are discoveries of what Lersch calls the "primal imagination" (*Urphantasie*).

In analysis we can see how the adult reacts to the deprivations and disappointments brought by daily life. One of the great gains of maturity, a sure sign of psychic health, is the ability to bear denials and refusals without resorting to compensating instinctual satisfactions. As a rule neurotics possess only a very small degree of this "frustration tolerance".[56] The neurotic is frustrated more than the healthy man because he claims and expects more, and he can tolerate his frustration less because he attaches more

[56] S. Rosenzweig, "An Outline of Frustration Theory", in J. McV. Hunt, *Personality and the Behavior Disorders*, New York, 1944, vol. 1, p. 379.

importance and significance to deprivation and disappointment. He has no capacity for abstention from pleasure or recovery from disappointment. The neurotic's whole psychic organism is hypersensitive and allergic to disappointment.

The healthy man can get over his disappointment that there is not enough housekeeping money for a glass of beer with dinner. The neurotic begins to torture himself: "I can't be any good or I would have enough money for beer—poverty is round the corner—my wife should have done without her new dress—she doesn't love me any more—she prefers the children—who gave her the right to take decisions over my head?" and so on. In short, he wants to cry or hit someone, take to his bed or suck a sweet, just as his young son did when he refused to get the train set out of the cupboard for him. And this is because a glass of beer, worldly goods in general, mean far too much to him in terms of prestige, security and satisfaction. If the neurotic is in any way disappointed during analysis, we can observe this kind of behaviour very clearly.

The neurotic's reaction to disappointment is even more important than the significance he attaches to it. Upbringing and the urge to conform usually place obstacles (Freud's "defensive attitudes" and "reaction-formation") to the reaction and prevent its complete development. Thus the real nature of the aggressive reaction may not appear; instead, we can observe a tearful mood, a striking unwillingness to work, or what Freud called a "conversion-manifestation" —a corresponding somatic-sensual feeling such as tiredness, stomach-ache or headache. But once spontaneity has been revived in analysis, the real nature of reactions will appear after a time. The course of the emotions becomes more clearly articulated. We can make out sequences: for example, disappointment—injured feelings —aggression—repression—depression—greed or desire. At the same time the picture changes. The developed emotions are no longer repressed, but consciously criticized. The glass of beer shrinks to its proper size. Imagination searches for other solutions, claims and expectations become more realistic and injuries become easier to bear. At first aggression mounts, but it cannot maintain itself in the general relaxation of tension; and depression declines proportionately. Thus in analysis we see how particular "mechanisms" or patterns in the course of experience gradually lose their power. The rigidity of a mechanical sequence grows elastic under the influence of reason.

We still know very little about all the various determinants of the development of fear and anxiety, feelings of guilt and depression.[57] It seems that anxiety can be produced by disappointments and by inhibited aggression and the stoppage of libidinal drives. But inhibitions of aggression can also lead to greed, manic be-

[57] There is a good analysis of "painful" experience in W. Daim, *Umwertung der Psychoanalyse*, Vienna, 1951, p. 143f.

haviour and depression. We have no precise idea of when and why aggression leads to these different results. Analytic observation does not lead to lightning solutions of all psychological problems; it merely gives us the opportunity to collect more and more material, and compare it, order it and gradually come to understand it.

CONFLICT

Neurosis begins in unresolved conflict. The neurotic is divided against himself. His psychic forces split him into two warring parts and the front lines are static. Will and counter-will, impulse and defence, damage each other or form compromises of various kinds.

According to Freud the hysterical symptom originates in a compromise between two conflicting emotional or instinctual movements. One of these tries to bring forward a component impulse or component element of the sexual constitution, and the other tries to suppress it.[58]

Freud describes the classical onset of neurosis as follows:

> These patients whom I analysed had enjoyed good mental health up to the time at which an intolerable idea presented itself within the

[58] "Hysterische Phantasien und ihre Beziehung zur Bisexualität", *Werke,* vol. 7, p. 196. This treatise gives the most concise account of the psychoanalytic theory of symptoms, resuming it under nine heads.

content of their ideational life; that is to say, until their ego was confronted by an experience, an idea, a feeling, arousing an affect so painful that the person resolved to forget it, since he had no confidence in his power to resolve the incompatibility between the unbearable idea and his ego by the process of thought.[59]

We now expect analysis as far as possible to clarify the conflict situation which follows neurosis. We know definitely that conflicts occur as soon as neurosis has begun. But what is *post hoc* is not always *propter hoc*, and the connection between conflict and the onset of neurosis is not self-evident. Viktor Frankl has suggested that a neurosis with an unknown (e.g., "endogenous") origin produces as its initial symptom an intensification of conflict or a decline in the neurotic's ability to deal with conflict, and that the more massive symptoms which follow later have no connection with this conflict.[60] The hypothesis seems improbable because it overlooks or underemphasizes two important facts. The first is that the various kinds of attacks which accompany fully developed neuroses and psycho-somatic illnesses can be ended by experiences involving

[59] "The Defence Neuro-Psychoses", *Collected Papers*, vol. 1, pp. 61, 62.

[60] Viktor Frankl, *Theorie und Therapie der Neurosen*, Vienna, 1956.

conflict.[61] The same applies to all symptoms which fluctuate in their intensity. The second fact is that analysis seems to alter the intensity of the conflicts which appear at the onset of neurosis: it can either encourage or remove symptoms and anxiety; distorted attitudes and behaviour and inner tension can grow rigid or they can disappear, sometimes permanently.

Analysis shows us human nature at odds with itself. The neurotic is unable to give himself over without anxiety to the course marked out by his own personal possibilities. He moves from conflict to conflict; and he has to learn to cultivate his untamed instinctual tendencies, observe the conditions of instinctual satisfaction and build limits and countervailing defensive and inhibiting forces into the structure of his personality. He has to learn and practise productive forms of mastering instincts and conflicts.

Neurosis shows that these structure-forming processes are absent or have remained incomplete. The neurotic cannot dispose of the proper "techniques" for mastering or appropriating experience, and as a result natural conflicts deepen and are either circumvented or approached in the wrong way.

It is a fundamental principle of psychoanalytic phenomenology and theory that neurosis is determined by conflict. But it does not

[61] F. Alexander, *Psychosomatic Medicine*, London, 1952; W. Bräutigam, "Über die psychosomatische Spezifität des Asthma bronchiale", *Psyche*, vol. 8 (1954–55), pp. 481ff.

follow that all conflict will necessarily produce neurosis. We cannot solve the problem of the general origin of neurosis just by pointing to typical conflict-situations; if we are going to do this we really need a theoretical psychological explanation.

In any case, "the neurotic patient presents us with a torn mind, divided by resistances".[62] The neurotic is unable to resolve his conflicts, and one of the main objects of analytic therapy is to help him to resolve them insofar as they are harmful and unfruitful. It is here that the success of analysis has been most convincing.

Neurotic conflicts are especially acute and bitter partly because they always protest against the determinate nature of existence (Schottlaender). As Freud says, the neurotic turns away from reality because he cannot bear it, either as a whole or in part.[63] He will not accept what has to be accepted. He bruises himself on the hard edges of reality. He protests against the fundamental data of the human condition: that he lives in time, that he has a body, a sexual nature, that he needs fulfilment through others and depends on others as a social animal.[64] He

[62] "Lines of Advance in Psychoanalytic Therapy", *Works,* vol. 17, p. 161.

[63] "Formulations of the Two Principles of Mental Functioning", *Works,* vol. 12, p. 218. Remarks like this show how far even Freud saw beyond the boundaries of sexuality and into the analysis of existence.

[64] Cf. F. Schottlaender, *Die Welt der Neurose,* Stuttgart, 1950, pp. 48ff.

protests against the existence of need and suffering, against the limits of his natural gifts and talents, against his inborn faults and defects. He protests against his spiritual nature and its implications: that there are such things as right and wrong, duty, wishes which cannot be fulfilled. He will not accept that the world is best as it is. He cannot bear the fact that he is necessarily dependent or contingent, and he wants to be God himself.

Processes, "Mechanisms" and Structures of Defence and Inhibition

"It will be an undoubted advantage, I think, to revert to the old term of 'defence', provided we employ it explicitly as a general designation for all the techniques which the ego makes use of in conflicts which may lead to a neurosis. . . ."[65] "Defence" covers all the means by which the ego defends itself against the demands of the instincts. And the analysis of conflicts asks three main questions: By which instinctual demands does the analysand feel that he is threatened? What are his motives for resisting these demands? And what tactical means does he employ to shelter and defend his ego against these demands? So-called "ego-analysis" and "resistance-analysis" are chiefly concerned with the last two questions.

[65] *Inhibitions, Symptoms and Anxiety,* trans. Alix Strachey, London, 1936, p. 155.

The ego can employ "techniques" or tactics when the corresponding structurally disposed functions or psychisms are available to it. The so-called "defence-mechanisms" are examples of these psychisms.

'The ego employs certain techniques" is perhaps not the best way to put it. If we say this, we tend to obscure the distinction between involuntary and for the most part unconscious processes, and behaviour according to conscious plans formed by the will. This distinction is characteristically obscured in neurosis. Hysterics are particularly adept at disguising their own actions as events over which they have no control and to which they must submit. This process of gaining without any personal responsibility what one does not consciously dare to want or do is itself a technique of circumventing conflict and was described by Freud. Adler appropriately termed it "arrangement". Repression and its various results are also described as defence-mechanisms, or means by which the neurotic controls his conflicts. The most important forms are conversion, displacement and false connection. Others are isolation, denial of reality, attempts to undo acts, transformation of instincts or forms of behaviour into their opposites, turning round against the subject's own self, projection and sublimation. Regression has a particular place of its own among defence-mechanisms.

Freud coined the two terms "reaction-formation" and "anti-cathexis" (or "counter-charge of energy") to indicate that defence was a definite part of the structure of the personality concerned with the habitual inhibition of instincts. Identification and introjection are not, strictly speaking, defence-mechanisms, but they can be employed in the defence against instincts and anxiety.

REPRESSION

The most important defensive process described by Freud is repression.[66] Freud was not, of course, the first to discover the existence of repression: it is obvious enough to be reflected in common language; and as a technical term it had previously been used by the psychologist Herbart.[67] Man has always known that he can to some extent encourage or conquer his feelings, impulses and thoughts. Social and religious and ethical systems, tradition and education rely on this assumption. Repression is man's original weapon in the fight against self, his tool for shaping, cultivating and exercising himself. Man

[66] Cf. "The Defence Neuro-Psychoses", *Collected Papers,* vol. 1, pp. 59ff.; "Repression", *Works,* vol. 14, pp. 141ff.; *Introductory Lectures,* pp. 242ff. Some of the most striking case-histories are in "Studies on Hysteria", *Works,* vol. 2, pp. xxixff., where one can also find the first constructions of theories.

[67] J. F. Herbart, *Psychologie als Wissenschaft, neugegründet auf Erfahrung, Metaphysik und Mathematik* (1824).

tends naturally towards cultivation and exercise (Greek, ἄσκησις). Repression gives one the power to live a human life, to free oneself as a person from the rule of the instincts. But this power has dangers which have also long been known. A man can overlook important matters, repress or ignore vital hints or clear insights: he can deceive himself and reject the truth. Such things were clearly described in Greek tragedies, in the dialogues of Socrates, in the accounts of the Pharisees and the unbelievers in the Gospels, the men who cannot see the beam in their own eye, "that strain out the gnat and then swallow the camel".[68] Theologians have therefore often described the kind of repression which produces this attitude. The psychology of errors plays a very important part in Freud's system; but before him, Augustine, St. Thomas and Descartes had explained errors, lack of faith, failures in the virtue of wisdom, as the results of hidden tendencies in the will leading the subject away from or obscuring his apprehension of reality. The theological term "ignorantia affectata" and the psychological term "repression" both describe tendentious error and interested ignorance. And theologians have seen how man can repress and deny what is fruitful and constructive or "spirit", as well as what is potentially uncontrollable and destructive or "flesh".[69] Man

[68] Matt. 23, 24.

[69] The contrast between "flesh" and "spirit" in the New Testament does not imply that man is divided into two

can repress his essence and deny the claims of reality. He can repress his better self, shut out the call to self-sacrifice and the voice of conscience.

Repression of this kind inevitably damages psychic life; it inflicts a permanent injury on the metaphysical narcissism or innermost life of the soul. It leads to "sickness unto death". (In the Old Testament this repression is described in various ways—blindness or hardness of heart, disobedience, lack of faith, extinction of the spirit, sin against the Holy Ghost. The basic doctrines of the theology of history in St. John's Gospel are partly concerned with the same thing. Christian prophecy turns us to what is repressed in the sense of "disregarded". Take heed, do not forget, remember—we can find these warnings and exhortations throughout the Old and New Testaments. The biblical writers saw that man had a constant tendency to distort and deny and repress truth and reality.)

Freud would have rendered an important service to psychology if he had done no more than coin the term "repression" to describe

---

parts. "Flesh" does not signify the vital, sensual, instinctual side of man as opposed to his rational side; it is the whole man, body, mind and spirit, as he exists by himself, with his natural tendency to place himself and his own in the centre of existence. "Spirit" is the holy, divine spirit which drives the whole man to live for God and not for himself. Flesh is *amor sui*, spirit *amor Dei*. Cf. G. Kittel, *Theologisches Wörterbuch zum Neuen Testament*, Stuttgart, 1933– ; R. Guardini, *Das Harren der Schöpfung*, *Würzburg*, 1940, p. 4.

what had already been discovered. A good terminology helps to order our thoughts and direct our attention; it can often do more than the most carefully extended description. But Freud discovered new facts about repression. In his early writings dating from before the turn of the century, he described repression as a conscious act of the will which aimed at the exclusion of painful elements from consciousness. He established that the first patients he analyzed had fallen sick shortly "after they had condemned, consciously repressed and forgotten some psychic movement".[70] Repression was therefore said to be "conscious forgetting", the rejection of some psychic movement from consciousness, and the prevention of its reappearance as a memory. The objects of repression, according to Freud, were movements of egotism and cruelty, which could be generally put down as wicked, and above all, movements of sexual desire.[71] Elsewhere he says: "Man's archaic heritage forms the nucleus of the unconscious mind, and whatever part of that heritage has to be left behind in the advance of the latter phases of development, because it is unserviceable to or incompatible with what is new and harmful to it, falls a victim to the process of repression."[72]

[70] "The Defence Neuro-Psychoses", *Collected Papers*, vol. 1; cf. "Studies on Hysteria", especially the case histories, *Works*, vol. 2.

[71] "Kurzer Abrisz der Psychoanalyse", *Werke*, vol. 13, p. 412.

[72] "A Child Is Being Beaten", *Works*, vol. 17, pp. 203, 204.

The main purpose of repression is to drive out painful emotions, to avoid pain. At first Freud was describing a conscious act of the will. But repression of this kind is an everyday experience which we recognize in ourselves. Freud said earlier that it did not normally have a pathogenic effect, and he later explicitly distinguished pathogenic repression from normal "condemnation and suppression". It is necessary and healthy for people to submit their psychic life to what Freud calls the "normal condemning judgement".[73]

Freud saw one of the objects of psychotherapy as the substitution of conscious judgement for blind repression. "There are several judgements of this kind which can bring, resolve and remove conflict and neurosis; sometimes they can be made in combination with each other. Either the patient's personality becomes convinced that the pathogenic wish has been wrongly rejected and induces him to accept it either completely or in part. Or the wish itself is re-directed towards a higher and therefore admissible object (we call this process sublimation). Or the patient recognizes that his rejection was justified and supplements the automatic and therefore insufficient mechanism of rejection *by a judgement employing his highest spiritual and intellectual powers: he achieves conscious control.*"[74]

[73] *An Autobiographical Study,* trans. James Strachey, London, 1935, p. 52.

[74] "Über Psychoanalyse", *Werke,* vol. 8, p. 25f. (our italics).

At first Freud understood pathogenic repression as a form of condemnation and suppression which was unsuccessful and remained incomplete[75]. Contradiction and conflict between two tendencies can only be resolved completely by condemnation and suppression, when the person clearly grasps the significance of the contradiction and creates a new climate of feeling by his adverse judgement. To do this, the person must not only have clear self-knowledge, but his judgement must be natural and justified, must correspond to his pre-existing human nature. Repression was seen as an incomplete impulse to drive away or flee from pain. But condemnation and suppression do not necessarily aim to avoid unpleasant feelings; they are often due to motives which are more than pleasure-seeking and pain-rejecting. A man may suppress certain pleasant fantasies because they hinder him from doing his unpleasant work or interrupt his concentration. This kind of suppression of inner and outer distraction which is a necessary part of normal life can be usefully distinguished by the term "repulsion" (*Abdrängen*).[76]

Condemnation and repression often involve self-denial and a certain amount of pain, but success brings freedom, a heightened sense of self-respect, an increase in personal "substance".

[75] "Three Essays on the Theory of Sexuality", *Works,* vol. 7, p. 171.

[76] A. Wellek, "Das Schichtenproblem in der Charakterologie", *Studium Generale,* 9 (1956), p. 246.

Freud never abandoned the kind of picture of the healthy personality which is suggested by the idea of condemnation. The healthy person learns to live critically with himself, the neurotic continues to rely on mere repression. And in the long run repression is incapable of controlling instincts and impulses. "We find that repression ... though it served a useful purpose to begin with, leads ultimately to a damaging loss of inhibition and mental control..."[77] The boundary between the conscious act of suppression and the involuntary process of repression is fluid. Repression can be conscious but nevertheless involuntary. At this point it starts to become a "psychic mechanism", a blind, impulsive process determined by the pre-personal structure. Some impulse or emotion or idea appears on the borders of consciousness which does not agree with the tendencies and ideas which rule the conscious mind. The ego involuntarily tries to escape the object of pain, anxiety or guilt, and turns its attention elsewhere. Moreover, "in the realms of fantasy, repression remains all-powerful, it brings about the inhibition of ideas in *statu nascendi* before they can be noticed by consciousness, if their cathexis (charge of energy) is likely to occasion a release of unpleasure".[78] We can best see involuntary and unnoticed pro-

[77] "The Interpretation of Dreams", *Works,* vol. 5, p. 617.

[78] "Formulations on the Two Principles of Mental Functioning", *Works,* vol. 12, p. 223. Freud refers here to facts which have since been experimentally established by Fried-

cesses of repression in the analysis of particular failures in performance like lapses of memory. The participation of affective defensive tones can often be seen as well.[79] Freud's treatment of the mechanisms of defence included both descriptions of directly observable facts (for example the repression with great difficulty of an idea in an attempt to forget it), and hypothetical interpretative models. Repression is a theoretical construction which is particularly closely based on empirical observation; other mechanisms are more purely hypothetical. Freud speaks of the "defensive disposition" when repression is a permanent habit inhibiting the development of the instincts and feelings rather than an actual process.

CONVERSION, SUBSTITUTION AND FALSE CONNECTION

Conversion, the process by which "a sum of psychic excitement turns into a physical phenomenon",[80] is a psychic or rather psychophysical "mechanism" which works in the same direction as repression and the defensive attitudes but

rich Sander's investigations of *Aktualgenese*; cf. U. Undeutsch, "Die Aktualgenese in ihrer allgemeinpsychologischen und charakterologischen Bedeutung", *Scientia*, 36 (1942).

[79] Numerous examples are given in "The Psychopathology of Everyday Life", *Works*, vol. 6.

[80] "The Defence Neuro-Psychoses", *Collected Papers*, vol. 1, p. 63.

seems to be independent of them. Conversion is one of the mechanisms which cannot be observed directly, but we can postulate it from the relation between observable movements of emotion and processes of repression, and the physical changes which follow or accompany them. The physical symptoms of neurosis change during treatment. These changes clearly correspond to the successive phases of analysis, and the correspondence needs some theoretical explanation.

Conversion is a particular instance of a general process by which psychic events can produce physical effects. Emotions can produce or be accompanied by crying, blushing, paling, nausea, spasms in the blood vessels and so on. There are storms of emotion which catch us up body and soul. But conversion appears only in the body; we do not experience any simultaneous inner feelings and tendencies whose connections with the bodily symptoms we can see for ourselves. The physical process replaces or represents the psychic process instead of accompanying it. Thus, for example, hysterical blindness can represent a repressed but connected desire to see such and such a forbidden object, or a desire not to have to see what must be seen. In this case the technique of defence provides for the physical expression of what is repressed. Conversion-symptoms symbolize or hint at repressed feelings, impulses, fantasies or memories in the same way that compulsive rituals symbolize repressed behaviour. This thesis can be justified by its ability to reduce all the complicated details of the conversion-symptom to a meaningful whole, when the fantasies which are assumed to lie behind the symptom, together with traumatic experiences and other preconditions, suddenly erupt into consciousness before any interpretation has been made and when, after this, the symptom changes or vanishes.

The conversion-mechanism is an hysterical characteristic. In compulsive neurosis we find the separate mechanism of "substitution" or "transposition".[81] These interchangeable terms describe how an emotion is detached from the idea to which it belongs and attached to some other idea against which no defensive measures need to be taken. The emotion is dislodged by habitual or intentional defence and misplaced in a new position. We can often see how neurotics attach great emotional significance to things which do not seem to warrant it. The pain which the emotion still continues to produce can be ended by discovering its proper and original but repressed object, restarting the conflict, and then resolving it by the effort of careful thought.

Substitution is a special case of "false connection".[82] In false connection the patient ascribes a false motive to a psychic process or condition and suppresses the real motive. In analysis we meet with this kind of self-deception very fre-

[81] "The Defence Neuro-Psychoses", *Collected Papers*, vol. 1, p. 69.

[82] *Works*, vol. 2, p. 67*n*.

quently. Sometimes the real motive suddenly appears in the course of free association, after the patient has given a series of false explanations of his feelings and behaviour.

ISOLATION, ATTEMPTS TO UNDO ACTS AND DENIAL OF REALITY

Isolation and attempts to undo acts are defensive techniques used as surrogates where repression fails.[83] They are particularly characteristic of compulsive neurosis. Isolation appears when pain is produced by belonging or by co-operation. By means of isolation ideas and memories can be separated from the emotions which are attached to them, or a separation can be made between pairs of connected feelings or tendencies, between for example love and hate for the father or sexual and defecatory pleasure. Both feelings remain conscious, but their mutual connections are severed.

Sometimes neurotics attempt to undo acts or to restore a lost order or recall an instinctual expression by magical means and symbolic behaviour.[84]

Denial of reality in the narrow sense is a psychotic mechanism; but in a broad sense it covers all neurotic defensive techniques; all neurosis involves a denial of reality.

[83] *Inhibitions, Symptoms and Anxiety*, London, 1936, p. 73.

[84] Ibid., p. 73f.

TRANSFORMATION OF INSTINCTS INTO THEIR OPPOSITES, TURNING UPON THE SELF AND PROJECTION

Embryo feelings and instincts can either develop naturally or their development can be distorted by defensive forces. Analysis suggests that distortions take certain typical forms. In this section we shall deal with three forms of distortion; sublimation will be treated separately.

The first form is what Freud called "transformation into opposites",[85] and it is based on findings such as the following. A mother is anxiously overdemonstrative and tender towards one of her children. She worries about the child for no apparent reason and spoils and makes a favourite of it. But when tension is removed under analysis she shows hostile, aggressive and competitive tendencies towards it. Later, feelings of tenderness develop again. The aggression is not just reversed; rather, the excessive tenderness expresses in some peculiar way the hidden aggression. The object of the tenderness often feels that it is really a form of aggression. In a similar way the very intensity of hostility can show repressed love. Thus it seems correct to distinguish transformation of instincts into their opposites from reaction-formation (to be considered later). In reaction-formation one set of feelings in an emotional split is intensified

[85] "Instincts and their Vicissitudes", *Works*, vol. 14, p. 126.

so as to hide the other set. Thus reaction-formation in the example given above would appear in the intensification of genuine feelings of tenderness so that they hide the feelings of hostility which are also present. This difference remains important even though it may not always be easy to see in practice.

We talk of turning round against the self,[86] when an embryo impulse turns on its owner after being unable to find a proper object. Self-torture may amount to rendering impulses harmless by directing them against the self; feelings of anxiety and guilt can be lessened by this kind of defensive technique. When painful sacrifices and prospects of humiliation are repeatedly avoided, this often shows that the impulse to love is directed towards the self. It will then take the form of narcissism and self-indulgence. A defence is set up against the dangers and possible pain which must be borne as a part of natural emotional development.

In projection "an internal perception is suppressed and instead its content, after undergoing a certain kind of distortion, enters consciousness in the form of an external perception".[87] In

[86] "Instincts and their Vicissitudes", *Works,* vol. 14, p. 216.

[87] "An Autobiographical Account of Paranoia", *Works,* vol. 12, p. 66f.; cf. also "Some Neurotic Mechanisms in Jealousy, Paranoia and Homosexuality", *Works,* vol. 18, pp. 221ff.; further: "Neurasthenia and Anxiety-Neurosis", *Collected Papers,* vol. 1, pp. 101, 2; "Further Remarks on the Defence Neuro-Psychoses", *Collected Papers,* vol. 1, p. 180; W. Hochheimer, "Über Projektion", *Psyche,* 9 (1955–56).

analysis we can observe projection primarily in connection with transference, which will be dealt with later. As a rule repressed feelings and attitudes are projected. For a time the analyst's friendly or objective approach is construed by the patient as hostility because of his own feelings of hostility towards the analyst. In the classic case the patient gives a complete inventory of his own repressed feelings, attitudes and conflicts in the belief that he is describing the character of the analyst (or that of other people with whom he may come into contact).

SUBLIMATION

The idea of sublimation involves some particularly difficult practical and theoretical problems. "Sexual . . . forces . . . are . . . sublimated, that is to say their energy is turned aside from its sexual goal and directed towards other ends, no longer sexual and socially more valuable."[88]

Sublimation is a particular case of the general rule that instincts are pliable in the sense that they are able to abandon their proper objects and accept substitute satisfactions. People have probably always been aware of practical examples of this rule.

The tension arising from sexual needs is no

[88] *Introductory Lectures*, p. 17; cf. "Über Psychoanalyse", *Werke*, vol. 8, p. 58; further, H. Lincke, "Bemerkungen zur Triebpsychologie der Ersatzbefriedigung und Sublimierung", *Psyche*, 7 (1953–4).

exception to the rule. It can be released or smothered by various satisfying kinds of activity and forms of experience, which may be favourable or unfavourable, considered from other points of view. As Freud would put it: Every interest employs and consumes libido, and therefore every kind of satisfaction can act as a substitute for sexual satisfaction. If the substitute is "higher"—that is, socially more valuable or serving intellectual or spiritual values—then Freud speaks of sublimation. If we discount the theoretical, metapsychological implications of this, we are left with an appropriate description of empirical findings which can in fact be theoretically interpreted in a number of possible ways. Freud's interpretation is that sexual tension is not merely lessened or removed by substitute satisfactions, in the way that a child's aggressive tendencies might be dampened down by exciting his curiosity. But the sexual libido can find traces of the specific quality of satisfaction which it seeks for itself in every possible kind of activity and experience, and therefore it can satisfactorily direct itself towards any possible kind of object. An instinctual experience of a particular kind is given. After certain activities and experiences the tension caused by the instinct abates. One way to explain this sequence is to assume that the activities and experiences contain something which corresponds to the specific quality of the given instinct, and are the expression and result of the instinct. This is, in fact, one of the fundamental assumptions of psychoanalytic theory. Although the assumption is often thought to be self-evidently justified, no attempt has so far been made to support it by really conclusive evidence. The sequence of observations could be equally well explained by saying that specific kinds of instinctual tension could be abated by activities and experiences which were independent of the instinct in question and in no way expressions of it.

On the Freudian assumption, the example given above would be interpreted as follows. The libido of the angry child is channelled in a sexual component instinct. Awakening curiosity means diverting the libido into the component instinct of sexual curiosity, which hopes to find sexual material, hints or symbols in everything which can be seen or known. This kind of substitute satisfaction would certainly be possible; but with a great many of the observations which Freud interpreted as cases of sublimation there seems to be no clear evidence that the substitute was sexual. In many cases the allegedly sublimated instinct merely introduces a person to an interest which is independent of that instinct. A child may turn to painting and modelling to find substitute anal satisfaction for the anal pleasure he gains from smearing excrement. But he may as a result experience the joy of artistic creation and become an artist; and his later artistic activity will not necessarily aim at anal satisfaction. A child can tear open his teddy-bear's belly or smash his toy car on a sadistic or destructive impulse. But as a result he can find the speaking-mechanism in the bear or the clockwork engine of the car, and in such ways begin a life-long interest in technology or physics; he need not always remain fixated on his destructive instinctual impulse.[89]

We have to remember that specific needs, which are not absolutely basic in the sense that their denial would cause death, are pressing not because they are specific but because their denial means that the person is emptier, poorer and less happy. Any kind of enrichment or fulfilment can lessen the pain of this denial. A child may long for an ice-cream at the fair, and if he cannot have one he will be less disappointed after a turn on the roundabout.

Freud's doctrine of sublimation can only be understood fully if we see that it depends on a metaphysical assumption as well as on empirical observations. The assumption is that in his basic instincts man is indistinguishable from the animals; he is ruled by the instincts of self-preservation and of the preservation of the species.[90] Freud set himself the difficult task of showing that all psychic life was either egotistical or sexual. As we can see from psychoanalytic

[89] Cf. G. Allport's doctrine of the functional autonomy of motives (*Personality,* New York, 1937).

[90] In various careful studies G. Portmann has shown that such principles are insufficient to order even zoological observations: see *Animal Forms and Patterns,* trans. Hella Czech, London, 1952.

theory, this involved some complicated constructions.

We can sum up by saying that Freud's concepts of substitute satisfactions and sublimations are based on three groups of propositions. Those in the first group are clearly true, those in the second probably true, and those in the third false.

(1) Many satisfying, pleasurable or interesting activities can dissolve or reduce instinctual tension. It is possible to escape from instinctual tension into other motivational spheres. And this possibility can be employed as a defensive technique.

(2) Instincts can be satisfied in different measures. Actions leading to orgasm are not the only relief from sexual tension. The sexual instinct can be satisfied for a time or permanently by hints of pre-pleasure, or by forms of expression which reduce tension but do not produce pleasure. If this is true, it is very relevant to symbol and symptom formations. A symptom could afford substitute satisfaction by expressing instinctual tension without itself affording pleasure, and in the extreme case without showing any trace of pre-pleasure. Specific instinctual tension also tends to incomplete expression in fantasies and forms of speech and behaviour which resemble the instinctual behaviour concerned and afford pre-pleasure. The satisfaction of instincts by speech and imagination can be called sublimation. If the Homeric heroes had

satisfied themselves with verbal battles, then these battles would have been a refined and sub limated form of real fighting. Aggressive and agonal needs can be satisfied in competitions of courage or in bardic contests. In these and similar cases it is not just that specific instinctual tensions are resolved by quite different kinds of satisfactions; also the specific instinct itself works and expresses itself in the liberating experience.

When some object can attract instinctual energy just because it is similar to the proper object of the instinct, then it is possible that sensual, biopsychic impulses and needs can find satisfaction in supervital or cultural activity. We understand this in a broad sense to include all social and cultural activity—politics, law, business, science, technology, art of all kinds, religion. Scientific controversies, surgical operations, lessons in school can give scope for the exercise of sadistic impulses. We can see the sadistic element when it is present, and we have no good reason to be surprised when we do see it.

(3) Human culture as a whole is the product and expression of either the self-preserving instinct, the sexual libido, the narcissistic libido, the object libido or the death-wish; these are the only components which can be revealed by the psychological analysis of culture. This proposition is not founded on psychoanalytic observation and there is no real evidence to support it.

We can now conclude by quoting an important consideration put forward by Romano

Guardini in his commemorative lecture on the centenary of Freud's birth.

Some of Freud's most important insights are contained in his theory of sublimation. According to this theory instincts are not predetermined to follow one particular course alone. They aim first at direct satisfactions. But they are pliable enough to be detached from their immediate object, transformed and redirected towards another object. This transformation serves society and produces works of art and metaphysical and religious ideas; it produces cultural activities which resolve instinctual tension.

But it is difficult to see how instincts can do all this by themselves, and on their own resources. There is a difference of kind as well as degree between culture and the immediate biophysical development. Instincts cannot simply develop into culture; there is a qualitative gulf which can only be bridged by great efforts. The analysis of creative activity shows that these efforts often entail some destruction of immediate instincts. Instincts as such do not have their own logic of development which leads them to grow out of themselves and into culture. There are similarities between the approaches towards the two kinds of object; but these similarities in no wise mean that the instinct is denying itself one satisfaction in order to achieve another.

Thus the instinct can really only be detached from its immediate object and lead to cultural achievement by the intervention of some force outside itself. The value of the "higher" object must be shown. There is no one-sided relationship. Mind and spirit must direct the instincts to the objects whose worth they demonstrate.[91]

REGRESSION

We know from a variety of everyday and clinical experiences that Freud's concept of fixation corresponds to psychic reality. Is this also true of the concept of regression, which presupposes fixation?

Various new values and sources of satisfactions present themselves at each stage of human development. People abstain from many of their previous satisfactions as new areas of experience are opened up. But forms of satisfaction which have been given up or have become relatively less valuable can be taken up again if the forms belonging to the new stage of development do not present themselves. Sweet-eating, an essentially childish pleasure, can become very important to adults if their own proper sources of satisfactions are blocked. People who are frustrated in one way generally tend to escape to the

[91] "Philosophische Anmerkungen zu Sigmund Freuds Psychologie", in *S. Freud, Gedenkfeier zur 100. Wiederkehr seines Geburtstages, Münchener Universitätsreden,* new series, 19 (1956), p. 33f.

opportunities for satisfaction which are still open to them. We often find specific preference for childish or juvenile, "oral" and "anal"[92] forms of satisfaction. Some patients have fantasies in which they see themselves as children again, being looked after and cuddled by their mother, smacked by their father, allowed to wet their beds and such-like. Similarly children will in certain situations revert to behaviour which they have really grown out of, for example bed-wetting or baby-talk.

Observations of this kind therefore suggest that there is a human tendency to escape from present difficulties into the compensations and sure boundaries of an outgrown form of life. Regression helps us to understand many otherwise inexplicable details of neurotic and psychotic behaviour. It therefore satisfies the requirements of a good hypothesis. This kind of "as-if" approach is also of great practical value.[93] It helps the analysand to achieve a certain distance from his own experience and behaviour; he can consider it as an intelligible object, and mark out the elements from which he must emancipate himself. Once they are understood for what they are, incongruous expectations or misplaced feelings and tendencies can be gradually and sometimes quite suddenly set to rights.

[92] See below, pp. 250ff.

[93] K. Jaspers, *Allgemeine Psychopathologie,* Berlin and Heidelberg, 1946 (4), pp. 254, 452.

REACTION-FORMATION AND THE ANTI-CATHEXIS OR COUNTER-CHARGE

One of the basic principles of analytical psychology is that the structure of human instincts is antithetical. People are forced by environment and reason to oppose their primitive instincts by conscience, shame, disgust and fear; and these feelings are as natural as the instincts they oppose. People finally build up lasting character traits which act as "psychic dams"[94] to guard against floods of impulse and emotion. Freud terms this process "reaction-formation".[95] Where energy is continually spent on defence against instincts, he speaks of "anti-cathexis" or "counter-charge".[96] The terms generalize the following findings. Neurotics often behave in an apparently unnatural, exaggerated and forced way. When the patient's attention is directed to this and free association is used to throw light upon it, one often finds two things. First, that the unnaturalness and exaggeration have originated in a break in development. An obstinate child suddenly becomes pliant and obedient, and a dirty child becomes rigorously clean and tidy, a delicate little girl becomes rough and noisy, a cruel or bullying child becomes tender and sympathetic. The second thing one finds is that the

[94] "Three Essays on the Theory of Sexuality", *Works*, vol. 7, p. 178.

[95] Ibid., *Works*, vol. 7, p. 238.

[96] *Introductory Lectures*, London, 1949 (2), pp. 301–2; *An Autobiographical Study*, London, 1935, p. 52.

patient tends suddenly to change his characteristics; there are sudden exceptions to the general trend of his behaviour. Remarkably modest and contented men suddenly behave in ways or have fantasies that show measureless greed and ambition. Polite, charming and co-operative analysands suffer from bursts of irrational defiance which surprise and alarm themselves. Character traits which are used to suppress and deny the instincts rather than to train and mould them make behaviour seem exaggerated, unstable, unnatural and rigid; the person becomes oversensitive towards criticism or even observation. There are some qualities which can be best understood when they are seen as defences against inner and outer dangers, against feelings of guilt and shame or possible external insults and injuries. Some people are constricted by the very completeness of the defences they have constructed. Wilhelm Reich described these defences as "character-armour", and he rather unhappily restricted the use of the term "character-analysis", introduced by Freud[97] to cover the analysis of these protective and defensive attitudes and the rigid and often incongruous forms of resistance which they produced.[98]

Freud gave self-will, greed and pedantry as examples of the character-traits which he re-

[97] "Three Essays on the Theory of Sexuality", *Works,* vol. 7, p. 238.

[98] W. Reich, *Character Analysis,* trans. T. P. Wolfe, London, 1950 (3).

garded as partly the expressions of instincts and partly reaction-formations. These three traits are often found in compulsive neurotics. By means of analysis we can construct a kind of genealogy of good and bad habits, real or apparent, which confirms the basic principles of Freud's doctrine of reaction-formation. We can see particularly clearly, by analysing children, how habits develop. A child represses the undue envy or hostility it feels towards its new brother or sister by means of obviously unnatural and excessive demonstrations of tenderness and considerateness. It reacts against its pressing need for love, its overpowering impulses of tenderness, with mean or rough behaviour. Children exploit their possibilities, and thus in the end form their characters so that the world that surrounds them is pleasant, or at least tolerable. Sometimes they are strong enough to exploit the surrounding world as well.

IDENTIFICATION AND INTROJECTION

When children try to bring their impulses into conformity with the threats and demands of the world, they learn from models. Identification is the process by which an individual, as the result of an emotional tie with a person, behaves as though he were that person; introjection[99] is a partial form of identification, by which chiefly the characteristics of other persons are absorbed.

[99] "Massenpsychologie und Ich Analyse", Werke, vol. 13, pp. 115ff.

Both these processes are of the highest importance in the formation of children. Freud also included them among the defence mechanisms. Identification can help to reduce instinctual tension by helping to bring the instincts under control, and can smother or even remove anxiety.

Freud described ten defence-mechanisms, but there is no reason why his list should be considered complete, as it sometimes is; there could be hundreds or thousands more mechanisms of which we know nothing. Progress can be made in this direction. Experimental studies can complement clinical observation; and psychoanalysis, with its biographical and phenomenological approach and acting in conjunction with normal introspection, is the best method for the investigation of motivation.

Perhaps it is rather misleading to talk of mechanisms at all. It is a question of alternative structural routes which the emotions and instincts follow when their normal routes of development are blocked by forms of inhibition and defence. Embryo instincts can also, in some circumstances, take alternative routes on their own account.

Freud's findings on inhibition remain of great importance. Because it is true that inhibitory structures and processes exert a decisive influence on the psychic life of neurotics and that they are so very often met with in analysis, inhibition finds a fundamental place in one form or another in all systems of depth psychology.

DEFENSIVE ATTITUDES AND THE SUPER-EGO

We have already seen that psychic processes are inhibited by both contrary processes and by structures built into the personality, "psychic dams",[100] "structural limits" (Wellek),[101] which obstruct the processes without being processes themselves. The analogy is of a moving vehicle which can be stopped by brakes or by the opposition of a brick wall. Defence is primarily a process, but defensive dispositions can become structurally organized. Defence in general covers everything that can be termed a structural limit; in neurosis these limits are falsely placed and over-rigidly maintained.

Psychoanalysis shows that with all neurotics defensive dispositions are organized in the super-ego, a structural unity that resembles the conscience and which gives rise to normative and imperative tendencies. Apart from the lasting, personal dispositions of the will there are also certain stable feelings and tendencies which are independent of the dispositions of the will, and although they usually agree with the latter, there can also be disagreements in which they are experienced as if they were movements of conscience. Freud's concept of the super-ego[102] ex-

[100] "Three Essays on the Theory of Sexuality", *Works,* vol. 7, p. 178.

[101] "Beiträge zu einer Strukturtheorie der Hypnose", *Psych. Rundschau,* 6 (1955), p. 39.

[102] "Group Psychology and the Analysis of the Ego", *Works,* vol. 18, pp. 109–10; *The Ego and the Id,* trans. Joan

presses the fact that these tendencies are organized in a dynamic structure which can be understood as a whole, and which is analogous to a bodily organ. Felix Krueger calls this whole a "partial structure"; Alexander Pfänder talks of "psychic organs".

Freud calls the super-ego a "psychic apparatus", a "psychic system", and so emphasizes the relative independence of the structure. The super-ego leads to conflicts between the ego and the instincts and produces feelings of pain and guilt which often have no rational connection with the conscious attitudes and values maintained by the person. Thus the super-ego as described by Freud is quite distinct from the conscience, from both the centre and intellectual superstructure of the person. It belongs in the pre-personal sphere; it originates in anxious social conformity and training rather than in intuition and insight into values.

The super-ego is usually formed on the model of the parents and by the training, especially pot-training, received in childhood. It is thus an infantile prefiguration of the conscience which has remained outside the development of the person to maturity. The neurotic suffers from the severity of his super-ego. As Franz Alexander put it, "his ego suffers rather than renounces, his super-ego punishes rather than prohibits". The subject of the super-ego must

---

Rivière, London, 1950, p. 34; *New Introductory Lectures*, pp. 78ff.

pursue a tyrannical and illusory ego-ideal, regardless of moral considerations.

These are negative aspects of the super-ego which are strikingly apparent in neurosis. But the super-ego can also contribute to the healthy development of the person. It is not superfluous when the conscience is mature and accurate: it usefully obviates the need for conscious thought in all the situations where taste and convention predetermine the appropriate. A well-formed super-ego inhibits its owner at the right times.

The opposition between the id and the super-ego[103] corresponds not so much to that between instinct and reason as to that between instinct and controlling habit. It is not so much a question of necessary tensions between what is possible and what is permissible, as of tensions within the pre-personal sphere which can involve no moral principle, but which nevertheless radically involve the neurotic because he cannot distinguish between super-ego and conscience. Freud seems to have recognized and explicitly mentioned the centre of the person and the conscience only in his earliest writings; his later interests were restricted for theoretical reasons to a single expression of the centre of the person, the defensive ego. But description of the facts

[103] Freud's "id" designates the primitive layers of the personality and its "endothymic base" (Lersch, "endothymen Grund") as the source of the instinctual tendencies and passions. "Its content is everything inherited, constitutionally established." Freud had an insufficient appreciation of the spiritual aspect of the person; cf. *The Ego and the Id*.

must sometimes go beyond the limits which theory has previously laid down. The super-ego, as understood by Freud, is to a large extent an organized form belonging to the primitive layers of the personality. We can say that the higher animals have a super-ego which is formed by the training we can give them. The super-ego represents to us the requirements and prohibitions and norms of behaviour of authorities which we love or fear. It does not tell us whether the demands of the authorities are justified. Conscience, following the natural order of the rational person, tells us to do what is good whether or not present or past authorities require it or like it. The imperative of the primitive conscience is absolute and unalterable, but each occasion or situation also requires its proper response. And in this realm of practical particular judgements there can be a great deal of apparent conflict and confusion between the conscience and the super-ego. We can be ashamed of doing what is right because it is "not done" in the circumstances, because it does not fall into the category of behaviour approved by a particular social group.

The opposition between the id and the super-ego is not the only one that tortures the neurotic. "In all psychoneuroses we can see that the tension between the vital and spiritual elements in human nature which characterizes puberty and adolescence has grown more acute and more difficult to deal with. We sometimes find in these cases that the neurotic believes he can make a proper allowance for his emotions, instincts and sensitivity and his desire to participate and to involve himself, only by declaring war on any kind of practical, calculating intelligence or logical exactitude. And equally often we find that the spiritual sphere tries to escape from and to deny all instinctual and emotional life. Usually the two opposing tendencies conflict within the bounds of the same personality, and their struggle obstructs both outward behaviour and inner development."[104]

All the neurotic characteristics which we have described are not only revealed by analysis but also act in it, and determine the relations between doctor and patient. The analytic situation brings out the details of neurosis so that we can see them clearly. The main elements and conditions of the course of neurotic experience can be seen in Freud's description of actual psychoanalytic treatment under the headings of transference and resistance. Psychoanalysis is not just a method of investigating psychic life; it is itself a part of psychic life which must be investigated. It is the psychic medium through which other psychic facts, the characteristics of neurosis, can be brought to light and understood. The neurotic elements in the patient's constitution become concentrated during psychoanaly-

[104] V. E. von Gebsattel, "Sigmund Freud und die Seelenheilkunde der Gegenwart", *Med. Klinik* (1946), p. 391.

sis and are reproduced, as it were, on a large scale in transference and resistance.

But before we turn to transference and resistance there is a final question to be dealt with. It might seem as though the forms of behaviour which we have been describing are really not specifically neurotic, but can be found in everyone. Everyone is to some extent inhibited or uncontrolled. No-one is completely free and spontaneous in his relationships with others. But one of the fundamental principles of Freud's theory of neurosis was precisely that all the psychopathological phenomena, all the psychic mechanisms, structures and processes which we can find in neurotics are also present in normal people. Neurotic phenomena differ in degree but not in essence from normal phenomena.[105] Almost everybody shows some neurotic characteristics. But in practice we only call people neurotic whose external behaviour and necessary psychic competence is importantly influenced by inhibition or pathological lack of control. So far as one can see, this thesis seems to confirm the findings of psychoanalytical observation. The neurotic forms of behaviour which are to be described in the next two sections can also to some extent be induced in normal people, for example in demonstrations of psychoanalysis.

105 "A Discussion on Masturbation: (II) Concluding Remarks", *Works,* vol. 12, pp. 252ff.

5

TRANSFERENCE AND THE RELATIONS BETWEEN DOCTOR AND PATIENT

PSYCHOANALYSIS is a conversation between two people, and the two people will stand in some kind of relationship. But their relationship is of a peculiar and unprecedented kind. It is not friendship or discipleship. It is not the relation of the teacher to his pupil, of the spiritual director to his charge, of the priest to the members of his flock or congregation. The analyst is neither a counsellor nor an experimental psychologist nor a doctor pure and simple. Psychoanalysis is not a saving personal encounter between one man who is neglected, suffering and confused, and another who is merciful, understanding and wise. All these, and particularly also family relationships, bear some resemblance to the relation between analyst and analysand, traces of all of them appear in the course of psychoanalysis and help or hinder the treatment. But a basic difference remains.

Something of the uniqueness of the relationship can be seen in the external arrangements of an analytical session. The patient lies down in front of the doctor, who can see his face without himself being seen by the patient. This emphasizes that the doctor is not a conversational partner, and so makes it easier for the patient to give up the habitual checks and defences which are attached to conventional conversation and to surrender himself to the free-play of his thoughts and feelings.

The analytic, like all human relationships, is bound by rules and has a specific form. Its end is to heal the patient, by means of allowing him to recognize and report what spontaneously occurs to him and by encouraging him to confront his hidden wishes and passions without instantly gratifying them. The patient will have faced many situations in which his only possible courses of action were repression and unconditional capitulation. The experience and exercise of psychoanalysis show him that there is a third possibility; it is possible to feel emotions without being carried away, to satisfy instincts without being overpowered by them, to tolerate tensions without being torn apart by them, and to solve conflicts by careful thought.

The rules of the analytic relationship are made clear by the analyst at the beginning of the treatment. Most emphatically, he does not say that everything will be permitted. Physical reactions are prohibited; the patient cannot be allowed to attack the analyst or to smash up his furniture. The patient is not normally allowed to get up from the couch during the session. He is not allowed to invoke the fact that he is under treatment as an excuse for acting against his conscience during or outside analysis; no man can require another to act in this way. The analyst will, however, have to tolerate many things which he has neither the right nor the power to permit or prevent.

The analyst cannot authoritatively sanction anything, because he abstains in principle from moral judgement and direction. If he does not abstain from them, then not only has he misunderstood the proper purpose of psychoanalysis, but he will also tend artificially to imprison the patient between the two alternatives mentioned above rather than liberate him from them. Psychoanalysis does not recommend that the patient get rid of his desires by satisfying them—say, by murdering his father and possessing his mother.[1] If neurotic symptoms can occasionally be removed by such means, it will only be at the cost of injuring the centre of the person and the conscience. One cannot deny that there are psychotherapists who work on this principle and are prepared to accept badness as a kind of psychic hormone preparation which can help the maturing process. But this has nothing to do with analytic freedom, which depends on the strict observation of certain safe rules and forms. We should also note Freud's requirement that his patients rigidly abstain from compensating satisfactions during analysis: "Analytic treatment should be carried through, as far as is possible, under privation—in a state of absti-

[1] *Introductory Lectures on Psychoanalysis,* London, 1949 (2), pp. 360, 1.

nence. . . . In all such situations activity on the part of the physician must take the form of energetic opposition to substitute satisfactions. . . . It is expedient to deny [the patient] precisely those satisfactions which he desires most intensely and expresses most importunately."[2]

Many things can be permitted in analysis which would be inadmissible in any other human relationship. The patient is entitled to tell the analyst everything without exception that occurs to him; and the analyst suspends his right to expect some measure of restraint and courtesy for the length of the analytic session, or rather for as long as the patient is lying down. But if the patient is to co-operate at all freely, his relationship with the analyst must have some basis of consideration and trust. He may abuse the analyst's family and friends, ask indiscreet questions, voice his suspicions, and so on, but only so long as he is on the analyst's couch. He cannot extend his relationship with the analyst outside analysis, intrude on his private life or ask him for financial, professional or social help. If the fee has to be lowered, it can be dangerous for the patient to think of the difference as a gift and of the new fee as excessively small. Ideas of this kind will detract from his sense of inner freedom. The analyst must avoid all philanthropic gestures, all the prudery of a bad conscience in money matters—nor, of

[2] "Lines of Advance in Psychoanalytic Therapy", *Works*, vol. 17, pp. 162, 164.

course, must he appear grasping. A clear, frank atmosphere in this respect prevents all kinds of possible unfavourable developments and helps to build a proper analytic relationship.

Let us imagine a highly sensitive and perceptive patient, of good character and high intelligence. He would meet the doctor, form an accurate estimate of him, and develop corresponding feelings towards him, feelings compounded of sympathy and antipathy, fear and trust, satisfaction and disappointment. At the same time the patient would grasp the nature of analysis. In short, the patient's attitude towards the doctor and the method of treatment would be as favourable as possible. Suppose the analyst were also almost ideal—good, mature, expert, with only a few minor faults. The two men would be similar enough to understand each other, different enough not to bore each other. When the two model men meet as doctor and patient they will form a real and positive relationship based on mutual trust, respect and inclination and containing no element of distortion.

Or we can suppose that the relationship is based on a proper perception of reality and on adequate feelings on both sides, but that the doctor is fundamentally selfish. The sensitive patient feels this and can therefore feel little respect for or trust in the doctor or inclination towards him; indeed, he may feel anger and repulsion. He may feel injured and disappointed because he thinks he has the right to expect warmth and friendliness. The doctor himself reacts against these feelings in the patient. Thus there are negative feelings on both sides which are based on accurate perceptions made by both partners. We can see from these two examples how important natural human feelings can be in the analytic situation. Depending on the character and personality and behaviour of doctor and patient, all possible kinds of positive and negative feelings can arise—all the feelings which human beings have experienced from Adam and Eve and Cain and Abel onwards. When such feelings occur in analysis they need no psychoanalytical explanation; and the course of treatment is thus often decisively influenced by the psychologically self-evident. If there is anything in the real relationship between doctor and patient which hinders analysis or leads to resistance, it must be dealt with apart from analysis. It need not and cannot be derived from the childhood experience of the patient. The natural relationship which underlies and determines analysis has to be stressed and remembered because it is so easy to lose sight of. The phenomenon of transference is more striking.[3]

A healthy and successful analysis requires that patient and doctor respect and trust each other and that the doctor has sufficient insight into

[3] Freud saw the difference between transference and the natural relationship between doctor and patient but he did not stress it. (Cf. "Analysis Terminable and Interminable", *Collected Papers,* vol. 5, pp. 322–3.)

the individual characteristics of the patient. It is too much to expect him to see the personal individuality of the patient clearly in all its aspects; there are few relationships of any kind in which we can find such a full measure of understanding. If the analyst imagines that he can see right into the heart of his patient, then he is deceiving himself.[4] Every error contains a grain of truth, and in every relationship, no matter how distorted, there is some truth in the estimates which the partners make of each other, and their feelings for each other are in some degree appropriate. But there are many factors which influence our relationships with others beforehand. Our perception and intuition of others is influenced, and can be distorted, by moods and feelings, inclinations and desires. If a man feels guilty, he will often falsely feel that others are judging him. If a man is unsure of himself, he will feel he is being criticized. This process, by which perception is distorted by the humour, feelings, or general condition of the subject and the condition of the subject ascribed to the object, was termed "projection" by Freud.[5] And it is obvious how projection can distort and overlie the picture which the analyst and the patient will form of each other.

[4] Cardiognosis, the charismatic faculty to do this, is a mystical phenomenon.

[5] "Neurasthenia and Anxiety-Neurosis", *Collected Papers,* vol. 1, pp. 101–2; "Further Remarks on the Defence Neuro-Psychoses", *Collected Papers,* vol. 1, p. 183; cf. above, pp. 153ff.

Human relationships are determined by past experience as well as present conditions. According to their associations in past experience, the different qualities which we can find in others attract us or repel us; patterns and models drawn from the recent or distant past are applied or "transferred"[6] to others in our present relations with them. We approach others with involuntary attitudes, expectations and dispositions.

There is nothing pathological about this process, distorting though it necessarily tends to be. On the contrary, if it were not for this kind of transference, every new person we encountered would be as unintelligible as a book written in some unfamiliar language; we could not even begin to appreciate the less obvious aspects of a person's character and personality. It is here that our past experience can influence our future. If a man's experience of others has been on the whole good, then he will enter into new relationships with feelings which will smother aggression and anxiety and encourage friendship. Transference is the channel between past

[6] Cf. with what follows: "On the Psychotherapy of Hysteria", *Works,* vol. 2, p. 255; "The Dynamics of Transference", *Works,* vol. 12, pp. 97ff.; "Remembering, Repeating, Working Through", *Works,* vol. 12, p. 145; *Introductory Lectures,* pp. 360ff.; "Observations on Transference-Love", *Works,* vol. 12, pp. 157ff.; "From the History of an Infantile Neurosis", *Works,* vol. 17, pp. 1ff.; "Analysis Terminable and Interminable", *Collected Papers,* vol. 5, pp. 322ff.; M. Steinbach, "Die Übertragung. Geschichte und Entwicklung einer Theorie", *Psyche,* 7 (1953–4); the lectures on transference delivered at the International Congress of Psychotherapy, 1955, *Acta Psychotherapeutica,* suppl. 3.

and future. Sometimes past experience is consistent with the undistorted apprehension of the present, but sometimes it can lead to mistakes. We can suffer from hallucinations and distortions of sensual perception, and in the same way transference can be pathological. The various possible forms of pathological transference occur whenever the "anticipated scheme" and the present perception fail to complement and correct each other. Pathological transference occurs in a particularly striking form in psychoanalysis, and it was in this particular form that it was discovered and described by Freud. In this form, but not necessarily in the others, it depends on the defence-mechanisms, especially repression. This dependence seems to make it particularly liable to run completely out of control; repressed tendencies use transference as an entry into fully conscious life.

The first description and theory of this pathological transference, which must always be carefully distinguished from the normal kind, is in the treatise "On the Psychotherapy of Hysteria"[7]:

> I have already admitted the possibility of the pressure technique failing, of its not eliciting any reminiscence in spite of every assurance and assistance.... This happens when the patient's relation to the physician is disturbed, and it is the worst obstacle that we can come across. We can, however, reckon on

[7] *Works,* vol. 2, pp. 301ff.

meeting it in every comparatively serious analysis. . . . In my experience this obstacle arises in three principal cases. (1) If there is a personal estrangement—if, for instance, the patient feels she[8] has been neglected, has been too little appreciated or has been insulted, or if she has heard unfavourable comments on the physician or the method of treatment. This is the least serious case. The obstacle can easily be overcome by discussion and explanation, even though the sensitiveness and suspiciousness of hysterical patients may occasionally attain surprising dimensions. (2) If the patient is seized by a dread of becoming too much accustomed to the physician personally, or of losing her independence in relation to him and even of perhaps becoming sexually dependent on him. This is a very important case, because its determinants are less individual. The cause of the obstacle lies in the special solicitude inherent in the treatment. (3) If the patient is frightened at finding that she is transferring onto the figure of the physician the distressing ideas which arise from the content of the analysis. This is a frequent, and indeed in some analyses a regular, occurrence. *Transference* onto the physician takes place through a false connection. I must give an example of this. In one of my patients the origin of a particular hysterical

[8] When he wrote the "Studies", Freud had treated only a few male neurotics.

symptom lay in a wish, which she had many years earlier and at once relegated to the unconscious, that the man she was talking to at the time might boldly take the initiative and give her a kiss. On one occasion at the end of a session a similar wish came up in her about me. She was horrified at it, spent a sleepless night and at the next session was quite useless for work. After I had discovered the obstacle and removed it, the work proceeded further; and lo and behold! the wish that had so much frightened the patient made its appearance as the next of her pathogenic recollections and the one which was demanded by the immediate logical context. What happened therefore was this. The content of the wish had appeared first of all in the patient's consciousness, without any memories of the surrounding circumstances which would have assigned it to a past time. The wish which was present was then, owing to the compulsion to associate which was dominant in her consciousness, linked to my person, with which the patient was legitimately concerned; and as the result of this *mésalliance*—which I describe as a "false connection"—the same effect was provoked which had forced the patient long before to repudiate this forbidden wish. Since I have discovered this I have been able, whenever I have been similarly involved personally, to presume that a transference and a false connection have once more taken place. Strangely enough, the patient is deceived afresh each time this is repeated.

In this case a repressed, traumatic experience which has been partly liberated by analysis tries, as it were, to force its way into the relationship between patient and doctor before it actually reappears as a memory. The repressed wish is expressed anew and transferred onto the doctor, and in the same way the defence against, and rejection of, the wish, all the self-hate and anger which it excites are expressed as aggression against the doctor. He is subjected to all the emotions which are produced by the wish.

Processes of this kind can be observed very frequently in the course of analysis. Memories of remote and repressed experiences which may have produced neurosis regularly occur in conjunction with the phenomena of transference; and they appear so clearly from one day to the next that it is impossible to overlook the inner connection. We can also observe in analysis that the way in which the patient apprehends the doctor—all his expectations, fears, wishes, feelings with regard to the doctor, the valuation he sets on him—that his approach to the doctor in all these respects is often identical to his approach to his parents. If, for example, the patient concludes from the fact that the analyst smokes a pipe that he is a poor man unable to afford cigarettes, then we can put forward the hypothesis that the patient's childhood was darkened by his father's poverty and threatened destitution. The remembered childhood experience resembles the corresponding disposition towards present experience; and we can therefore conclude that it is the childhood experience which has formed the disposition and will cause the appropriate reaction to all experiences which resemble the childhood experience. Often, indeed, spontaneous memories occur shortly after a reaction which they explain has distorted the relationship between doctor and patient. We see this in the example from Freud quoted above. Thus, repressed experiences influence present experience and behaviour through the structures they form before they can break the bounds of repression and reappear as conscious memories. In transference the present is experienced in the pattern of the forgotten past. The past is in a sense re-lived but not, as it should be, remembered.[9] At first psychoanalysis could offer only a rather over-simplified explanation of the trauma, but as it developed, the theory of transference grew more complex. In the example given above, where Freud describes the actual discovery of transference, a concrete experience is transferred onto the doctor and afterwards clearly and completely remembered. It is a question of a single experience. But it later appeared that attitudes and tendencies and feelings which had influenced a whole phase of a person's life could also be

[9] Cf. *Introductory Lectures,* p. 360.

transferred. And the term "transference" therefore came to cover all kinds of rigid dispositions taking their origins in childhood experience and producing stereotyped and persistent forms of experience and behaviour, regardless of whether or not these dispositions could be derived from single experiences. Transference thus denotes a general repertoire of clichés which one can see determining the relationship between doctor and patient,[10] and also a process by which a man's attitude towards and judgements of other people is influenced by infantile values and prejudices. With its reference extended in this way, the analysis of transference comprises a broad investigation of all infantile patterns of experience and behaviour and their disordered or inappropriate consequences in all kinds of internal and external situations.

Here we reach the transition between Freud's analysis of transference and the analyses of appropriateness and "character-analysis",[11] which have developed since Freud's death. Modern work places less and less emphasis on the connection between transference and the repression of single traumatic experiences. This change of emphasis could already be seen in Freud's work and it is already hinted at in the "Studies on

[10] Cf. "The Dynamics of Transference", *Works,* vol. 12, p. 100.

[11] The term was introduced by Freud (*Werke,* 5, p. 140). Cf. W. Reich, *Character Analysis,* trans. T. P. Wolfe, London, 1950 (3); Karen Horney, *New Ways in Psychoanalysis,* New York, 1939.

Hysteria".[12] Jung developed the theory of transference by completing Freud's work on projection. He showed that the patient's picture of the doctor is distorted not just by the projection of parental images but also by that of unconscious psychic distortions (the "shadow"), by the projection of all kinds of undeveloped dispositions and unfulfilled hopes and wishes. "The doctor becomes some kind of substitute figure, an object for the projection of all the longings which neurosis encourages and prevents from being even partially fulfilled".[13]

There is an obvious objection to Freud's formulation of the doctrine of transference (see above, pp. 183–5). One can object that the woman's wish that Freud should kiss her can be sufficiently explained by the actual situation, quite apart from her previous experience. However detached the doctor may be, there is an intimacy and trust in the analytic atmosphere that could be conducive to erotic feelings, and these feelings could afterwards be transferred back onto memories of previous experiences. Surely, therefore, one cannot simply say that transference is taking place every time inappropriate or extra-clinical feelings enter into the relationship between doctor and patient.

The objection is perfectly valid. Freud always

[12] *Works,* vol. 2, p. 304.

[13] P. Dessauer, "Ärztliche Psychotherapie und priesterliche Seelsorge", in "Geist und Leben", *Zeitschrift für Aszese und Mystik* (1951), p. 443.

tended to generalize too hastily and broadly and brilliantly. This enabled him to schematize a wealth of observation, but sometimes at the cost of neglecting what would not fit into the scheme. This particular generalization has great heuristic value. It helps to relate all the phenomena of neurosis and psychoanalysis to repression. The phenomenologist may object to the procedure, but it helps practical analysis. The simplification and reduction of the phenomena helps the analyst to take a definite position in the midst of the difficulties of his relationship with the patient.

We should carefully note the sentence in the account quoted above, in which Freud talks of presuming that a transference had taken place whenever he was involved personally. Freud was a passionate man, and it must have been difficult for him to come to terms with himself and give such an impression of external stability. He must have grasped readily enough where he could find security against illegitimate demands on his position as a doctor. This sentence is itself an example of transference and resistance by the analyst onto and against his patients. Freud transfers what he experienced on one occasion onto all future patients and situations in order to protect himself.

Uncontrolled transference is onc of the most striking and important of neurotic symptoms; and Freud saw this, even if he reached his conclusions for the wrong reasons. Nothing would endanger an analysis more than to neglect or to misinterpret this phenomenon. Freud saw much more clearly than all his opponents the degree of attention, reflection and self-control that is necessary in order to preserve the proper relationship between doctor and patient. No doubt he neglected the natural aspect of the relationship and interpreted all inappropriate feelings as necessarily no more than the projected repetition of repressed experiences. In the quotation given above Freud does make a distinction between transference and other kinds of disturbances in the relationship. But later he extends the categories of transference and counter-transference to include any feelings of trust, respect or sympathy between doctor and patient. We can see here an evolutionist disposition to make all later experience into a repetition, or at best a compound, of previous elements, whereas this is only true of some neurotic experience.

Counter-Transference

One of the most important principles of psychoanalysis is that the observing therapist will himself tend to influence the process which he observes: Freud saw that the infantilism and distorted attitudes of the analyst as well as the neurosis of the patient can distort the relationship between the two. He took seriously the jest that it is only a white coat and a chair to sit on that distinguish the analyst from his patient.

This was a natural consequence of his belief that the difference between health and neurosis is only one of degree. One cannot expect too much of a man just because he is medically qualified and free from gross neurotic symptoms. (Freud himself suffered from a neurosis with a profusion of symptoms, and managed to overcome it to a large extent by analysing himself.) He therefore assumes as a matter of course that the analyst can repress his experience, develop a pathological transference and be provoked by the transferences of his patients. Even if perfectly healthy analysts really existed, they would be liable to this last danger. The analyst's defence-mechanisms ensure that either he does not see, or sees only, the things that he represses in himself. His unresolved conflicts and uncorrected distorted dispositions will prevent him from attentively listening to the patient and making an accurate diagnosis of his condition. They will make his reaction aggressive, competitive, over-sensitive and sentimental; he will have false expectations of the patient. Freud's general term for all these and many other possible reactions was "counter-transference".[14] Most failures in analysis can be attributed to the fact that misunderstood transference and uncontrolled counter-transference have prevented the development of an atmosphere and relationship

[14] "The Future Prospects of Psychoanalytic Therapy", vol. 11, pp. 144–5; cf. W. Kemper, "Die Gegenübertragung", *Psyche*, 7 (1953–4).

capable of reducing tension and anxiety and liberating the patient from the grip of his neurosis.

In order to moderate the effects of counter-transference, Freud required that all analysts begin their training by being analysed themselves. One cannot expect this analysis to make up for deficiencies of character or competence, or even to ensure that the analyst will make no gross mistakes of judgement in his treatment of the patient. But it will greatly help the careful and conscientious analyst to come to proper terms with the patient and with himself, and it will enable him to experience for himself the peculiar nature and the dangers of the analytic process.

6

RESISTANCE

THE examination of spontaneous mental experience is not a psychoanalytical innovation. Just as the analyst tells his patient to report everything that occurs to him, hoping by this means to discover the roots of his illness, so teachers of the inner life have traditionally enjoined us to pause often during the day and consider ourselves; to ask, "Where is my heart? What are the ends and motives of my feelings and desires?" By this simple means one can gain an accurate insight into one's interior disposition. And anyone who examines himself honestly over a long period in this way will come to see that he can himself become conscious of many so-called unconscious processes.

This kind of self-examination is difficult, and so also is the observation of the train of thought in psychoanalysis. The patient may be so overwhelmed by the richness of his train of thought that he does not know where to begin to report it. Or it may appear as a kind of undulating waste in which it is impossible to grasp any particular details. But the usual obstacle is a feeling that the contents of the train of thought are too trivial, incongruous or painful; the patient feels that it is unnecessary to repeat what he has already reported, or that certain things are not fit to report at all. Often he finds it impossible to overcome emotional inhibitions, and has to break his undertaking to report everything without exception. The patient can neither overcome these inhibitions nor surrender to them. He interrupts the train of thought and changes its course. Sometimes his dilemma becomes so unbearable that he will try to break off the analysis on some pretext, or turn it into a conversation or discussion or quiz. In short, his intention to report what occurs to him meets with all kinds of emotional resistance.[1]

Each different person resists reporting different kinds of things. One man will try to avoid talking about his achievements, another about his religious attitudes, another about the analyst or about his childhood or his family, and so on. And in the same way resistance to the expression of certain forms of experience will differ from person to person; irritation, friendly sympathy, erotic feelings, pretensions and disappointments, critical censures of the analyst, exaggerated self-esteem and feelings of envy or injury, can all remain hidden. Others can say what they feel but are unable to communicate the accompanying emotion. In fact, all neurotics disguise or displace emotion in certain characteristic ways;

[1] "The Psychotherapy of Hysteria", pp. 267ff. "The Future Prospects of Psychoanalytic Therapy", *Works*, vol. 11, pp. 144ff.; "The Dynamics of Transference", *Works*, vol. 12, pp. 97ff.; *Introductory Lectures*, p. 242; *Inhibitions, Symptoms and Anxiety*, London, 1936, pp. 143ff.; Anna Freud, *The Ego and the Mechanisms of Defence*, London, 1937.

they resort to irony towards the self, humour or rationalization, or they completely drive out the emotion by aggressiveness or sudden bursts of anger. Analysis also shows us certain individual forms of resistance which distort and re-form the spontaneous tendency.

A spontaneous tendency can be resisted after it has been completely experienced and its nature fully grasped; but it also seems to be true that there are kinds of resistance which prevent the conscious recognition, or even the preconscious crystallization, of spontaneous tendencies.[2] These tendencies can be resisted at various stages in their development. Thus we sometimes find that a problem which has intensively preoccupied the patient for a long period does not occur to him during the actual analytical session. Or again, the patient may not notice some feeling which has an important influence on his relationship with the doctor and which appears quite clearly in his behaviour. Or an injury or insult takes on definite shape as a memory only some days or weeks after it has been received, and after it has led to a general depressive or aggressive mood. Many patients only allow themselves to recognize their opinion of the analyst months or years after the analysis has taken place, even though they formed their opinion at the beginning of analysis.

[2] "Formulations on the Two Principles of Mental Functioning", *Works,* vol. 13, p. 223.

Normal Resistance

Freud interpreted resistance in relation to his theory of neurosis. He held that once the neurotic obstacles had been removed, the patient should be able to observe the rules of analysis without difficulty, and that resistance was a repetition and representation of repression. But in fact some resistance to analysis is to be expected as a normal matter of course. It is natural, for example, to resist pain and humiliation. And this normal resistance can "generalize itself"[3] and work against spontaneous tendencies other than those originally resisted.

It is also natural to conceal psychic life; and it is exceptional for the conditions of trust to be fulfilled under which the hidden elements of psychic life can be revealed. When a man opens himself to the world he becomes vulnerable. If audience and circumstances are unsuitable, a man exposes his mental life to danger simply by expressing it. Human words are dangerous; they can compromise decisions and obligations, bludgeon tender growth. Lies and half-truths disintegrate the inner life. It is just as difficult to speak out the plain, frank, complete and unequivocal truth in analysis as it is at any time. So long as men are imperfect, self-revelation will always tend to produce humiliation. A man's self-confidence and self-respect need to be defended

[3] Cf. P. R. Hofstätter, "Psychotherapie und die Theorie der Lernvorgänge", *Psyche,* 7 (1953–4), p. 329.

against painful and guilt-laden memories and fantasies. People naturally take precautions when they open their innermost life to others. Their confidence may not be returned, and the onesidedness may make them feel humbled and humiliated.

And so it is natural to find resistance to humiliation in every analysis. Each patient will find different kinds of things humiliating. Each patient will have a different sense of honour, showing how he feels he should be, or at least how he feels he ought to appear to the analyst. These feelings are often quite independent of moral norms. Often patients find it much more difficult to reveal, for example, sexual deficiencies and lapses of taste than serious guilt. Resistance can show us the values which make up the super-ego or ego-ideal.

The patient is told that he has to try to respect both the analyst and himself. But he will know that this respect is bound to be difficult to maintain and that the suspension of judgement in analysis is also bound to be partial and precarious. Only people of exceptional maturity are able to refrain from judging others in normal life, and the doctor will not find it so very much easier in analysis. This can, however, be a good sign. There is a false kind of tolerance which disguises the lack of any firm values.

Fear of humiliation is not the only motive for resistance. The patient may fear that if he says everything he will lose the respect of the analyst and forfeit his good will and friendly interest. Most neurotics are already isolated and would find this an intolerable loss and a terrible confirmation of their conviction that they are unlovable. The patient is afraid of displeasing the analyst. And he therefore tends to suppress the things that are inconsistent either with his ideal of himself or with what he imagines are the ideals of the analyst. And this tendency to conformity leads to resistance wherever self-revelation could produce tension or displeasure or differences of opinion.

People know instinctively that what is alien attracts hate as well as interest. People may take for granted certain modes of behaviour and personal, family, national or religious characteristics. If the stranger is convinced of the superiority of his own mode of behaviour, he may find the behaviour of others pretentious or overbearing; if he is not, then he may feel ashamed and consider himself an outcast. He will know that his peculiarity can be offensive. Thus conformity, mimicry and disguise are spontaneous measures of defence. And when these measures cannot be adopted, as for example in analysis, we can expect resistance. No analyst can be completely free from feelings of aggression towards strange and unfamiliar behaviour; the controversies between the various schools of depth psychology are enough to show this. In our civilization these considerations are particularly important in the religious sphere. Many patients are able to report painful sexual experiences without too much difficulty, but find it almost impossible to reveal the innermost recesses of the person because here they cannot be sure of sympathetic understanding. And their hesitation is often justified.

When the patient reports his experience to the doctor he expects an intervention in his innermost life which will help and direct him. But he will know or have some sense of the great risk which he is running, that he has no strict evidence of the reliability of the doctor and that he is open to misdirection. Even if he has heard excellent reports of the doctor's professional competence, he may still feel that psychic life is too essentially mysterious for analysis to be really safe.

When we look at the matter from this point of view it may seem surprising that anyone should submit to psychoanalytical treatment at all. But what is even more surprising is the automatic confidence which some psychotherapists have in their own reliability, and the automatic way in which they interpret any resistance as a sign of neurotic inhibition, when so much of this resistance can obviously be due to a healthy sense of the doubtfulness of the analytical situation. Such resistance must not be overpowered forcibly by either doctor or patient, because it springs from a natural sense of the vulnerability of the soul. There is a particular danger of this in hypnotic and narcotic analysis, but attempts to force the pace of any method of treatment should be avoided. There is no sure guarantee that the analyst will keep his promise of discretion and good-will, refrain from sitting in at least tacit judgement on the patient or that he will really be able to resist the temptation to exploit the patient's natural instability and dependence. Sometimes the patient may be in a better position to know about these things than the analyst himself. The patient will also need to make sure that the analyst is in fact able to understand the subtler kinds of experience before he begins to report them.

Apart from this, there is also no guarantee that the patient's moral constitution is sufficiently strong to withstand analysis. He can be sure neither of himself nor of the doctor. What he fears is not just injury and humiliation, but guilt. He senses that analysis can set all kinds of passions in motion, and he may doubt whether he will be able to withstand them. He is afraid of being carried away by hate, anger, desire for revenge or desire to deny God and his commandments. He may feel that the doctor's request for him to reveal his spontaneous experience is irresponsible or even a deliberate temptation. He senses that there are dangers attached to his revelations. "Flectere si nequeo superos, acheronta movebo". Freud had good reason to choose this as the motto to his *Interpretation of Dreams.* The patient will know that guilt begins in the heart, in words and thoughts rather than in deeds, and that the analytic method can call forth certain responses which can take on the character of temptations. And if he is at all concerned to follow a code of ethics or to live according to his conscience, then he will produce a normal and healthy resistance to what he experiences as a genuine danger.

But there is no point in exaggerating these dangers, and they do not constitute a fundamental objection to psychoanalysis. We are obliged, morally or otherwise, to do many things which are dangerous. We must always try to eliminate danger beforehand, but we cannot always hope to avoid it.

Thus there is a normal resistance to the analyst and the analytic situation as such; and normal resistance may also arise from circumstances within the course of analysis and go on growing as long as analysis lasts. If, for example, the patient realizes that the analyst is too concerned with himself to give him his full attention, or if the analyst loses his patience or loses the thread of the analysis, then there will be resistance of this second kind. The patient will sense whether the analyst is able to maintain the fundamental goodwill that he needs in order to begin the treatment. He will sense whether his aggressive criticism has really found a weakness in the analyst. He will recognize tension in the tone of the analyst's voice and in his silences. Certain kinds of people seem to prevent either very subtle or very crude things from occurring to us, or prevent us from expressing these things. A conceited analyst will rarely hear a really accurate and appropriate personal criticism of himself. There will be something about him which will frustrate the patient's impulse to say what he thinks. A cynical analyst will not recognize the movements of conscience or the intimate religious problems of his patient because the patient will sense that the atmosphere is inappropriate. The over-sensitive analyst will only occasionally, or only with certain patients, hear aggressive or crudely sexual elements in the train of thought. Thus the personality of the analyst limits the analytical experience of the patient. The analyst assures the patient that he can tell him everything without risk, but the analyst can never be in a position to guarantee that he will be able to abide completely by his assurances.

Finally, resistance can be a sign of the patient's fundamental moral health. We can see resistance of this kind when the analyst mistakes the patient's conscience for his super-ego or for the manifestations of his "neurotic ideologies" (Schultz-Hencke), and tries to overcome his conscience and direct him towards morally doubtful behaviour. This resistance grows out of a spiritual intuition that the dimension of personal existence is being overlooked or misunderstood. And it can be fortunate for the patient when it succeeds in blocking the course of analysis. This kind of resistance cannot be removed by psychoanalysis. Its root is clear enough without analytic reduction, and the analyst has therefore nothing to contribute to its explanation.

But there are also kinds of non-neurotic resistance which are unjustified. A man may be unwilling to recognize unpleasant truths about himself or to give up a convenient but false mode of life. And he may be unwilling, not because he is a neurotic personality but because of his human nature. He may not want to face the painful or burdensome consequences of truth or of an alteration in his mode of life. He can resist the conscious recognition of inconvenient truths and the conscious recognition of himself he can, in Kierkegaard's words, "despairing, refuse to be himself".

It is difficult to decide in practice when resistance from such motives is in fact neurotic. For example, in some cases a "personal resistance"[4] replaces a neurotic resistance. The patient loses his symptom and perhaps overcomes his neurosis altogether. But the analysis is falsified by a more refined form of self-deception: the patient tries to exculpate himself from mistakes and failures for which he is really responsible, by explaining them analytically. The analyst can unconsciously assist the patient to take refuge in analysis from the unbearable knowledge of his own guilt. Guilty acts are remembered by way of neurotic

[4] V. E. von Gebsattel, "Die Person und die Grenzen des tiefenpsychologischen Verfahrens", in *Prolegomena einer medizinischen Anthropologie,* Berlin, 1954, p. 329.

inhibition, are "understood" in terms of analysis and excuse themselves automatically. The more the analyst uses his theories to remove the free guilty act from the conscious sphere, the more this is likely to occur. If both doctor and patient do not keep an alert conscience, then there is a danger that analysis will encourage moral decline.

Thus one can see that the analyst must be particularly careful when he is dealing with resistance. It is no part of his duty to still his patient's doubts and questions. He must recognize that they may be justified. He must recognize that his method has its dangers and his knowledge its limits, and that he himself is no more than human. He must make it clear that he has no competence or authority as a spiritual director, and that as a psychotherapist he can offer no world-view or road to salvation. He can help the patient towards clearer self-knowledge, but he cannot direct his conscience. In this way the patient will realize the risks attached to analysis, and he will see that it cannot really be used as an escape from personal responsibility.

This is important, because the kind of people who visit the psychotherapist are not just sick but are also unsure of where they stand in the most important matters of life. They do not know what they should be and what they should do. They are not clear about the end and purpose of life and the means towards it, and they are afraid that they will never be clear. Or they may be clear about these things but involved in difficulties that they are unable to overcome. People in this situation are particularly ready to trust others; they are in constant hope of finding an authority who can enlighten them about the object of life and show them the way to reach it. Disappointment or disillusion will not remove this hope. They will be prepared to trust the most doubtful people, and to trust specialists and experts of various kinds implicitly. Healthy resistance can often be overcome by this unhealthy need to trust in authority, and it is important for analysis that the patient should have reasonable and healthy motives for overcoming his resistance and trusting the analyst. The patient should be able to grasp by intuition that the analytical situation which the doctor describes to him offers him some possibility of recovery, offers him protection from himself and creates a sphere of freedom in which he can move more easily without abolishing his personal responsibility. Often he can grasp the situation very clearly, and as if at a single glance, in the first session. This allows a proper human relationship to develop, based on trust and reality and free from pathological transference. Normal resistance can then be overcome by the cooperation of doctor and patient. If this kind of personal trust is lacking, no mere proficiency in psychoanalytic technique can establish a healthy and flexible relationship between doctor and patient.

Flight and defensive resistance are not the only possible human reactions to danger. Life is full of danger and insecurity, but it is not a perpetual defensive retreat. Hope and courage can lead to positive action. The hope of being cured is often an important reason for undertaking analysis in the first place. And we can also suppose that every patient has a need to confide in others, to seek the help of his fellow beings, and that he has a natural conviction that there will somewhere be someone who can provide a remedy for his sufferings.

Psychic distortions do, of course, produce certain impulsive tendencies which will also lead people towards psychoanalysis. The instinct to self-expression is distorted into gross exhibitionism, consuming self-pity, or the tendency to make oneself the subject of endless dissection and cross-examination. Or we can find the demand for easy absolution from oppressive feelings of guilt, an absolution requiring neither restitution nor a change of conduct. The analyst can appear as the judge and avenger of sins. And there are many other reasons for entering upon analysis. A man may be trying to find some authority who can give meaning and direction to his life. A man may be so isolated that psychoanalysis seems to be the only means by which he can involve another person in his life. Such motives are frequently present, but fortunately they seldom predominate. If they were completely absent, psychoanalysis would be superfluous. The analytic process must always partly be set and maintained in motion by "perverted" and unhealthy tendencies. This is unavoidable, and it remains unobjectionable so long as these tendencies are not strengthened by the analyst in the false hope that he is overcoming the neurosis.

Neurotic Resistance

The kinds of resistance which have been described so far were not completely neglected by Freud. But he was not really interested in them. He seems to have found it easy to win the trust of his patients; and he took it for granted that he should do so, even though the dream which gave him the basic idea for his theory of dreams[5] was concerned with important misgivings about his professional trustworthiness. But besides reasonable and justified resistance to the analyst and to psychoanalytic treatment there is also neurotic resistance. This has to be interpreted in terms of the psychology of neurosis, and it was with this that Freud was chiefly concerned.

RESISTANCE DUE TO REPRESSION

The patient sometimes encounters an insurmountable inner obstacle which prevents him from reporting some part of his train of thought; and the obstacle cannot be sufficiently explained

[5] "The Interpretation of Dreams", *Works,* vol. 4, p. 106.

by the nature of the train of thought. Sometimes it may be painful, sometimes the patient would need to stand in a particularly favourable relationship with the analyst in order to report it, but sometimes it appears to be completely harmless.[6] The patient finds all kinds of reasons not to report this part of his train of thought to the analyst. If he does manage to reveal it, it will be found to be either a memory of the traumatic situation itself, or a representation of the movements repressed in that situation, or it will at least offer a bridge back to the traumatic situation. "Experiences like this made me think that it would in fact be possible for the pathogenic group of ideas, that were after all certainly present, to be brought into light by mere insistence; and since this insistence involved effort on my part and so suggested the idea that I had to overcome a resistance, the situation led me at once to the theory that by means of my psychical work I had to overcome a psychical force in the patients which was opposed to the pathogenic ideas becoming conscious (being remembered). A new understanding seemed to open before my eyes when it occurred to me that this must no doubt be the same psychical force that had played a part in the generating of the hysterical symptom and had at that time prevented the

[6] There is a good example in "From the History of an Infantile Neurosis", *Works,* vol. 18, p. 91, and there are more examples in "The Psychopathology of Everyday Life", *Works,* vol. 6.

pathogenic idea from becoming conscious. That force was repression."[7]

When the movements of free association lead the conscious mind into areas where there are repressed emotions and tendencies, it halts and refuses to penetrate any further as soon as it realizes that these repressed elements are present. It will resist even repressed elements which are in an early stage of *Aktualgenese* and are too amorphous to be fully grasped. This avoidance of contact with repressed elements leads to ill-humour and defensive tensions which halt the flow of free association, and often also "generalize" and spread to the whole of present experience. The patient's relations with himself and with the analyst are affected by moods of aggression, depression or anxiety. This is the connection between the two poles or stages of resistance described by Freud: at first it represents repression,[8] and then regularly turns to "fear, defiance and suspicion" directed against the analyst as the author and spectator of the unpleasant process.[9]

RESISTANCE DUE TO TRANSFERENCE

Freud observed that in their resistance to the doctor patients adopted attitudes and emotions which resembled those which they would have

[7] *Works,* vol. 2, p. 268.
[8] Cf. *Works,* vol. 2, pp. 166, 267ff.
[9] "The Future Prospects of Analytic Therapy", *Works,* vol. 11, p. 144.

shown when they were children to their parents and the other members of the family. There was a "regression" to childish attitudes. In resistance "fear, defiance and suspicion of the father" or of the mother is transferred onto the analyst.[10] The patient does not himself know that this transference is taking place.[11] "Resistance from transference" results directly from the painful emotions which appear in so-called negative transference (that is, among others, defiance, fear and suspicion), and from the tendency to resist these emotions. Many patients find it extremely difficult to admit to the aggressive, erotic or sometimes purely sexual feelings which they experience towards the analyst.

Freud also held that resistance from repression could employ transference for its own purposes. In an extreme case the patient loves or hates the analyst in order to make a pretext for diverting the course of analysis or even for breaking it off altogether. And there is another more intimate connection between transference and resistance from repression: "If we now follow a pathogenic complex from its representation in the conscious (whether this is an obvious one in the form of a symptom or something quite inconspicuous) to its root in the unconscious, we shall soon enter a region in which the resistance makes itself felt so clearly that the next associa-

[10] "The Future Prospects of Analytic Therapy", *Works*, vol. 11, p. 144.

[11] Cf. *Introductory Lectures*, p. 242.

tion must take account of it and appear as a compromise between its demands and those of the work of investigation. It is at this point, on the evidence of our experience, that transference enters on the scene. When anything in the complexive material (in the subject-matter of the complex) is suitable for being transferred onto the figure of the doctor, that transference is carried out; it produces the next association, and announces itself by indications of a resistance—by a stoppage, for instance. We infer from this experience that the transference-idea has penetrated into the consciousness in front of any other possible associations because it satisfies the resistance. An event of this sort is repeated on countless occasions in the course of an analysis. Over and over again, when we come near to a pathogenic complex, the portion of that complex which is capable of transference is pushed forward into consciousness and defended with the greatest obstinacy."[12]

This inner relationship between transference and resistance makes it necessary to repeat some of the points which we have already made in the section on transference.

In many cases the resistance which occurs in analysis cannot be understood simply as a reaction to a specific situation in which the patient finds himself for the first time. Often old patterns of behaviour are repeated in new circum-

[12] "The Dynamics of Transference", *Works*, vol. 12, pp. 193–4.

stances; the patient clings to old habits or reveals the repressions which were formed in his childhood. People need to hold onto the things that are familiar to them just as much as they need to advance into the unknown and to adapt themselves in new ways to new circumstances, new people and new stages of life. Resistance shows the lack of this adaptive ability; the patient can only move along the old familiar paths, whether they really lead anywhere or not; nothing new ever occurs to him. He relies on the old childish ways of dealing with situations. His resistance to analysis reflects the whole of his behaviour.

But this is only one side of the phenomenon. The patient fights against the new situation because he regards it as a repetition of the old one; but he also fights against it because it is different from the old one, because the analyst is not the father and does not make the same demands as the father. Resistance is not just defiance, fear and suspicion against the father; it is also defiance with the father against someone who refuses to be the same as the father (or mother). This is a characteristic neurotic dilemma. Equally the co-operative, submissive or conformist attitude towards the analyst which one often finds can represent a compulsive repetition of childhood submission to the father.[13]

[13] ". . . [the patient] repeats everything that has already made its way from the sources of the repressed into his manifest personality—his inhibitions and unserviceable attitudes and his pathological character-traits." ("Remembering, Repeating, Working Through", *Works*, vol. 12, p. 151.)

This repetition hinders the development of individual feelings and an individual capacity for judgement. Lack of resistance to the analyst can mean that there is powerful resistance to the process of self-development. Such "identification-resistance" stems from fear of the father; excessive identification is usually partly due to fear. And "defiance of the father" has to be understood as representing the whole scale of aggressive feelings: hatred, revenge, envy, resentment and self-assertion. All these feelings can lead to resistance to the analytic process and the ends which it is trying to achieve. In the same way when we talk about "suspicion" we should recognize that it represents not just excessive scepticism and criticism, but also the desire to delve into the private life of the analyst in the hope of finding something objectionable.

RESISTANCE DUE TO ATTACHMENT TO ILLNESS

The psychotherapist will often have to content himself with modest aims. He will have to say to the patient, as Freud did, "... you will be able to convince yourself that much will be gained if we succeed in transforming your hysterical misery into common unhappiness. With a mental life that has been restored to health you will be better armed against that unhappiness."[14] But many patients will not be convinced by this assurance, sometimes with good reason.

[14] This is Freud's last word in his first book, *The Psychotherapy of Hysteria* (*Works*, vol. 2).

Many neurotics resist the progress of analysis because for various reasons their neurosis has become dear to them and useful to them, or at least it appears to them to be the lesser of two evils. Health and "common unhappiness" seem to bring burdens which are far harder to bear than the ones that go with neurosis and "hysterical misery". Very little co-operation can be expected from patients who feel like this.

RESISTANCE AND RELEASE FROM INHIBITION

Not all resistance is due to repression, defence and transference. It can also occur when the defensive dispositions fail to prevent an invasion of aggressive impulses from the primitive layers of the personality. Hate-feelings which were previously repressed and blocked up are liberated and directed against the nearest object. In analysis this is the analyst and his intentions. Resistance due to repression can turn into this kind of resistance. And many cases of resistance from transference should also be interpreted in this way.

Resistance as the result of release from inhibition is not mentioned in Freud's works but only described in one of his letters:

> An idea about resistance has enabled me to put back on the rails all the cases of mine which look like breaking down, with the result that they are now going on satisfactorily

again. Resistance, which in the last resort is the thing that stands in the way of the work, is nothing but the child's character, its degenerative character, which has or would have developed as a consequence of those experiences which one finds in conscious form in so-called degenerate cases; in these cases, however, degenerative character is overlaid by the development of repression. In my work I dig it out, it rebels, and the patient, who started by being so civilized and well-mannered, becomes vulgar, untruthful or defiant, a malingerer, until I tell him so, and thus make him able to overcome this degenerative character. Resistance has thus become an objectively tangible thing for me, and I only wish I had also grasped what lies behind repression.[15]

FIVE KINDS OF RESISTANCE

Freud completed his doctrine of resistance in the great revision of his system which is contained in the treatise *Inhibitions, Symptoms and Anxiety*.[16] Here he distinguishes five kinds of resistance: the three forms of resistance by the ego already dealt with—resistance from repression, from transference and from attachment to illness; and then two kinds of resistance which

[15] *The Origins of Psychoanalysis. Letters to Wilhelm Fliess, Drafts and Notes:* 1887–1902, trans. E. Mosbacher and J. Strachey, London, 1954, p. 240.
[16] London, 1936, pp. 149ff.

were discovered later—resistance by the id (also rather misleadingly called resistance by the unconscious); and resistance by the super-ego. These distinctions rest on the following findings.

In some cases analysis, especially of resistance by the ego, has very clear and immediate effects. The symptoms either vanish or they become more acute; one can see changes in personality structures and in established patterns of behaviour and forms of relationship with the outside world. In Freud's terms, the libido frees itself from fixations, flows towards new objects and returns to the disposal of the ego. But in other cases analysis moves round in circles. Certain connections seem to be indissoluble; there is compulsive repetition of the patterns of experience and behaviour which have for a long time governed the patient's course of life. Such patterns reappear unchanged although the libido adheres to the points of fixation, and the chief characteristic of the neurosis becomes repetition-compulsion. Freud's explanation of this rigidity is that it is determined by inherited characteristics and due to the particular strength of the component instincts which resist attempts at organization and control. Some people certainly have more rigid personality-structures than others. These differences are not just a matter of age (the child's personality is obviously more flexible than that of the adult): there are also individual differences which cannot be explained sufficiently by the ego and its motives.

"The fifth [variety of resistance], belonging to the super-ego and the last to be discovered, is also the most obscure, though not always the least powerful, one. It seems to originate from the sense of guilt or the need for punishment; and it opposes every move towards success, including, therefore, the patient's own recovery through psychoanalysis."[17] The analysis of certain patients reveals an excess of guilt-feelings and a corresponding need for punishment which can mount to the point of a masochistic desire for pain. A correct analysis of this kind of patient produces a negative reaction. Every advance in insight or emotional development must be paid for with an increase in neurotic sufferings. Neurosis is used as a hairshirt in penance for imaginary sins. The patient is frightened and worried by success or good luck as if he were threatened by the envy of the gods. He will not obstruct the course of analysis so long as it remains painful; and he will continually devise new ways to make the analyst adopt the attitude of the stern father who punishes his child. Because the demand for punishment is insatiable there is no end to neurosis or analysis. There is a painful satisfaction to be gained from the recognition that the case is hopeless.

In general, experience of analysis makes the patient more sensitive to the pain which it involves; and in most cases his reaction is to divert and obstruct the course of analysis by

[17] *Inhibitions, Symptoms and Anxiety,* pp. 149–50

subtle tactical manoeuvres. It soon becomes apparent that "character tactics" of this kind merely represent special applications of a practised capacity long employed by the patient for dealing with critical inner situations. Freud described resistance as if it were the work of a second self skilfully defending consciousness against the incursion of painful memories and using other more mysterious methods of self-deception in order to prevent even the approach of danger. What in fact happens is that whenever the patient remembers something particularly painful, and also whenever he apprehends a danger of remembering something of this kind without consciously grasping what it is, then a whole variety of factors conjoin to obstruct the course of analysis. Resistance employs all kinds of tensions arising between doctor and patient and all possible routes of escape in order to frustrate the analysis. According to Freud, resistance acts as an intelligent independent subject. It plans its campaign. It plans to make the patient's relationship with the doctor erotic or to intensify or weaken the symptoms simply in order to obstruct the treatment of the neurosis. And because it seemed to Freud that resistance represented an organizing psychic force and not just a collection of disparate instincts, he derived it theoretically from an organizing structural principle in the shape of the (defensive) ego.[18]

[18] *Inhibitions, Symptoms and Anxiety*, pp. 149ff.

The Analysis of Resistance

The analytic method changed direction on encountering resistance. It began by investigating repressed experiences and instincts and forcing them up into consciousness. But its attention shifted more and more from the repressed to the repressing elements, to the defensive dispositions which work through the various forms of resistance. It became the chief task of the analyst to master resistance and to understand its genetic conditions and immediate context. According to Freud,[19] psychoanalysis is the analysis of resistance, and when it succeeds as such the repressed elements are able by their own force to integrate conscious experience and the personal sphere. Alfred Adler's technique can in part also be seen as the analysis of resistance. On Adler's theory the patient's behaviour is entirely determined by masculine protest against (feminine) feelings of inferiority. He tries to establish his complete dominance in analysis and to bring the analyst under his submission either by force or cunning. This motive of "defiance of the father", as Freud described it, is only one of many which can cause resistance. But if the motive can be worked through and brought under control, then this will certainly often be enough to bring the analysis of neurosis to a satisfactory conclusion. From the point of view of psychoanalysis the therapy used

[19] See below pp. 279–80.

in Individual Psychology is a particular form of the analysis of resistance.

The concept of resistance generalizes psychic phenomena of various kinds and origins. It is useful in psychotherapy because it groups together the obstructions that analysis encounters; it makes it easier for the patient to see these obstructions as a whole, and for the analyst to keep a sense of direction and concentrate on the most important phenomena amongst the profusion of free association. In this way the doctor can see the attitude which the patient adopts towards the contents of his free association, and the way in which he has formed, distorted or overlaid his natural character by failure and omission or in accordance with private or cultural norms. By concentrating on the sources of obstruction the analyst will develop a capacity to discriminate between those of the patient's reports which show that he is moving towards the centres of psychic tension and those which show that he is tending to avoid them. Even if the factual findings cannot be completely contained in the theoretical formulation of the concept, Freud's description, classification and interpretation of resistance are all useful in psychotherapy.

Like other technical terms, "resistance" is open to misuse. It can seem to imply that all resistance to analysis is due to neurosis and should therefore be overcome. This is dangerous because, as we have seen, what may seem to be implied here is not always the case; resistance can also be due to well-grounded and conscientious doubts about the doctor himself or the possible consequences of following his instructions. Freud himself showed how many possibilities there are of misusing the analysis of resistance. He wrote:

> What means have we at our disposal for overcoming this continual resistance? Few, but they include almost all those by which one man can ordinarily exert a psychical influence on another. In the first place, we must reflect that a psychical resistance, especially one that has been in force for a long time, can only be resolved slowly and by degrees, and we must wait patiently. In the next place, we may reckon on the intellectual interest which the patient begins to feel after working for a short time. By explaining things to him, by giving him information about the marvellous world of psychical processes in which we ourselves only gained insight by such analyses, we make him himself into a collaborator, induce him to regard himself with the objective interest of an investigator, and thus push back his resistance, resting as it does on an affective basis. But lastly—and this remains the strongest lever—we must endeavour, after we have discovered the motives for his defence, to deprive them of their value or even to replace them by more powerful ones. This no doubt

is where it ceases to be possible to state psychotherapeutic activity in formulas. One works to the best of one's power, as an elucidator (where ignorance has given rise to fear), as a teacher, as the representative of a freer or superior view of the world, as a father confessor who gives absolution, as it were, by a continuance of his sympathy and respect after the confession has been made.[20]

This was written in the early days of psychoanalysis, and in a later period Freud's formulation would have been more cautious. But he describes things which tend to happen in psychoanalysis even if the analyst explicitly sets out to avoid them. One can well ask what right the analyst has to overcome the patient's resistance, to act as the representative of a more comprehensive or superior view of the world or as a confessor and absolver of sins. Nevertheless, all psychotherapy does depend on a view of the world insofar as it needs to distinguish between health and sickness, true and false, good and evil, appropriate and inappropriate. The psychoanalytic method can be separated from Freud's particular view of the world, and worked with reference to the assumptions of a different philosophy of man; but it will always need to work from some such suppositions, and we can see them latent in a great deal of the literature of depth psychology. Even the supposition that it

[20] "The Psychotherapy of Hysteria", *Works,* vol. 2.

is legitimate to report the train of thought in free association is, as we have seen, by no means self-evident. It implies a partial answer to the question of man's end and purpose. Freud himself had a very precise idea of right and wrong and health and sickness, and he refused to treat people who did not approach his ethical ideals, or have a "dependable character".[21] And no-one will deny that Freud's principles determined his practice, his devaluation of defensive motives, and his general activity "as elucidator, teacher, as representative of a freer or superior view of the world, as a father confessor who gives absolution".

The analysis of resistance tries to elucidate a man's inner life, and the conduct of this inner life depends on a person's view of life as a whole and on the exercise of his conscience. So that the analysis of resistance is concerned with values, and it can never be a mere technique for making unconscious elements conscious. And because it is concerned with the fundamentals of existence it can be misused to convert the patient and to destroy his convictions. The analyst can score a series of easy victories for his own ideas, and the danger is that he will adopt psychoanalysis as a substitute religion with a hidden claim to universal conformity.

But *abusus non tollit usum*, and provided the analyst is competent, and aware of his own motives and of the limits and dangers of the

[21] "On Psychotherapy", *Works*, vol. 7, p. 263.

method, the analysis of resistance can be put to its proper and necessary use. Unjustified and neurotic resistance springs from an emotional misapprehension of the analyst, and the analytic situation can be dealt with and justified and normal resistance can be softened by explaining the course of analysis to the patient and by making the analysis as transparent and straightforward as possible.

INTEGRITY OF METHOD

Psychoanalysis is the analysis of resistance and "re-education in overcoming internal resistances",[22] and it might seem that this re-education would involve the analyst in active intervention and suggestive distortion.

But this is not necessarily the case. Some patients grasp the meaning of the analytic rules very clearly and realize when they are infringing them. They experience the various characteristic kinds of resistance from transference—defiance, fear and ungrounded suspicion—but they realize what is happening and embark on a course of introspection which leads them to some knowledge of their dispositions. They overcome the resistance and resume the report of free association after only a short intermission of defiance or anxiety. But even when the patient is unable to overcome resistance by himself the

[22] "On Psychotherapy", *Works,* vol. 7, p. 267.

analyst must not sacrifice the integrity of the method. Some kinds of intervention involve no danger of distortion, or only a small danger which can be safeguarded against. If, for example, a patient obstructs free association and, despite good intelligence, can or will not understand why analysis has been interrupted, then it is quite legitimate for the analyst to draw his attention to the inner obstacles which are causing this resistance. The resistance is as manifest a phenomenon as one could wish for. Or if a usually punctual patient regularly begins to arrive late for sessions, then it would not be suggestive or distorting for the analyst to ask the patient to use this behaviour as a starting-point in free association. If in free association a patient makes only very vague, indistinct or general references to, say, his financial circumstances or his career, then one is certainly entitled to ask whether the patient has "edited" the things that occurred to him, or substituted abstract formulas for what was originally precise and concrete. This kind of abstraction is a favourite defensive technique of intelligent patients. There is a whole repertoire of devices for circumventing the analytic rules but fortunately at least some of these are unambiguous and easy enough to detect. Often if the patient's behaviour is described to him, he will be able to recognize its defensive tendency for himself and from his emotions. It is a further sign of resistance if the patient surrenders immediately to unconscious resistance without the slightest reflection or introspection. The psychotherapist can make very little progress with completely unconscious processes. Analysis has to begin where there is a possibility of admitting and recognizing sometimes very subtle emotional and instinctual movements which have previously been rejected or denied.

But it is, of course, possible to misuse the analysis of resistance by suggestion. For example, when nothing occurred to Freud's patients he would suggest that they were unconsciously concerning themselves with the analyst. "For our experience has shown us—and the fact can be confirmed as often as we please—that if the patient's free associations fail the stoppage can invariably be removed by an assurance which is concerned with the doctor himself or with something connected with him."[23]

This kind of procedure and interpretation is not completely circular. It can lead to the discovery of other things beside one's own original suggestion. The technique of porcelain manufacture was discovered in an attempt to make gold. Freud often made new discoveries with daring hypotheses. And suggestive devices are very much a part of psychoanalysis.[24] But it does nevertheless remain true that long silences and interruptions

[23] "The Dynamics of Transference", *Works,* vol. 12, p. 101.

[24] Freud, like Polonius, wanted to catch the carp of truth with a bait of falsehood. ("Constructions in Analysis", *Collected Papers,* vol. 5, p. 363.)

in analysis are also partly determined by the actual relationship between the patient and the analyst.

In general, methodological purism does not help a psychology concerned with the basic interrelations of human life. The exact scientific methods which can be employed to deal with measurable quantities have only a very limited sphere of application in the pathology of psychic development. The rigour of psychoanalytic method lies elsewhere. It is under the necessity of avoiding over-anxiety and frivolity and carelessness, and steering a middle course of careful observation and sober reflection. Properly practised, the analysis of resistance can have this kind of rigour and furnish insights and findings which are not distorted.

7

SOME REMARKS ON THE ANALYSIS OF DREAMS

IN ANALYSIS patients report their dreams as well as their waking life.[1] Often patients quite independently take dreams as starting-points for trains of thought. And it is of course also open to the analyst to relate the patient's free association to a dream or fragment of a dream. Freud distinguished various technical procedures which could be used for interpreting dreams in analysis:

> One can (a) proceed chronologically and get the dreamer to bring up his associations to the elements of the dream in the order in which these elements occurred to him in his account of the dream. This is the original, classical method, which I still regard as the best if one is analysing one's own dreams.

[1] For what follows: "The Interpretation of Dreams", *Works,* vol. 1 and 5; "On Dreams", *Works,* vol. 5; "A Case of Hysteria", *Works,* vol. 7, p. 7ff.; "The Handling of Dream-Interpretation in Psychoanalysis", *Works,* vol. 12, p. 89; "A Metapsychological Supplement to the Theory of Dreams", *Works,* vol. 14, p. 217; *Introductory Lectures on Psychoanalysis*; *New Introductory Lectures on Psychoanalysis*; "Remarks on the Theory and Practice of Dream-Interpretation", *Collected Papers,* vol. 5, p. 136; H. Schultz-Hencke, *Lehrbuch der Traumanalyse,* Stuttgart, 1949; M. Boss, *The Analysis of Dreams,* trans. Arnold J. Pomerans (London, 1957); W. von Siebenthal, *Die Wissenschaft vom Traum,* Berlin, 1953.

Or one can (b) start the work of interpretation from some one particular element of the dream which one picks out of the middle of it. For instance, one can choose the most striking piece of it, or the piece which shows the most striking clarity or sensory intensity; or, again, one can start off from some spoken words in waking life.

Or one can (c) begin by entirely disregarding the manifest content and instead ask the dreamer what events of the previous day are associated in his mind with the dreams he has just described.

Finally one can (d), if the dreamer is already familiar with the techniques of interpretation, avoid giving him any instructions and leave it to him to decide with which associations to the dream he shall begin. I cannot lay it down that one or other of these techniques is preferable or in general gives better results.[2]

These procedures can produce valuable results by themselves quite apart from any actual interpretation of the dreams. We might, for example, want to find out what part of the previous day's experience left an emotional impression on the patient. If we hear his report of what he dreamed during the previous night after his account of the experiences of the previous day, and then ask him if this dream reminds him of anything

[2] "Remarks on the Theory and Practice of Dream-Interpretation", *Collected Papers,* vol. 5, pp. 136–7.

that happened during the previous day, he will often be able to relate a number of particulars which were missed out of his original account. And if these additional particulars are examined more closely they will often be found to represent precisely those inhibitions, difficulties and distortions from which the patient is suffering. Usually this only becomes apparent after the particulars have been considered in a broad context.

The same procedure can be used on a larger scale to fill in gaps in the patient's account of his life-history. Sometimes the dreams themselves seem to contain the missing experience in a more or less disguised form. Dreams have a liberating effect on blocked-up memory-dispositions and structures. They contain emotionally charged memories of experiences which have not been mastered or integrated, or they give access to such experiences. If the patient surrenders to the dream without trying to interpret it, then it will stimulate not just his memory but every sphere of his personality. But as the emotions and the neurotic structures seem to be stimulated most, dreams can give powerful assistance to free association.

The dream is the royal road to the unconscious; the associative meditation of dreams leads back to characteristic conflicts and problems, to difficulties in day-to-day life and in life as a whole and to the centres of tension in neurotic illness. Dreams either represent or arouse memories of critical periods in the patient's development and critical moments in his daily experience. These memories show us the patient's characteristic failures and problems, but above all they reveal his unconscious fantasies. "At bottom dreams consist of complex, disguised fantasies which reappear every day but are misunderstood by the conscious mind."[3]

Fantasies in dreams, like all fantasies, are produced by desires. But the chief concern of the psychotherapist is not to determine whether every dream is wish-fulfilment (as Freud held) but to use the dream in order to discover emotions, wishes and impulses that were previously hidden. These things often become apparent by themselves, and there is no need for a theoretical interpretation of the dream. Psychic spheres from which the patient has become alienated can be catalyzed into activity by dreams.

Our knowledge of chronic hysteria and compulsive neurosis supports Freud's thesis that severe traumatic experiences reappear over and over again in dreams. In these experiences the child may have felt shock, terror, anxiety, frustration or passion; it may have suffered cruelty, malice, lack of love or humiliation, and been subjected to violent emotions like anger, envy or sexual desire. Thus *dreams are in part distorted memories of rejected experience, and they give access to, and stimulate, the psychic struc-*

[3] "Hysterische Phantasien und ihre Beziehung zur Bisexualität", *Werke,* vol. 7, p. 192; cf. *Werke,* vol. 2, p. 336.

tures which are related to this experience. This is a well-established thesis which makes a useful basis for both psychotherapy and research.

All psychological schools can offer plausible interpretations of dreams, but they can never strictly prove them. It might even be objected that it is always open to us to piece together an imaginary dream (we might make a surrealist juxtaposition of fragments of various types of films) and recount this to the analyst. He will, of course, detect symbols, displacement, reversal, abstraction, representations through opposites, and so on. But this possibility is not really a valid objection to the interpretation of dreams as such. The dreams which a person actually has are determined by his past experience and psychic structures, and they throw light on his development and present psychic condition. Yet it is certainly true that understanding a person from his dreams is to a large extent an intuitive art rather than a technique based on distinct and rational principles. The analyst has to know a great deal about the analysand apart from the actual details of his dream in order to make an interpretation. It is possible to understand dreams without knowing exactly what all their details represent. The patient can realize that his dream has been understood and, what is perhaps more important, that he himself has been

[4] A. Mitscherlich gives many non-theoretical but intuitive and appropriate analyses of dreams in his *Ursprung der Sucht,* Stuttgart, 1947.

understood through his dreams. Some analysts are gifted with the ability to reach this understanding.

The validity of the psychoanalytic method does not depend on whether or not it can always give convincing interpretations of dreams. When the analyst is dealing with certain kinds of neurosis and resistance it may in fact be better for him not to attempt any interpretation. It is true that the rules of dream-interpretation set out by Freud amount to more than suggestions for guiding the operations of intuition; and it is also a fact that one can often establish that the childhood experiences reconstructed from dreams really did take place. Freud gave a fascinating description of how he first recognized his own childhood in his dreams and how the memories of his old mother enabled him to correct and verify the interpretative reconstructions he had made.[5]

In other cases the details of the dreams and the thoughts which they stimulate in the patient combine in complex ways to make up a simple pattern of meaning which is most unlikely to be a pure accident.[6]

But these are rare strokes of luck, and the techniques of interpretation mentioned above are much more important. The first dream that

[5] *The Origins of Psychoanalysis*, pp. 218ff.

[6] There is a very good example in E. H. Erikson, "Das Traummuster der Psychoanalyse", *Psyche*, 8 (1954–5), p. 572f.

Freud interpreted[7] was one of his own. He noticed in it a tendency to question his reliability and competence as a doctor. His interpretation was that he had been unconsciously concerned with doubts of this kind. Thus the patient can come to recognize preconscious processes, tendencies and dispositions through dreams; and this is sufficient justification for using dreams in analysis. But suggestion must be avoided. It is a general psychoanalytical rule that interpretations of any phenomena should only be given when the latter are so near to consciousness that it is really a question of drawing the patient's attention to what he has not yet noticed. "Deep" interpretations of vigorously repressed psychic elements are to be avoided on the whole, and only to be made for grave reasons.[8]

[7] "The Interpretation of Dreams", *Works,* vol. 4, pp. 118ff.

[8] Cf. E. Glover, *The Technique of Psychoanalysis,* London, 1955, pp. 275ff.

8

FORMATION AND DEVELOPMENT OF THE PERSONALITY IN THE LIGHT OF PSYCHOANALYSIS

THE "formation" of the personality is used here as a general term to describe the various ways in which psychic structures are determined by experience. Freud occasionally used the term in this sense,[1] which has also been found useful in recent work on the psychology of animals. The genetic approach in psychoanalysis[2] shows us that fixation, trauma, instinctual conflict, identification, repression and the formation of the

[1] "A Case of Homosexuality in a Woman", *Works,* vol. 18, p. 169.

[2] Cf. many of the essays in *The Psychoanalytic Study of the Child* (London, 1945); especially H. Hartmann and E. Kris, "The Genetic Approach in Psychoanalysis" (vol. 1); H. Hartmann and R. M. Loewenstein, "Comments on the Formation of Psychic Structure" (vol. 2); H. Hartmann, "Psychoanalysis and Developmental Psychology" (vol. 5); "Comment on the Psychoanalytic Theory of the Ego" (vol. 5); E. Kris, "Notes on the Development and on Some Current Problems of Psychoanalytic Child Psychology" (vol. 5); also: E. H. Erikson, "Wachstum und Krisen der gesunden Persönlichkeit", *Psyche,* 7 (1953–4); R. Spitz, *Die Entstehung der ersten Objektbeziehungen,* Stuttgart, 1957. A. Dührssen gives a good general account of the results produced by various methods of research in *Psychogene Erkrankungen bei Kindern und Jugendlichen,* Göttingen, 1954. For a philosophical interpretation of early development which also throws a great deal of light on the findings of psychoanalysis see G. Siewerth, *Metaphysik der Kindheit,* Einsiedeln, 1957.

super-ego are all processes which can form psychic structures. Genetic analysis is concerned with the disposing forces and phases of the development of the ego and the instincts, and with all the particular events, experiences and processes that leave an impression on the personality, including successful or unsuccessful personal encounters with the world.

We shall try to describe the forming processes (especially those which distort the personality) which can be hypothetically reconstructed from the memories of the patient and identified through the observations of developmental psychology and the findings of child psychotherapy. It is easy enough to establish the picture that the patient himself has of his childhood, but psychoanalysis alone cannot tell us whether this picture really represents the facts. In particular the analytic method cannot give us a sufficiently reliable account of the actual genesis of the personality and of neurosis. Child psychology has probably succeeded in showing that we are unable to remember events of early childhood not so much because of repression but because there is a qualitative difference between adult and early childhood experience. The very young child is aware of the world, but he does not yet consider it as a patterned object and himself as a subject. And our memories are determined by the present form of our consciousness; if we are not remembering things that we have experienced after we have already attained a mature form of consciousness, we translate our experience into this mature form. We should be confused and astonished if we could remember the experience of early childhood as we actually experienced it.

The experience of the child and the situations in which it finds itself are said to form psychic structures because they correspond in certain ways to adult experience. But one can always object that it is a pure coincidence that the patient remembers certain things in analysis out of the whole variety of his experience and that these things seem to correspond to his present psychic condition. Or one can say that the patient is not neurotic because he has experienced a trauma, but has experienced a certain event as a trauma because he is already neurotically disposed; his present condition and his childhood seem to correspond simply because they are both determined by the same native disposition. The argument would then go on: A man is not homosexual because he has been corrupted or because his instinctual structure has been distorted in a certain way; rather, he has a native disposition to homosexuality, and this will become manifest at the first opportunity. All memories which relate to his perverted disposition will have an emotional tone.

Thus it might seem as though the childhood memories of the patient can be used to support any theory one wants to put forward. But this difficulty has been removed by recent studies in a number of fields; by systematic and comparative study of the development of twins and of children in general; by study of the psychological consequences of the last war; by ethnological research on the relations between culture and character[3]; and by research in animal psychology (which has some analogical value). All these studies have emphasized the importance of the formation and malformation of the personality by outside experience. René Spitz[4] has shown, for example, that children brought up in prison by their own mothers develop more favourably, and are less likely to sicken and die, than children who are deprived of their mothers and brought up from an early age in excellently staffed and equipped orphanages. Psychoanalytic assumptions on the formation of the personality in early childhood have been partly confirmed and partly extended and altered by research in other fields.[5]

C. G. Jung has called the Freudian method "conjuring with memories". If this remark were taken literally, it would hardly testify to his knowledge of psychoanalysis. The Freudian therapist does not set out to heal the patient by

[3] Geza Roheim, *Psychoanalysis and the Social Sciences,* New York, 1947.

[4] "Hospitalism, an Inquiry into the Genesis of Psychiatric Conditions in Early Childhood", in *The Psychoanalytic Study of the Child,* vol. 1, London, 1945; *Die Entstehung der ersten Objektbeziehungen.*

[5] Cf. John Bowlby's general report "Maternal Care and Mental Health", *Bulletin of the World Health Organisation,* Geneva, 1951.

filling in the gaps in his memory; he tries to overcome defences and structural obstacles of all kinds, and restoration of the memory is no more than a sign that he is on the way to success. The memory is only one among several spheres of the personality which are liberated when defensive obstacles are overcome. In some cures the restoration of the memory is relatively unimportant. Jung's remark is based on a misunderstanding implicit in the thesis of the *Preliminary Report* that hysterics "suffer from their reminiscences".[6] Later, when his system was fully developed, Freud would have said that hysterics suffer habitual tension from conflict, and that one of the ways in which this is expressed is in repressed memories. Jung's remark is unfair, because it does not take into account that psychoanalysis developed from a cathartic method for investigating traumas into a method for the analysis of the defences offered by the ego in resistance and transference.

But the memories of the neurotic remain important. It is difficult to find a single formula which is comprehensive enough to cover all the various factors appearing in the neurotic's picture of the past and determining his personality.[7] Schultz-Hencke is certainly right when he says that almost always neurotics will have been subjected as children to excessive strictness or to

[6] *Works,* vol. 2, p. 8.

[7] G. Pfahler, *Der Mensch und seine Vergangenheit* (Stuttgart, 1950) is a basic authority on this question.

spoiling, or to an arbitrary alternation of both.[8]

We find all the abnormalities of experience and behaviour which have been set out above in the descriptions of neurosis in the childhood environment of the patient. His parents and the other people concerned with his upbringing are more or less neurotic and abnormal. The family atmosphere is often horribly unfeeling, brutalized or charged with anxiety. We often find, as Karen Horney says, "an emotional hothouse atmosphere surrounding all members of the family or including some members and excluding others who are regarded with animosity".[9]

The conclusion is often drawn that neurosis is hereditary. But this is just as false as it is to say that tuberculosis is hereditary because several members of a family suffer from it. We can see this by considering cases of neurotics who, though coming from healthy families, have been brought up as foster-children in neurotic families and have then developed neurotic symptoms (cf. R. Spitz).[10] The rapid increase in neurosis in children during the War and in the

[8] *Der gehemmte Mensch,* Stuttgart, 1947, p. 43. Freud, too, wrote: "Psychoanalysis often allows one to see the part played by a pointlessly harsh upbringing in the generation of nervous diseases". ("Das Interesse an der Psychoanalyse", *Werke*, vol. 8, p. 420.)

[9] *New Ways in Psychoanalysis,* New York, 1939, p. 82.

[10] It seems to be true that an experienced psychotherapist could induce neurosis in any small child. Neurotic conditions and psychosomatic diseases have been produced experimentally in animals: cf. R. W. Russell, "Experimentelle Neurose", *Fortschr. d. Neurol. Psychiat.*, 21 (1953), pp. 78–93.

immediate post-war period points in the same direction. The symptoms of neurosis in children depend to a large extent on the crises, tensions and neurotic behaviour of the parents, and the neurosis frequently vanishes of its own accord after the parents have found some solution to their problems.

The study of neurosis in children also shows us that the memories of adult neurotics, however distorted, are likely to contain a solid kernel of truth. The elaborations and distortions of the truth are likely to drop away in the course of treatment without any active intervention on the part of the analyst. The patient often begins his account of himself with the claim that his childhood and home life were happy and harmonious. Then a quite different picture begins to develop, with much more precise and convincing details; and it often becomes clear that the neurosis in fact developed in childhood.

It is very common to find that neurotics have been brought up in a pronounced religious or moral atmosphere[11] in which the mistakes and

[11] C. G. Jung's statement is often quoted, that among all his patients he has hardly ever had a believing Catholic. There are several possible reasons for this; but Jung's explanation that there are few neurotics among Catholics as a whole seems implausible. This kind of simple equation of religion and psychic health is unacceptable. The bearing of psychoanalysis on the psychology of religion and the problems it raises have only been hinted at in this study and will be dealt with in a further work. Cf. A. Görres, "Heilung und Heil; zur Kritik der Psychoanalyse", *Hochland*, 45 (1952), p. 38.

weaknesses of the parents are clothed with the authority of God and in which no love or humour can penetrate the armour of selfrighteous piety. Even when they are not distorted in this way, one should always remember that Christian ideals of life do not automatically make everything simpler, but increase tension and lead to conflicts which are not always easy to resolve. A neurotic atmosphere can represent the price which is, and perhaps has to be, paid for the gains of Christianity. It is a biological law that small doses of stimulation increase vital activity, larger ones disturb it, and still larger ones destroy it altogether. But with Christianity a smattering does much more harm than good; the kind of Christian family atmosphere that brings warmth and openness and joy, the kind of atmosphere that usually the neurotic has never experienced, must be won by labour and self-sacrifice. Many parents are not prepared for this; and they take refuge in pseudo-religious compensations, pious structures, of puritanism or pharisaism, racked with tension, heartless, and based on a dark and sinister image of God. *Corruptio optimi pessima.* In this kind of atmosphere the child often encounters a spiritual meanness or even brutality which stands in gross contrast to the ideals that are proclaimed.

It is impossible to typify the great variety of situations in which a child's mind can be so badly wounded or distorted that he becomes neurotic or develops a disposition to neurosis.[12] In neurotic families children are often regarded as intruders, enemies or competitors or as objects for spirtual exploitation. It is quite common to find parents guilty of despotism, senseless restriction of the children's freedom, injustice, unreliability or lack of understanding; and all these things, even in their most subtle forms, can leave a deep mark on a child. What is lacking is selfless interest, respect, frankness, trustworthiness and warmth.[13] In most cases we find a disturbed relationship with the mother, who because of her own difficulties is unable to offer the child security and freedom from anxiety. We sometimes find the kind of mother, without any warmth of feeling, who is no more than a policewoman to her child, prohibiting, scolding and punishing. Or there is the mother with a neurotic desire for cleanliness, whose children are terrified of getting anything dirty; or the mother who proudly boasts that one look is enough to reduce her children to obedience; or the over-anxious, over-protective mother who is determined to shield her child from the slightest possible danger and so prevents his gaining experience and developing; or the mother who expects her child to make up for the disappointments of her emotional life, spoils it and begins

[12] Detailed descriptions of a large number of such determining situations are to be found in H.Schultz-Hencke, *Der gehemmte Mensch,* and in A. Dührssen, *Psychogene Erkrankungen bei Kindern und Jugendlichen*, Göttingen, 1954.

[13] Cf. Horney, *New Ways in Psychoanalysis,* pp. 72ff.

an early over-emphasis of the erotic; or the ambitious mother who demands that her child shall reach the peaks of talent, beauty or achievement that have eluded her husband. Or the mother who does not like being a woman, and will therefore make her daughter into a boy at any price. Or the prudish mother who is unreconciled to the fact that her children have a sex at all and who either makes an anxious retreat from anything to do with sex or pursues it with an over-intense mixture of curiosity and disgust. Or the mother who has no time for her children and appeases her conscience by spoiling them and overwhelming them with substitutes for her affection at irregular intervals, between the times when her feelings of guilt lead to aggression towards them. The father can injure the child in the same ways. The destiny of the child lies in the personality of the parents and the atmosphere of the family.[14]

The early environment of the child deprives it of the assistance that it needs for the healthy development of its personality. And besides, it puts positive obstacles in the way of this development, which the child is too young to be able to overcome. These are the two conclusions which come from comparing the biographies of neurotics.

We have formulated all this in adult concepts. The child experiences things in a different way.

[14] Cf. F. Schottländer, *Die Mutter als Schicksal*, Stuttgart, 1948.

It adapts itself in its own way to the worlds of environment and of relations with others, which are both experienced emotionally rather than conceptualized, and tries to use these worlds as far as it can for its own purposes. Often it proves the stronger. In this way an inner original mode of experiencing, meeting and mastering the world is formed, which makes an imperceptible basis for later experience. These original human experiences and reactions are difficult to grasp as memories which are verbally communicable or have a definite shape. They are only faintly discernible in adult experience and behaviour. But memories, even of events which took place at a later time, and present experience, can arouse them; we can feel that what we are experiencing has already gone before but is yet still present. It is only by recognizing this feeling that we can recognize and understand our very early experience.

Often the permanent injuries that the personality has received are gathered up into a single memory, or "screen memory",[15] composed of many similar experiences. Or there is an attempt to conceal the painful experiences by portraying their opposites in defensive memories. There are, of course, acute individual traumas which can have a powerful distorting effect on the personality and, as we should expect, isolated experiences of a sexual nature are likely to be especially significant. Thus, patients

[15] "Screen Memories", *Collected Papers,* vol. 5, pp. 47ff.

suffering from conversion and anxiety hysteria and other conditions give convincing accounts of sexual experiences in early childhood. Often it is a case of assault or interference, not uncommonly by the father but also by older children. "Playing at doctors" is widespread, and in this game children often examine each other's private parts. These childhood experiences frequently have a perverted character.

It is not really possible to get a statistical idea of the frequency of sexual traumas, or to assert that children are as a rule sexually misused. We are not absolutely sure that they do not occur with equal frequency in adult life, only to be repressed without further consequences. Nor can we be sure that memories of this kind do not occur just as often in the analysis of healthy people as in the analysis of neurotics. Freud held in his early work that hysteria was ultimately derived from childhood seduction or experiences resembling coitus.[16] But he later explicitly changed his opinion[17] and interpreted memories of seductions as fantasies designed to hide childhood masturbation.[18] We can certainly admit, as Freud in fact did,[19] that he probably provoked at least some of these fantasies himself. But it still remains true that it is relatively frequent

[16] "Further Remarks on the Defence Neuro-Psychoses", *Collected Papers,* vol. 1, p. 156.

[17] In a note added to the 1924 German addition of this treatise, *Werke,* vol. 1, p. 385.

[18] *The Origins of Psychoanalysis,* p. 196.

[19] *An Autobiographical Study,* p. 61.

for neurotics to report early and drastic sexual experiences which can quite often be shown to have actually taken place. One may object that any particular suggestion by the analyst is superfluous, because the diffuse suggestion of psychoanalytic popularization is sufficient to produce sexual memories. But although this may be so in some cases, it is not enough to explain the facts mentioned above. Nor does it explain the fact that neurotics report sexual and perverted fantasies, often carefully guarded, which date from all periods of their lives.

Memories of childhood fantasies serve various purposes. The patient may have a busy curiosity about the mysteries of birth and early life, and the anatomical differences between the sexes. Or they may be due to the association of sexual pleasure with inadequate and inappropriate experiences and images characteristic of all perversions. It may appear from the patient's accounts that even before about school age he obtained specifically sexual sensations of pleasure from experiences and images concerned with defecation and excrement or with suffering or inflicting pain. As we have already said, Freud derived his theory of sexual development from findings of this kind. Empirical observation has established beyond doubt that as young children many neurotics receive sexual pleasure, often intentionally, from urethral, sadistic, masochistic, incestuous, and other pregenital and genital experiences and fantasies. These are facts, not

Freudian theories or hypotheses. Psychoanalytic experience has been able to refute the objection that it is the adult neurotic himself who adds the sexual element to his memories of childhood.

These findings might not be confirmed by psychotherapists of all schools. And they are in fact bound up with psychoanalytic method (though not in the way that critics suppose). For the patient can only produce memories of this kind in the analytic situation, if the analyst can listen patiently over a long period. There must be a securely based relationship of mutual trust; and it may need many sessions, sometimes as many as a hundred, before this can be established. Certain methods of psychotherapy do not give the patient enough time to develop his memories peacefully, but from the outset begin to lead him in a definite direction with hints and interpretations. In the same way, childhood memories do not very often occur to the patient when he is being treated by an ordinary doctor or psychiatrist using non-psychological methods. It is, of course, true that therapists using psychoanalysis can also intervene actively in the patient's free association. Indeed, Freud began by using the method in this way. As late as 1928 he wrote, "This material [the contents of free association] did not itself reveal the forgotten experience. But it gave such clear and pregnant hints towards it that the doctor was able to reconstruct the forgotten experience by means of certain additions and interpretations."[20] We now know that the forgotten experience can come to light without this kind of interpretation and reconstruction if the analyst is prepared to wait long enough.

Thus the development of the libido and of the instincts plays a central part in Freud's analysis; and he gives a very simple basic account of the formative factors which produce neurosis.

We shall now briefly consider these findings from the genetic aspect.[21] The most fundamental formative process is that of the *fixation* of the instinct on some particular kind of pleasurable experience which exercises a constant attraction on the instinct. But the development of the instincts and emotions through childhood leads to unpleasant encounters with environment, and can lead to pain, punishment, fear, deprivation of love, and misery, as well as to experiences of pleasure. Formative processes can be produced by fixation on the trauma,[22] instinctual conflict, particularly strong inhibition, defensive attitudes, and dispositions towards self-protection and avoiding painful experience (reaction-formations)[23] and, finally, by regression[24] to well-tried

[20] "Kurzer Abrisz der Psychoanalyse", *Werke,* vol. 13, p. 411.

[21] Having already considered them from the structural aspect.

[22] *Introductory Lectures,* p. 231.

[23] *Introductory Lectures,* p. 314.

[24] *Introductory Lectures,* pp. 257–9; *New Introductory Lectures,* p. 86.

childish sources of pleasure and compensation. As the result of these fixations, the emotions and impulses which arise in situations resembling those of childhood will be experienced either permanently or for a long time according to childish patterns.

The kinds of situations which lead to fixation and inhibition in a wide range of neurotic conditions—perversion, depressions, compulsive neuroses, phobias, hysterias, chronic psychosomatic illnesses, and "character neuroses"—were placed by Freud in three categories: oral, anal, and Oedipal or genital. The categories were derived from his theory of the phases of development of the libido.[25] According to this theory, sexual experience and behaviour, neurotic conditions, and indeed the whole human personality, are determined by the small child's experiences of pain and pleasure in feeding (oral phase), in defecation and at the time of pot-training (anal phase), and its relations with its parents, involving both conflict and tenderness (Oedipal or genital phase).

Freud held that sexuality, or the libido, was expressed in all these processes. He tried to organize all human instincts into two comprehensive groups, and to explain the whole of psychic development from their conflict and co-

[25] "Three Essays on the Theory of Sexuality", *Works,* vol. 7, pp. 123ff.; *Introductory Lectures,* pp. 255ff.; "Psychoanalyse und Libidotheorie", *Werke,* vol. 13, pp. 219ff.; "The Infantile Genital Organisation . . .", *Collected Papers,* vol. 2, pp. 244ff.

operation. He supposed that human beings, like animals, are governed by two great instincts: the reproductive instinct and the instinct of self-preservation, or, in Freudian terminology, the sexual instinct and the ego instinct. He later saw these two as fundamentally homogeneous and as composing the "life-instinct" or Eros, and set this against the "death-instinct" or Thanatos.[26] The attempt to explain human existence and experience by means of these two biological forces alone leads to an extension of the term "sexuality" to cover all human spiritual emotions, impulses and aspirations. "Sexuality" has to include Eros and love in the broadest sense,[27] as well as all the various forces which assist in the formation or perversion of sexual life. Karen Horney and Schultz-Hencke have shown that it is possible to interpret the factual findings of psychoanalytical investigation in quite a different way, and that Freud's theory of the libido in any case lacks a sufficient factual basis. But these investigators have confirmed the prevalence of oral, anal and Oedipal themes in the formative processes. Freud concentrated attention on the critical points at which the process of emotional development is especially liable to be disturbed. The main disturbance

[26] *The Ego and the Id,* London, 1950, pp. 7ff.; pp. 54ff.; *New Introductory Lectures*, pp. 173–4.

[27] "In its origin, function and relation to sexual love, the 'Eros' of the philosopher Plato coincides exactly with the love-force, the Libido of psychoanalysis . . . " ("Group Psychology and the Analysis of the Ego", *Works,* vol. 18, p. 91.)

comes from situations in which the child becomes fixated or involved in painful conflicts with the demands and prohibitions of his environment.

It is only rarely that we find conscious memories dating from the first year of life. Our knowledge of the very earliest, "oral" phase of the child's life and of the set of diffuse feelings which makes up its earliest view of the world, is derived from speculation and from direct observation of the young child. It is reasonable to suppose that children of this age gain a good deal of basic experience in their oral world—"Mundwelt" (Spranger). They experience need and assistance, pain and consolation, continuity and interruption, rest and haste, success and failure in their own activities and all kinds of pleasure and pain. These early formative experiences certainly help to determine the form and content of the later influences which they presuppose.

The child's psychic life will differ according to whether it has been brought up by its own mother or by alternating shifts of nurses in a children's home; whether it has been breast- or bottle-fed; whether it can get milk from its mother easily or not, and whether or not its mother treats it lovingly and attentively. Red Indian mothers smack their babies' heads until they scream with rage, in order to make them into good hunters; Korean babies are in close and constant contact with their mothers, strapped tightly onto their backs throughout the day, and they are given the breast whenever they want it; European mothers may follow a rigid and old-fashioned programme of feeding at four-hour intervals. In each case these differences of upbringing will mean that the children will experience the world in a different way. They will experience different combinations of pain and pleasure, hope and fear, and they will develop different kinds of reaction to the basic types of experience. These reactions are formed above all by experiences of pleasure, which the child tries to have again, and experiences of pain, which the child tries to avoid or make less unpleasant. The child becomes fixated in certain characteristic directions.

Fixations become dangerous when they make a person stick to certain definite forms of life and in so doing resist all change. Certain parents, for example, are captivated by their child when it is very young and treat it lovingly, patiently, justly; but as soon as it has outgrown its cot they lose their love and patience. The result may be that the child's experience of pleasure will be restricted to oral satisfactions and it will remain fixated on this kind of satisfaction. The child will spend as long as it can sucking its thumb, sucking sweets and feeding itself, enjoying experiences which correspond to passive pleasure from parental care in infancy. This in turn will produce unfavourable reactions in the parents, and the child will be involved in conflict. The further it goes towards satisfying its own desires, the further it will estrange itself from its parents' love. It is easy enough to see that this conflict will produce feelings of guilt, hatred and fear. And the stronger the fixation on the instinctual satisfaction, the more difficult the child will find it to resolve the conflict by abandoning the fixation and turning to new and more legitimate forms of satisfaction.

Instinctual conflicts should also be seen as formative processes because their resolution involves changes in the structure of the personality. The child has to inhibit, and often to suppress, his natural tendencies, whether or not they are strengthened by fixation. In some cases the result is a personality in which either inhibition or fixation is predominant; in most cases we find both. Children and adults are said to be orally fixated when they can find satisfaction only in forms of experience which resemble those characteristic of the first year of life. They feel really contented only when other people are caring for them without demanding anything in return, and when all their wishes are granted, however many and difficult to gratify they may be. A man with unconscious demands and expectations of this kind will be in a constant state of disappointment. He will need oral compensations—that is to say, he will react with essentially oral and infantile self-indulgence: greedy eating, drinking and smoking and childish bad temper. In the same way, his sexual life will not be an equal balance of giving and receiving, but more passive, narcissistic or auto-erotic.

It seems that we can also find *fixation on the oral trauma.* This is derived from the infant's reaction to oral deprivation and appears in the tendency to react to disappointments either with loud protest or tearful resignation, or in any case without properly organized activity directed towards a definite object. This kind of behaviour may possibly be the result of abrupt weaning or the premature failure of the mother's milk. Infantile depression produced by the child's prolonged separation from its mother is well-known and has dangerous psychophysical effects.[28]

Oral inhibition occurs when a child's oral instincts are repressed too violently by its parents. Whereas the orally fixated person is only satisfied by patterns of behaviour characteristic of earliest childhood, for the orally inhibited person these patterns are charged with anxiety, shame and disgust. He finds all feelings and impulses of an oral nature extremely unpleasant and may even try to suppress them altogether. The orally fixated child is, of course, especially liable to suffer from oral inhibitions because his fixation is likely to attract parental disapproval. This can limit the freedom of experience very severely.

The orally inhibited man has needs which give rise to especially severe tensions; but he is

[28] There is a careful description in R. Spitz and K. M. Wolf, "Anaclitic Depression", in *The Psychoanalytic Study of the Child,* vol. 2, London, 1946.

unable to express his needs, often even to himself. He is unable to ask and receive, to enjoy good fortune happily, to bear the friendly help which other people offer or to tolerate his own longings and accept their fulfilment.

Oral memories and impulses outlast the first year of life. Family occasions can renew rivalries, envy and jealousy between brothers and sisters, and the fear of falling short of the others and becoming the unwanted child. Struggles over oral desires also begin later, after the child has attained the maturity which is necessary for real instinctual conflict. It is difficult to place the phases described by Freud in definite periods of the child's life. Oral themes are the earliest to appear, and they become less significant later, although they do not die out completely.

The anal phase is especially important for several reasons. Many analysands can remember fragments of the experience belonging to this phase. This is the phase in which the child is expected to do things of its own accord, is faced with demands, prohibitions and threats of punishment. The child learns to exert some control over its body and to walk and speak. It is no longer passively moved by its own impulses; it begins to direct them and bring them under control. It begins to experience conflicts and react towards them and to experience the first feelings of guilt. Finally, many of the impulses and tendencies which characterize this phase run against the proper course of human development, cannot be put to any later use and are therefore vigorously opposed.

This applies both to anal tendencies in the literal sense—that is, pleasure-seeking interest in the evacuation of the bowels and a concern with dirt and excrement—and to all powerful impulses of cruelty and destructiveness towards things, animals and other children, and impulses of hate and hostility directed against the people the child loves, or might be expected to love (for example parents, brothers and sisters). Frequent feelings of intense hatred and aggression, which can be provoked as well as brought under control by an overstrict upbringing, lead to fixations on hatred as a source of pleasure or to excessive inhibition of aggressive instincts. And this fixation and inhibition can affect the whole personality. Attacks of rage and hatred are not infrequently accompanied by sexual excitement.

When pot-training is carried through too strictly and rigidly the child seems to experience a terrifying revolution in its relationship to the world. The oral world of the very young baby yields or refuses but does not demand or prohibit; it is a matter of "I take, you give; I want something, you must do something." Now there is a sudden change: "You want something, I must do it; you forbid it and I must obey." This change is, of course, experienced in a diffuse and emotional way. But although the contrasts only gradually become definite and distinct, the process will have gone a considerable way by the time the child is two or three years old. The child is deprived of the pleasure which, according to Freud, it gains from actively withholding its stool, and instead it is required to behave according to a definite, regular pattern, to perform a duty. Moreover, it will experience the contrast between self-will and the will of others, order and liberty, one's own wishes and the demands and prohibitions of authority. The expression of the child on its pot sometimes means a great deal: it can show that the child is consciously asserting its own will against the grown-ups on the one occasion when it cannot be coerced, and in the one respect it which it is "stronger". It has discovered that it can irritate and annoy its parents and that it can gain satisfaction from fighting and resisting superior power. Perhaps on this account the anal element always produces aggressive and insulting behaviour. At the same time the parents praise the child's docility and express pleasure when it performs its duty, as if it were rendering some priceless service. There is a clear connection between the child's behaviour with its own excrement and its later attitude towards money and possessions, between the experience of pot-training and certain kinds of personality and neurosis (for example the "anal personality" and the triad avarice, pedantry and excessive tidiness and egotism). The experience of pot-training can also lead to localized and recurrent psychosomatic symptoms and to chronic functional disturbances. The connection is in fact often borne out with neurotics by painful memories, fantasies and dreams, and by conspicuous difficulties when it comes to giving and saving money or other possessions. With many neurotics, anal matters in the literal sense are charged with astonishingly strong emotional obstacles.[29]

Excrement and dirt have a very special significance for the child who grows up in the sterile linoleum world of an urban home without access to any kind of material, such as earth or even sand in a pit, which it can form for itself. Children who dirty themselves or play with excrement will give up these habits from one day to the next if they are allowed to knead wet clay or smear paint freely over big sheets of paper. This kind of therapy can also produce good results with adults (for example, with depressives). Children need access to material which they can form and use for expressing their energy, imagination, emotions and sensitivity.

Development in this sphere is disturbed by anal inhibition and anal fixation. Both are usually more or less clearly visible. Anal inhibition produces guilty and anxious responses to any kind of spontaneous behaviour which suggests the attraction that anal experience once held. It is too dangerous to renew the forbidden

[29] "Character and Anal-Eroticism", *Collected Papers,* vol. 2, pp. 45ff.; "Instincts and their Vicissitudes", *Works,* vol. 14, pp. 109ff.; "On the Transformation of Instincts, with Special Reference to Anal-Eroticism", *Collected Papers, Works,* vol. 2, pp. 401ff.

pleasures of the anal phase, and the corresponding impulse is inhibited. It is impossible to resist other people's orders, or to refuse their demands and requests. It is painful to talk or dispute about money, or other kinds of possessions, and these subjects have to be avoided. Any kind of self-assertion or even defensive opposition has to be disguised. Frequently, there are conspicuous difficulties in behaving creatively, and will-power and self-respect are broken. It is too frightening and dangerous to act independently of the orders and instructions of authority. Sometimes pedantry and scrupulosity, the feeling that all material things are bad, and tendencies towards angelism and hypochondria can be observed.

An anally fixated person, on the other hand, longs for the renewal of anal triumphs and satisfactions. He clings tightly to his money and possessions and obstinately refuses to give way to anyone else or take their wishes into account when they clash with his own. He always works according to his own ideas regardless of the circumstances. He can never fit into other people's plans. He always comes into conflict with laws and authorities. He feels an overbearing impulse to behave in an arbitrary way. He is rude, bullying and aggressive, and in extreme cases addicted to playing with dirt and excessively fond of anal jokes and stories.

These symptoms are by no means all entirely attributable to the way the baby may have behaved on the pot. Anal fixations seem to be especially liable to develop if the child's development is not assisted by a proper environment. The fixations, in such cases, do not produce neurosis, but rather a corruption and brutalization of character in which certain anal elements are evident. Again, a whole childhood may be penetrated, especially in certain particularly vulnerable situations, by the parents' neurosis or by other peculiarities of the family atmosphere. Later experience may confirm and deepen the original experience. The "corrective experience"[30] may be lacking which is so important for healthy development, and which may have been more easily available in the larger family communities of earlier times than it is in present-day conditions. Thus pot-training and the memories of it which occur in analysis do not make up the single traumatic root of early psychic development. They are one particularly significant element in a process which always lasts longer than a year and may extend over ten, twenty or more years.

It is, of course, easy enough to dismiss all this as mere imagination. But if one does this, one is obliged to find some alternative hypothesis which accounts more satisfactorily for the astonishing findings produced by the analysis of both children and adults. There is less evidence of the processes which we have described in the

[30] F. Alexander, "Analyse der therapeutischen Faktoren in der psychoanalytischen Behandlung", *Psyche,* 4 (1950–1), pp. 407ff.

development of children who have been brought up in a reasonable and loving way in a healthy environment. Pot-training is less liable to lead to great difficulties when it is carried through patiently and sensibly in a secure and peaceful atmosphere, and traumatic effects are unusual in these circumstances. Pot-training only becomes charged with emotion in neurotic families. In order to realize how potent a source of traumas this kind of experience can be, one needs to see the kind of tragi-comedy which a neurotic mother can build up round her child when it is sitting on its pot. In a healthy environment the phases succeed each other smoothly, and this may be why the significance of these processes can easily be underestimated by developmental psychologists.

There is one fundamental characteristic of human development which appears especially clearly in the anal phase. The child's environment either approves and encourages its spontaneous feelings and tendencies or disapproves and takes up a limiting and restricting position. And the child is more concerned to be at peace with its environment than to satisfy its actual instincts. It can oppose its own desires for fear or love of its parents, and this opposition can become a permanent feature of its personality. The phases in the development of the instincts are matched by phases in the formation of structures which inhibit and divert these instincts. Freud called such structures defence-mechanisms, and their organizing and integrating centre the ego and super-ego. The most powerful and important process which forms and distorts the ego-structures is identification.[31] In this process the person falls in love with some pattern and tries to make it into himself and model himself upon it. Identification forms the defensive ego, works directly on the instinctual structures and determines the personality in all its aspects.

Identification can be the result of love and admiration, or it can represent the conformity demanded by fear or feelings of guilt. We know that children can so assimilate themselves to their environment that even their organic functions are changed. "Wolf-children" apparently become able to see in the dark like wolves, they almost cease to perspire, and their general character and habits of life become wolf-like.[32]

Human beings develop according to models. If the tendency to appropriate these models is interrupted by fear or hate, if the person cannot therefore love and value the models which lie before him, or if the process of identification is forced and strained by unsureness, feelings of guilt or overmastering passion, then the result will be tension within the personality. The person will have identified himself with an ego-ideal which runs counter to his natural possibili-

[31] "Group Psychology and the Analysis of the Ego", *Works*, vol. 18, pp. 105ff. According to Max Scheler identification is one of the most valuable of all psychoanalytic formulations.

[32] J. A. L. Singh and R. M. Zingg, *Wolf-Children and Feral Man*, New York, 1942.

ties and estranges him from his natural self. He will become afraid of the ideal and quickly abandon it. The excessive masculine identification of the young girl with her father or brother makes a classical example; the ideal self organizes defensive dispositions against all feminine tendencies.

The part played by identification in psychic development can be reconstructed from the patient's memories and from his present behaviour. And the patient can help to dissolve the distorted dispositions due to identification by reflecting on the way in which they were formed.

Under the pressure of upbringing, instinctual conflicts, fears and feelings of guilt, and under the influence of environment and identification, the child turns to the defence-mechanisms as naturally available means for coming to terms with his instincts. Different children will find certain mechanisms more effective than others, and rely chiefly on these. They will rely chiefly on repression, projection, displacement, sublimation or some other defensive technique according to the stage of maturity that they have reached, the nature of the conflict that they have to deal with, and which of these mechanisms they find easier to employ. This experience and consequent fixation on one or more of the mechanisms will have a permanent formative effect on the structure of the personality.

Freud described further formative processes under the heading of "object attachment". This describes passionate attachment to people as a result of love, hate, fear or feelings of guilt. Object attachments exert to some extent constant influences over the world of the child and form a background to psychic movements. Their influence begins soon after birth, and is especially significant during the Oedipal phase.

Freud showed that sexuality becomes an important human concern long before puberty, and in fact from the beginning of life onwards. "Sexuality" is used here to describe everything connected with the facts that people are male and female and that they only become men and women after a difficult and dangerous process which involves many conflicts. As soon as a child is born his parents may take up a definite attitude to its sex, and when the parents are psychically unhealthy their attitude will be distorted. The neurotic mother may refuse to nurse her children or even to look at them for days on end because they belong to the wrong sex; or the parents may obstinately ignore reality and treat their child as if it belonged to a different sex.[33] Parents can take up a false and negative attitude to the sex of their children for many kinds of reasons. In this atmosphere it is impossible for the child to form the healthy self-respect which is such an important basis for the total development of its personality.

[33] Rilke's hysterical mother brought him up and dressed him as if he were a girl for several years, and after this preparation sent him to a military school, where he was tormented on account of his middle name ("Mizzo").

But the attitude of the child to its parents' sex can also become problematic. If the child's father is anxious and weak and his mother a strong woman in every way, then he will have no incentive to pattern himself on the masculine model. If the model for identification is lacking, then the child will have to develop masculine aspirations, feelings and modes of behaviour by himself, and often in the face of great obstacles. Human beings, unlike most animals, do not tend to do this naturally, and although they sometimes succeed, they often fail.

Sometimes the child lacks the possibility of forming "object relationships" with its parents or brothers and sisters. This threatens the development of the child's own sexual character and tends to prevent it from learning the way to form relationships with people of the opposite sex. If a young boy has no warm and heartfelt relationships with his mother and sister (or girl with her father and brother), then he will have difficulties in his later sexual relations. The child also experiences the parents' relationship with each other in their marriage; and this last experience can likewise have repercussions (which are sometimes fatal) on its power to love and on its marital relations.

Thus there are many ways in which the child's sexuality in the sense of its sexual role can be determined by its relations with its parents, brothers and sisters. Every child has periods when it prefers one parent to the other and approaches him or her with special tenderness; sometimes it also jealously rejects the other parent. Often enough in the early history of neurotics it appears that this normal tendency will have become exceptionally intense and taken on a distinctly sexual quality. Sometimes this quality derives from the parents' own behaviour: they or other adults may deliberately seduce or corrupt the child—or, more commonly, the child's sexual feelings may be prematurely awakened by the too passionate tenderness often displayed by mothers neglected by their husbands; but it can also develop on its own without external assistance. This is the "classical Oedipus situation" of psychoanalysis. The results of the situation can be seen most clearly in hysteria: there is an intensive and ambivalent libidinous-aggressive attachment to the parents, which is usually complicated by expiatory identification. The parents remain the measure of everything; behaviour is never independent, and either conforms to the parental pattern or reacts against it. And the distorted image of the parents in turn distorts all human relationships through transference. Love of a kind is only possible to neurotics of this sort when their partner is prepared to act as a substitute father or mother and to accept them in an infantile role. But the neurotic cannot maintain the infantile role for long, and the attachment ends in disaster. Oedipal fixation and formation is the root of many perversions, neuroses and difficulties in marriage and other kinds of relationships. Freud's "Oedipus complex" does exist, and it is not so very difficult to find examples of it in everyday life.

When the Oedipus element appears in dreams and memories and in discussions with the doctor it is sometimes possible to trace other problems lying behind it. We may find that the patient has difficulties in perceiving and recognizing his own moods and feelings. Or we may see the "Anima" described by Jung, appearing in dreams as a motherly woman; or the problem of how a person can integrate the spiritual and rational spheres of his nature from which he has become estranged. This kind of problem can also be expressed symbolically in a dream of union with the mother or of a fight with the father. Although Freud himself did not see the new aspects and dimensions of the psychoanalytical findings which appear at this point, he at least opened the way to their later discovery.

The threat of castration is another formative process belonging to the Oedipal phase. As is well known, Freud held that this threat, and the feelings of anxiety and guilt which flow from it, constitute one of the severest traumas of childhood. Freud's successors debated as to whether or not castration-anxiety was a special case of a general fear of being injured or damaged, an expression of the fact that human beings are vulnerable in the broadest sense and need many things which they can be deprived of. Many analysts consider that the original trauma is caused when the child is deprived of its mother's breast during weaning, or even when it loses the security of the uterus when it is born. Whichever of these opinions is correct, it remains true that parents sometimes explicitly threaten children with castration or cutting off their hands when they have been playing with their genitals, and that anxious dreams, memories and fantasies corresponding with this event occur in analysis. Mutilation is an important theme in many fairy-stories and children's books (for example, *Struwelpeter*); and the theme is often hinted at, and sometimes appears very clearly, in the analysis of children and in their games and drawings. It is obvious that genetic theories of neurosis can interpret these facts in a number of ways. But the psychoanalytical view that the fear of painful injury and mutilation is one of the most important ways in which psychic development can be disturbed does seem to be very probably true.

The personality can be determined, and neurosis produced, by deficiencies and deprivations as well as by positive formative processes. When a child does not find what its "primal imagination" (above, p. 133) naturally leads it to expect from its parents and environment—interest, attention and respect, incentives and some freedom of action, warmth, rest, security and love—then it will be frustrated, and this will allow and encourage fixations, traumas, regression and false identification. A man who is frustrated in early childhood will form a level of expectation which is essentially oral and insatiable and leads to an endless series of disappointments and a constant greedy hunt after all kinds of substitute satisfactions. This is passion in the broadest sense, "le complex d'abandon",[34] the oral-captative disposition (Schultz-Hencke). Such people approach God and the world and other people bearing a claim which was valid but never met in childhood but which is now too much out of date ever to be honoured. It is especially difficult for them to see, as they need to, that every neurotic personality shows traces of deprivation and deficiency.

In this chapter we have described the decisive formative processes which Freud discovered in his patient's memories and by observing children and which he used to explain the neurotic personality and the symptoms of neurosis. These processes are responsible for the faults in the structure of the personality which permit symptom-formation. Psychoanalytical observation does not itself show us how this works out in detail—how, for example, structural faults in the personality account for compulsive neurosis. Nor can psychoanalysis itself tell us whether there are any important factors which we have failed to take into consideration.

There are several questions to which our

[34] G. Guex, *La Névrose d'abandon*, Paris, 1950; A. Mitscherlich, "Öedipus und Kaspar Hauser", *Der Monat*, 25 (1950), 3, p. 11.

answers are still largely incomplete. We do not know whether, and how far, the form and genesis of neurosis have been influenced by the overstrain from which children suffer in large towns, by nights in air-raid shelters, or by changes in social and family structure and in accepted values and the cultural climate since the First World War. The suspicion is not always completely unfounded that we interpret neurosis and psychosomatic illness according to the psychology of our grandfathers. But the development of analytical phenomenology and theory does show that the method has not remained bound to Freud's own findings. Freud's theory of phases should not be seen and judged as an attempt at a comprehensive characterology of development. Its perspective is too limited; Freud viewed the personality as a psychopathologist. And psychoanalysts are in any case now constructing a more inclusive psychology of development, based especially on the psychology of the ego and on the observation and treatment of children.

9

THE EFFECTS OF ANALYSIS

We have already referred many times to processes which can be seen as effects of analysis, and in this last section we shall try to set these processes out together.[1]

One important effect of analysis is to strengthen and stimulate the natural freedom and spontaneity of experience. Freud held that the patient should practise analytic meditation daily. This attention to the details and characteristic patterns of everyday life was a new departure in psychological research. But we can find it also in some of the directions for the examination of conscience given by teachers of the inner life, for example in St. Ignatius Loyola's *Spiritual Exercises*: "... to review the time hour by hour, or period by period, from the moment I rose down to the present examination, and to demand account of my soul, first of my thoughts, then of my words, lastly of my actions ..."[2] Free association can set up strong psychic movements if it is practised daily, or at the least three times a week. If one is obliged to report exactly what

[1] This is not the place for a properly detailed description of the therapeutic and rehabilitatory workings of analysis; a separate account is in preparation.

[2] *Spiritual Exercises*, trans. John Morris and others, London, 1952, no. 43.

is passing through one's mind, one will regard psychic processes more closely than one would otherwise do, and these processes will themselves take on a more definite shape. Perceptions become more precise, memories more distinct, and fantasies—which, especially with neurotics, are liable to vanish from consciousness without a trace once they are in any way interrupted—become more deeply impressed and maintain themselves longer. One can see the articulation of subtle and almost indiscernible sequences of experience. Indistinct and habitual judgements become explicit, and their invalidity becomes obvious. Personal attitudes previously too dangerous to recognize come more sharply to the fore. When psychic life is set out in words, tensions and antinomies appear which have previously been hidden. One is surprised to discover that one's desires and preferences sometimes become stronger once they have been put into words, and sometimes they abruptly vanish or change almost immediately.

As we might expect, emotional life is particularly strongly affected by these movements. It is difficult to investigate emotional life because it is so allergic to introspection. Reflection destroys it or changes it. But although the analytic method cannot completely escape this difficulty, it does seem that the relaxed and detached contemplation and assembly of one's own experience which is practised in analysis permits, and even effectively encourages, emotional life to unfold itself. Free association is, above all, a means for the development of emotional life. When Freud was enumerating the types of experience which the patient has to report, he placed emotional experience, the most difficult to express in words, at the head of the list. Free association discovers emotions and makes them grow stronger and deeper. And we also find the opposite. Free association can smother emotions and even destroy them. This is to be expected as a part of the therapeutic process.

We ought to note here that neurotics reflect about themselves much too much anyway, and that some people also think that it is their excessive self-concern that has made them sick in the first place. Is not the doctor's object to liberate the patient from himself, and divert him away from himself and towards other people and his vocation in life? This may sound convincing, but a careful study of neurosis will show that people are not neurotic because they think too much about themselves, but are forced to think about themselves only because they no longer understand themselves and their psychic life. Analytic reflection increases the patient's understanding and redirects his psychic forces from himself and towards the outside world. At the same time, there are neurotics who are extremely extroverted and who do not reflect about themselves enough.[3]

[3] E. Michel, "Zur anthropologischen Deutung der Hysterie", *Stud. Generale*, 3 (1950), pp. 292ff.

There are many reasons for supposing that neurosis, and many distorted dispositions of the personality which are structurally similar to neurosis, are derived from obstructions and distortions in the development of emotional life. If this were true, psychotherapy would be emotional rehabilitation working according to the laws of emotional life. And it would be easy to explain how various and very dissimilar methods of depth psychology, each resting on mutually contradictory theoretical bases, have each been able to report therapeutic successes. (Successes do not, of course, by themselves prove the correctness of either the method or the theory.)

If the patient carefully, and over a long period, reports his train of thought, then as a rule his behaviour will change both in analysis and in his day-to-day life. Embryo experience will develop and habitual patterns of experience will be abandoned. A tendentious and stylized picture of the past will be modified in many respects by things remembered in analysis, and the past will appear in a completely new light; subtle additions will be made, darkness will lighten and shadows appear when the picture is too light. Cherished attitudes to the past will have to be revised. In the present, too, the patient's images of other people and attitudes towards them will have to be completed and corrected; and this will often be very painful. The patient who has seen his father as a kind of god may suddenly have to see him as a human being; the mother who has appeared as a hateful witch may become human and even lovable. The patient will see himself in a different way as well. Emotions, impulses, judgements, wishes and modes of behaviour appear which would earlier have been unthinkable. Fantasies, feelings and tendencies unfold in a way which suggests that the patient wants to return to some early childhood phase; his experience and behaviour regress. The neurotic imagines himself as a child and the doctor as his father or mother, and despite strong resistance infantile modes of behaviour frequently gain the upper hand and penetrate his life. It is difficult for the neurotic to recognize this infantile behaviour. It may be a matter of regression from resistance, an escape from the burdens and duties of everyday life into a dream world. Or regression may mean the rediscovery of an unformed part of the personality and quickly lead the patient to better terms with reality. Regression is a sign that the patient has power to regenerate his psychic life when he has seemed in every other way emotionally dead and drained of spirit and imagination.

As we have already said, analysis tends to restore the continuity of experience and incongruous feelings and emotions to their proper place. It reveals the hidden motivation of many kinds of behaviour; rational interrelations gradually begin to reappear where before fears, aggression and depression, attraction and repulsion had succeeded each other without apparent reason. The process is independent of the analyst's direction. Psychic life tends of itself towards completeness, unity, order and rational articulation, and once conditions are created in which the soul can come to terms with the disintegrating forces of repression and self-deception this order will be restored of its own accord. It is precisely the abstention from outward direction and the surrender to the spontaneity of one's own psychic life that allow repressed and unconscious experience to develop and unfold itself.

Once psychic life has been liberated from its paralysis we can see a marked improvement in the whole personality. The hidden side of ambivalent attitudes to people and things becomes visible. Emotional life flows in new directions. Petrified spheres of the personality are restored to life, and their restoration stimulates the growth of other areas which were previously neglected. The new growth follows rational laws. The soul rejects chaos. Moving cautiously, it begins to take up new attitudes to the world, and to discard infantile patterns of behaviour. It experiences and judges things in a more genuine and adult way. If neurosis is a form of psychic blindness, the soul also has a natural intuition of the true nature of things. Analysis makes the patient realize that this intuition has become obscured or been neglected and helps him to learn how to cultivate it once again. The rational ordering of the world, the true shape of life and its natural duties, have an extraordinary power to dissolve distorted attitudes and dispositions once they have been understood and thoroughly appropriated by the soul. Human beings do not willingly and consciously live falsely.

The patient very rarely talks to the analyst about the things he sees clearly and experiences in an ordered way. The soul has a natural knowledge of its own needs. The analyst is not concerned with a piece of psychic apparatus which he can set right simply by applying the appropriate technical knowledge. Analysis is a human living process, in which the patient's conscious reason combines with and assists the other elements of his psychic life. Freud belonged very much to the rationalist and technological times in which he lived. But despite his materialist metaphysics and all his talk of psychic mechanisms and apparatus, he had at least some idea of the living formative power of the soul. He wrote, on one occasion, that he had a kind of certainty that a patient would recover and everything somehow sort itself out.[4] And if something is to sort itself out it must in some way know by itself where the parts belong. A dismantled watch can never sort out its own parts and put itself together again. The following passage illustrates both Freud's recognition of this truth and the particular kind of sober pathos that is so typical of his work and of the man himself.

[4] *Works*, vol. 2, p. 160.

"We have *analysed* the patient—that is, separated his mental processes into their elementary constituents and demonstrated these instinctual elements in him simply and in isolation; what could be more natural than to expect that we should also help him to make a new and better combination of them?

But I cannot think . . . that any new task is set us by this psychosynthesis. . . . What is psychical is something so unique and peculiar to itself that no one comparison can reflect its nature. The work of psychoanalysis suggests analogies with chemical analysis, but it does so just as much with the intervention of the surgeon or the manipulations of the orthopaedist or the influence of the educator. The comparison with chemical analysis has its limitations: for in mental life we have to deal with trends that are under a compulsion towards unification and combination. Whenever we succeed in analysing a symptom into its elements, in freeing an instinctual impulse from one nexus, it does not remain in isolation, but immediately enters into a new one.

In actual fact, however, the neurotic patient presents us with a torn mind divided by resistances. As we analyse it and remove the resistances, it grows together; the great unity which we call his ego fits into itself all the instinctual impulses which before had been split off and held apart from it. The psycho-synthesis is thus achieved during analytic treatment without intervention, automatically and inevitably."[5]

Analysis releases spontaneity, sets feelings and emotions in their proper place, develops embryo experience and opens up areas of the personality which for one reason or another are undeveloped. And it does all this primarily through the relationship between doctor and patient. The analytic relationship, although limited and of a very special kind, enables the patient to practise his way into the ability to behave maturely towards himself and towards other people. It gives him freedom to experiment in being himself and in thinking of other people as well as himself; freedom to dare to do certain things without having to face the consequences. It places him in a stable relationship which can be cleared of fear, suspicion and hostility without haste or panic. If the patient can really involve himself in this relationship and face sympathy and anger, expectation and disappointment frankly and honestly, if he can dare to admit and express his real feelings, then the healing forces will grow strong, penetrate his psychic life and restore him to his natural self.

[5] "Lines of Advance in Psychoanalytic Therapy", *Works*, vol. 17, pp. 161ff.

LIST OF WORKS REFERRED TO IN THE TEXT

Abraham, Karl, *Psychoanalytische Studien zur Charakterbildung*, Leipzig, 1925

Ach, Narzisz, *Analyse des Willens*, Berlin and Leipzig, 1935

Adler, Alfred, *Understanding Human Nature*, trans. W. B. Wolfe, London, 1928

The Neurotic Constitution, trans. Bernard Glueck and John E. Lind, London, 1921

Die Technik der Individualpsychologie, Berlin, 1928

Alexander, Franz, *Psychoanalyse der Gesamtpersönlichkeit*, Vienna, 1927

Psychosomatic Medicine, London, 1952

"Analyse der therapeutischen Faktoren in der psychoanalytischen Behandlung", *Psyche*, 4 (1950–1)

Alexander, Franz and French, T., *Studies in Psychosomatic Medicine*, New York, 1948

Allers, Rudolf, *Über Psychoanalyse*, Berlin, 1922

The Psychology of Character, trans. and with an introduction by E. B. Strauss, London, 1939

"Versuch über individualpsychologische und psychoanalytische Charakterologie. Charakter als Ausdruck". *Jahrb. d. Charakterologie* (Berlin, 1924)

"Medizinische Charakterologie", in Brugsch and Levy, *Die Biologie der Person*, 2 (1931)

Allport, Gordon W., *Personality*, New York, 1937

Anschütz, Georg, *Psychologie*, Hamburg, 1953

Aster, Ernst von, *Die Psychoanalyse*, Bern, 1949
Bally, Gustav, *Der normale Mensch*, Zürich, 1952
Beauvoir, Simone de, *The Second Sex*, trans. H. M. Parshley, London, 1953
Behn, Siegfried, "Psychol. Methoden der Traumforschung", in *Abderhaldens Hdb. d. biol. Arbeitsmeth.*, 6, 2, Vienna, 1925
Bernard of Clairvaux, *Sermones de Diversis* (Migne, *Patrologia Latina*, vol. 183)
Bernfeld, Siegfried, *The Psychology of the Infant*, trans. Rosetta Hurwitz, London, 1929
Binswanger, Ludwig, *Ausgewählte Vorträge und Aufsätze*, Bern, 1947 and 1955, 2 vols.
Grundfragen und Erkenntnis menschlichen Daseins, Zürich, 1953
Erinnerungen an Sigmund Freud, Bern, 1956
Bollnow, Otto Fr., *Das Verstehen*, Mainz, 1949
Die Methode der Geisteswissenschaften, Mainz, 1950
Das Wesen der Stimmungen, Frankfurt-am-Main, 1956 (3)
Boss, Medard, *Sinn und Gehalt der sexuellen Perversionen*, Bern, 1952 (2)
The Analysis of Dreams, trans. Arnold J. Pomerans, London, 1957
Psychoanalyse und Daseinsanalytik, Bern and Stuttgart, 1957
Bovet, Theodor, *Die Person, ihre Krankheiten und Wandlungen*, Bern, 1946
Bowlby, John, "Maternal Care and Mental health", *Bulletin of the World Health Organisation*, Geneva, 1951
Bräutigam, Walter, "Über die psychosomatische Spezifität des Asthma bronchiale", *Psyche*, 8 (1954–5)

Breuer, Josef and Freud, Sigmund, *Studien über Hysterie,* Vienna, 1895

Brun, Rudolf, *General Theory of Neuroses,* trans. Bernard Miall, New York, 1951

Brunner, August, "Philosophisches zur Tiefenpsychologie und Psychotherapie", *Stimmen der Zeit,* 144 (1949)

Bühler, Karl, *Die Krise der Psychologie,* Jena, 1929 (2)

Caruso, Igor, *Religion und Psychotherapie,* Innsbruck, 1946

Psychoanalyse und Synthese der Existenz, Freiburg, 1952

Cavé, Madeleine, *L'Oeuvre paradoxale de Freud,* Paris, 1945

Daim, Wilfried, *Umwertung der Psychoanalyse,* Vienna, 1951

Dalbiez, R., *Psychoanalytic Method and the Doctrine of Freud,* trans. T. F. Lindsay, London, 1941, 2 vols.

Dembo, Tamara, "Das Ärger als dynamisches Problem", *Psych. Forschg.,* 15, 1931

Dessauer, Philipp, "Ärztliche Psychotherapie und priesterliche Seelsorge", in *Geist und Leben, Zeitschrift für Aszese und Mystik,* 1951

Dollard, J. L. W., et al., *Frustration and Aggression,* New Haven, 1939

Dorer, Maria, *Historische Grundlagen der Psychoanalyse,* Leipzig, 1932

Dührssen, Annemarie, *Psychogene Erkrankungen bei Kindern und Jugendlichen,* Göttingen, 1954

Dunbar, Flanders, *Psychosomatic Diagnosis,* New York, 1945

Emotions and Bodily Changes, New York, 1949

Duykaerts, François, *La Notion de normal en psychologie clinique*, Paris, 1945
Eiff, A. W. von, *Grundumsatz und Psyche*, Berlin, Göttingen and Heidelberg, 1957
Erikson, Eric H., *Wachstum und Krisen der gesunden Persönlichkeit*, Stuttgart, 1953
"Das Traummuster der Psychoanalyse", *Psyche*, 8 (1954–5)
Fairbairn, W. R., *Psychoanalytic Studies of the Personality*, London, 1949
Fenichel, Otto, *Perversionen, Psychosen, Charakterstörungen*, Vienna, 1931
Problems of Psychoanalytic Technique, New York, 1941
The Psychoanalytic Theory of Neurosis, New York, 1945
Ferenczi, Sandor, *Bausteine zur Psychoanalyse*, Vienna, 1927
Feuling, Daniel, *Das Leben der Seele*, Salzburg, 1940 (2)
Fodor, Nandor, "Freud", in *Dictionary of Psychoanalysis*, New York, 1945
Frankl, Viktor E., *Ärztliche Seelsorge*, Vienna, 1947
Theorie und Therapie der Neurosen, Vienna, 1956
Freud, Anna, *The Ego and the Mechanisms of Defence*, trans. Cecil Baines, London, 1937
"Psychoanalyse und Entwicklungspsychologie", *Psyche*, 11 (1956–7)
Freud, Anna with Fenichel and Glover, *The Psychoanalytic Study of the Child*, London, 1945–
Freud, Sigmund, *Complete Psychological Works*, trans. and ed. James Strachey and others, London, 1956–, 24 vols.

Gesammelte Werke, London, 1940–
Collected Papers, various translators, London, 1924–, 5 vols.
An Outline of Psychoanalysis, trans. J. Strachey, London, 1949
Introductory Lectures on Psychoanalysis, trans. Joan Rivière, London, 1949 (2)
New Introductory Lectures on Psychoanalysis, trans. W. J. H. Sprott, London, 1949
An Autobiographical Study, trans. J. Strachey, London, 1935
The Ego and the Id, trans. Joan Rivière, London, 1950
Inhibitions, Symptoms and Anxiety, trans. Alix Strachey, London, 1936
The Origins of Psychoanalysis, Letters to Wilhelm Fliess, Drafts and Notes: 1887–1902, trans. E. Mosbacher and J. Strachey, London, 1954
The Question of Lay Analysis, trans. Nancy Procter-Gregg, London, 1947

Fromm-Reichmann, Frieda, *Principles of Intensive Psychotherapy*, Chicago, 1950

Gebsattel, Viktor Emil, Frhr. von, "Sigmund Freud und die Seelenheilkunde der Gegenwart", *Med. Klinik*, 1946
Not und Hilfe, Freiburg, 1947
Prolegomena einer medizinischen Anthropologie, Berlin and Heidelberg, 1954

Gesell, Arnold, Ilg, F. W. et al., *Infant and Child in the Culture of Today*, London, 1945

Glover, Edward, *Freud or Jung?*, London, 1950
"Forschungsmethoden in der Psychoanalyse", *Psyche*, 6 (1952–3)

The Technique of Psychoanalysis, London, 1955

Görres, Albert, "Heilung und Heil. Zur Kritik der Psychoanalyse", *Hochland*, 45 (1952–)

"Die Technik der Psychoanalyse", *Psyche*, 9 (1955–6)

"Über die Gewissensprüfung nach der Weise des hl. Ignatius von Loyola", *Geist und Leben*, 29 (1956)

"Personale Psychoanalyse?", *Psyche*, 11 (1957–)

"Person, Psyche, Krankheit", in *Jahrb. f. Psychologie u. Psychotherapie—Festschrift für V. E. Frhr. von Gebsattel zum 75. Geburtstag*, 1958

Grodzicki, W. D., "Neue Wege in der Psychoanalyse?", *Psyche*, 10 (1956–7)

Gruhle, Hans W., "Kritik der Psychoanalyse", *Studium Generale*, 3 (1950)

Guardini, Romano, *Welt und Person*, Würzburg, 1939

Das Harren der Schöpfung, Würzburg, 1940

"Philosophische Anmerkungen zu Sigmund Freuds Psychologie", in *S. Freud, Gedenkfeier zur 100 Wiederkehr seines Geburtstages, Münchener Universitätsreden*, Neue Folge, 19 (1956)

Gueux, Germaine, *La Névrose d'abandon*, Paris, 1950

Hartmann, Heinz, *Die Grundlagen der Psychoanalyse*, Leipzig, 1927

"Ichpsychologie und Anpassungensproblem", *Int. Zeitschr. F. Psychoanalyse*, 24 (1939)

"Psychoanalysis and Developmental Psychology", in *The Psychoanalytical Study of the Child*, London, 1945–, vol. 4

"Comment on the Psychoanalytic Theory of the Ego", ibid.

Hartmann, Heinz and Kris, E., "The Genetic Approach to Psychoanalysis", *The Psychoanalytical Study of the Child*, vol. 1

Hartmann, Heinz, Kris, E. and Loewenstein, R. M., "Comments on the Formation of Psychic Structure", *The Psychoanalytical Study of the Child*, vol. 2

Heinen, Wilhelm, *Fehlformen des Liebesstrebens in moralpsychologischer Deutung und moraltheologischer Würdigung*, Freiburg, 1954

Heiss, Robert, *Allgemeine Tiefenpsychologie. Methoden, Probleme, Ergebnisse*, Stuttgart, 1956

Hellpach, Willy, *Klinische Psychologie*, Stuttgart, 1946

Hengstenberg, Hans E., *Philosophische Anthropologie*, Stuttgart, 1957

Herbart, J. F., *Psychologie als Wissenschaft, neugegründet auf Erfahrung, Metaphysik und Mathematik*, Königsberg, 1884

Hochheimer, Wolfgang, "Über Projektion", *Psyche*, 9 (1955–6)

Hofstätter, Peter R., *Einführung in die Tiefenpsychologie*, Vienna, 1948

"Psychotherapie und die Theorie der Lernvorgänge", *Psyche*, 7 (1953–4)

Hollenbach, Johannes M., *Der Mensch als Entwurf*, Frankfurt, 1957

Hoppe, Ferdinand, "Erfolg und Misserfolg", *Psych. Forschung*, 14 (1930)

Horney, Karen, *The Neurotic Personality of Our Time*, New York, 1939

New Ways in Psychoanalysis, New York, 1939

Our Inner Conflicts, New York, 1945
Neurosis and Human Growth, New York, 1951
Hunt, J. McV., *Personality and the Behaviour Disorders*, New York, 1944
"Experimental Psychoanalysis", *Harriman's Encyclopedia of Psychology*, New York, 1946
Ignatius of Loyola, *Spiritual Exercises*, trans. John Morris and others, London, 1952 (5)
International Congress of Psychotherapy, Zürich, 1954, on Transference; *Acta Psychotherapeutica*, Suppl., 3 (1955)
Jaspers, Karl, *Allgemeine Psychopathologie*, Heidelberg, 1946 (4)
Zur Kritik der Psychoanalyse, Heidelberg, 1950
Wesen und Kritik der Psychotherapie, Munich, 1955
Jones, Ernest, *Sigmund Freud, Life and Work*, London, 1953, 3 vols.
Jores, Artur, "Was ist Krankheit?", *Medizin heute*, 1 (1952)
Der Mensch und seine Krankheit, Stuttgart, 1956
Jung, Carl Gustav, *Versuch einer Darstellung der psychoanalytischen Theorie*, Zürich, 1955 (2)
Keller, Wilhelm, *Psychologie und Philosophie des Wollens*, Munich, 1954
Kemper, Werner, "Die Gegenübertragung", *Psyche*, 7 (1953–4)
Der Traum und seine Bedeutung, Hamburg, 1955
Kittel, Gerhard, *Theologisches Wörterbuch zum Neuen Testament*, Stuttgart, 1933–
Klages, Ludwig, "Bemerkungen zur sogenannten Psychopathie", *Nervenarzt*, 1 (1928)
Kolle, Kurt, "Zur Kritik der sogenannten Psychoso-

matik", *Mschr. für Psychiatrie und Neurologie* (1953)

Kranefeldt, W. M., *Die Psychoanalyse*, Berlin, 1930

Kretschmer, Ernst, *Hysterie, Reflex und Instinkt*, Stuttgart, 1948

Psychotherapeutische Studien, Stuttgart, 1949

Kris, E., "Notes on the Development and on Some Current Problems of Psychoanalytic Child Psychology", in *The Psychoanalytic Study of the Child*, vol. 5

Krudewig, Maria, *Vom Stand der Psychologie des Gefühls und von ihrem bleibenden Ertrag*, Berlin, 1942

Krueger, Felix, *Zur Philosophie und Psychologie der Ganzheit (Schriften aus den Jahren 1918–1940)*, Berlin, 1953

Kubie, Lawrence S., *Psychoanalyse ohne Geheimnis*, Hamburg, 1956

Künkel, Fritz, *Let's Be Normal! The Psychologist Comes to his Senses*, tr. Eleanore Jensen, New York, 1929

Kunz, Hans, *Die Anthropologische Bedeutung der Phantasie*, Basel, 1946

Die Aggressivität und die Zärtlichkeit, Bern, 1946

"Zur Theorie der Perversion", *Mschr. f. Psychiatrie*, 105 (1942)

"Zur Frage nach dem Wesen der Norm", *Psyche*, 8 (1954–5)

Landauer, Carl, "Passive Technik", *Int. Ztschr. f. Psychoanalyse*, 10 (1924)

Lao-Tse, *Tao-Te-King*, trans. Richard Wilhelm, Jena, 1911

Lersch, Philipp, *Aufbau der Person*, Munich, 1954 (6)

Lewin, Kurt, *Die Entwicklung der experimentellen Willenspsychologie und die Psychotherapie*, Leipzig, 1929

A Dynamic Theory of Personality, New York, 1935

Lincke, Harold, "Bemerkungen zur Triebpsychologie der Ersatzbefriedigung und Sublimierung", *Psyche*, 7 (1953–4)

Lorand, S., *Technique of Psychoanalytic Therapy*, New York, 1946

Lorenz, Konrad, "Die angeborenen Formen möglicher Erfahrungen", *Ztschr. f. Tierpsychologie*, 5 (1943)

Massermann, J. H., "Experimente über psychodynamische Probleme", *Psyche*, 6 (1952–3)

Matussek, Paul, *Metaphysische Probleme der Medizin*, Berlin, 1950 (2)

McClelland, D. C., *Personality*, 1951

Metzger, Wolfgang, *Psychologie. Die Entwicklung ihrer Grundannahmen seit der Einführung des Experiments*, Darmstadt, 1954 (2)

Michel, Ernst, "Zur anthropologischen Deutung der Hysterie", *Studium Generale*, 3 (1950)

Rettung und Erneuerung des personalen Lebens, Frankfurt-am-Main, 1951

Mitscherlich, Alexander, *Vom Ursprung der Sucht*, Stuttgart, 1947

"Oedipus und Kaspar Hauser. Tiefenpsychologische Probleme der Gegenwart", *Der Monat*, 3 (1950)

"Kritische Anmerkungen zur Problementfaltung in der Tiefenpsychologie", *Psyche*, 5 (1951–2)

(Ed.) *Entfaltung der Psychoanalyse*, Stuttgart, 1956

Mittenzwei, Kuno, "Versuch einer Darstellung und Kritik der Freudschen Neurosenlehre", *Ztschr. f. Pathopsych.*, 1–3 (1911–14)

Morgan, Charles, *The Flashing Stream*, London, 1948

The Voyage, London, 1940

Mühle, Günther W., "Zur Psychologie des Symbolischen", *Studium Generale*, 6 (1953)

"Rückgriff und Regression", *Studium Generale*, 9 (1956)

Müller-Suur, Hemmo, *Das psychisch Abnorme*, Berlin, 1950

Murphy, Gardner, *Personality*, New York, 1947

Neumeister, Heddy, "Säkularisierte Passion und Ketzerstolz", *Frankfurter Allgemeine Zeitung*, 28.2.1957

Newman, John H., *An Essay in Aid of a Grammar of Assent*, London, 1870

Nuttin, Joseph, *Psychoanalysis and Personality*, trans. George Lamb London, 1954

Petrilowitsch, Nikolaus, *Zur Charakterologie der Zwangsneurotiker*, Halle, 1956

Pfahler, Gerhard, *Der Mensch und seine Vergangenheit*, Stuttgart, 1950

Der Mensch und seine Lebenswerkzeug, Stuttgart, 1954

Pfänder, Alexander, *Die Seele des Menschen*, Halle, 1933

"Grundlagen der Charakterologie", *Jahrb. der Charakterologie*, 1 (1924)

Pfister, Oskar, *The Psychoanalytic Method*, trans. Charles Rockwell Payne, London, 1917

Pieper, Josef, *Die Wirklichkeit und das Gute*, Leipzig, 1935

Happiness and Contemplation, trans. Richard and Clara Winston, London, 1959
Porphyry, *Vita Plotini*, in *Plotini Opera*, vol. 1, ed. P. Henry and H. R. Schwyzer, Paris and Brussels, 1951
Portmann, Adolf, *Animal Forms and Patterns*, trans. Hella Czech, London, 1952
Zoologie und das neue Bild des Menschen, Hamburg, 1956
Rahner, Karl, *Geist in Welt*, Münich, 1957 (2)
Schriften zur Theologie, 3 vols., Einsiedeln, Zürich and Cologne, 1954 (vol. 1 translated as *Theological Investigations*, London, 1961)
Rank, Otto, *Die Technik der Psychoanalyse*, Leipzig, 1926
Reich, Wilhelm, *Character Analysis*, trans. T. P. Wolfe, London, 1950 (3)
Rieffert, J. B., *Methoden und Grundbegriffe der Charakterologie, Bericht über den 13. Kongresz der Deutschen Gesellschaft f. Psychologie*, Jena, 1934
Riemann, Fritz, "Über neurosenspezifische Anwendung der psychoanalytischen Technik", *Psyche*, 6 (1952–3)
Rogers, Carl, *Client-centred Therapy*, Boston, 1951
Roheim, Geza, *Psychoanalysis and the Social Sciences*, New York, 1947
Rosenzweig, S., "An Outline of Frustration Theory", in Hunt, *Personality and the Behaviour Disorders*
Rudert, Johannes, "Genetische Schichtung der Person", *Jb. f. Psychologie und Psychotherapie*, 3 (1955)
Russell, Roger W., "Experimentelle Neurose", *Fortschr. d. Neur., Psychiatrie*, 21 (1953)

Sacherl, Karl, *Die Pedanterie*, Göttingen, 1958

Sander, Friedrich, *Experimentelle Ergebnisse der Gestaltpsychologie*, Jena, 1928

Scheler, Max, *Der Formalismus in der Ethik und die materielle Wertethik, Ges. Werke*, vol. 2, Bern, 1954

The Nature of Sympathy, trans. Peter Heath, London, 1954

Schneider, Kurt, *Die psychopathischen Persönlichkeiten*, Vienna, 1943 (6)

"Kritik der klinisch-typologischen Psychopathenbetrachtung", *Nervenarzt*, 19 (1948)

Klinische Psychopathologie, Stuttgart, 1952 (3)

Schöffler, Herbert, *Deutsche Geist im 18. Jahrhundert*, Göttingen, 1956

Schottlaender, Felix, *Die Mutter als Schicksal*, Stuttgart, 1948

Die Welt der Neurose, Stuttgart, 1950

"Das Ich und seine Determinanten", *Psyche*, 5 (1951–2)

Schultz-Hencke, Harald, *Der gehemmte Mensch*, Stuttgart, 1947

Lehrbuch der Traumanalyse, Stuttgart, 1949

Lehrbuch der analytischen Psychotherapie, Stuttgart, 1951

Schwidder, Werner, "Die Technischen Schriften Freuds und die Weiterentwicklung der psychoanalytischen Behandlungstechnik", *Ztschr. f. psychosom. Med.*, 2 (1955–6)

Sears, R. R., *Survey of Objective Studies of Psychoanalytic Concepts*, New York, 1943

Seemann, Walter F., "Über Symptombewegung bei vegetativen Störungen", in *Wiedergeburt des Einzelnen*, Stuttgart, 1956

Siebenthal, W. von, *Die Wissenschaft vom Traum*, Berlin, 1953

Siegmund, Georg, *Der Mensch in seinem Dasein*, Freiburg, 1953

Siewerth, Gustav, *Metaphysik der Kindheit*, Einsiedeln, 1957

Singh, J. A. L. and Zingg, R. M., *Wolf-children and Feral Man*, New York, 1942

Sonnemann, Ulrich, *Existence and Therapy*, New York, 1954

Speer, Ernst, *Der Arzt der Persönlichkeit*, Stuttgart, 1949

Spehlmann, Rainer, *Sigmund Freuds neurologische Schriften*, Berlin, 1953

Spitz, René, "Hospitalism", in *The Psychoanalytic Study of the Child*, vol. 1, London, 1945

Die Entstehung der ersten Objektbeziehungen, Stuttgart, 1957

Spitz, René and Wolf, K. M., "Anaclitic Depression", in *The Psychoanalytic Study of the Child*, vol. 2, London, 1946

Steinbach, Margarete, "Die Übertragung, Geschichte und Entwicklung einer Theorie", *Psyche*, 7 (1953–4)

Stekel, Wilhelm, *Technique of Analytical Psychotherapy*, trans. Eden and Cedar Paul, London, 1950 (2)

The Interpretation of Dreams, trans. Eden and Cedar Paul, New York, 1943, 2 vols.

Stern, Karl, *The Third Revolution*, London, 1955

Stierlin, Helm, "Verstehen und wissenschaftliche Theoriebildung in der Psychoanalyse", *Psyche*, 6 (1952–3)

Strachey, James, "The Nature of the Therapeutic

Action of Psychoanalysis", *Int. Journal of PSA*, 15, 127 (1934)

Sullivan, Harry, *Conceptions of Modern Psychiatry*, Washington, 1947

Thomae, Hans, "Die biographische Methode in den anthropologischen Wissenschaften", *Studium Generale*, 5 (1952)

Persönlichkeit, Bonn, 1955 (2)

Thompson, Clara, *Psychoanalysis: Its Evolution and Development*, London, 1952

Toman, Walter, *Dynamik der Motive*, Frankfurt-am-Main and Vienna, 1954

Tournier, Paul, *Krankheit und Lebensprobleme*, Basel, 1955

Uexküll, Thure von, "Die Naturwissenschaften und unsere Vorstellungen von der Seele", *Psyche*, 11 (1957–8)

Undeutsch, Udo, "Die Aktualgenese in ihrer allgemeinpsychologischen und ihrer charakterologischen Bedeutung", *Scientia*, 36 (1942)

Vetter, August, *Natur und Person*, Stuttgart, 1950

Die Erlebnisbedeutung der Phantasie, Stuttgart, 1950–

"Strukturanalyse und Tiefenpsychologie", *Psyche*, 5 (1951–2)

Weiss, Edward and English, O. S., *Psychosomatic Medicine*, Philadelphia, 1947

Weitbrecht, Hans Jörg, *Kritik der Psychosomatik*, Stuttgart, 1955

Weizsäcker, Viktor von, *Studien zur Pathogenese*, Wiesbaden, 1946 (2)

Körpergeschehen und Neurose, Stuttgart, 1947

Der kranke Mensch, Stuttgart, 1951

Wellek, Albert, *Die Polarität im Aufbau des Charakters,* Bern, 1950
Das Problem des seelischen Seins, Meisenheim, 1953 (2)
"Die Genetische Ganzheitspsychologie", *Neue Psycholog. Studien,* 15, 3 (1954)
Ganzheitspsychologie und Strukturtheorie, Bern, 1955
"Beiträge zu einer Strukturtheorie der Hypnose", *Psychol. Rundschau,* 6 (1955)
"Das Schichtenproblem in der Charakterologie", *Studium Generale,* 9 (1956)
Werner, Heinz, "Einführung in die Entwicklungspsychologie", *Münich,* 1953 (3)
Zutt, Jürg, "Die innere Haltung", *Mschr. f. Psychiatrie und Neurologie,* 73 (1929)

INDEX

(*Note: This index does not cover the bibliography, which is arranged in alphabetical order of authors*)